Come my friends.
'Tis not too late to seek a newer world.
Push off, and sitting well in order smite
The sounding furrows; for my purpose holds
To sail beyond the sunset, and the baths
Of all the western stars, until I die.

Ulysses - TENNYSON

NEW SMYRNA

An Eighteenth Century Greek Odyssey

BY

E. P. PANAGOPOULOS

HOLY CROSS ORTHODOX PRESS

Thanks are due to the University of Florida Press for their kind permission to republish *New Smyrna.*

© 1978 by Holy Cross Orthodox Press
50 Goddard Avenue
Brookline, Massachusetts 02146

ISBN 0-916-586-13-8

First published by the University of Florida Press, Gainesville, Florida in 1966.

Printed in the United States of America

Library of Congress Cataloging in Publication Data

Panagopoulos, Epaminondes P
    New Smyrna: an eighteenth century Greek odyssey.

    Bibliography: p.
    Includes index.
    1. Smyrna, Fla.—History.   2. Greek Americans—Florida—New Smyrna.
3. Turnbull, Andrew, d. 1972.
I. Title.
F319.N5P3 1977   975.9'21   77-16303
ISBN 0-916-58613-8
ISBN 0-916-58614-6 pbk.

FOR

Beata Maria

Acknowledgments

A GRANT FROM THE American Philosophical Society, which made my research in England possible, and a similar one from the Saint Augustine Historical Society, which enabled me to visit Minorca, were indispensable for the writing of this book. To both Societies I wish to express my sincere thanks.

I am also deeply obligated to a number of kind persons who either in their official capacities or as colleagues and friends helped me in many ways to complete this study. I am particularly grateful to Mr. John Griffin, Regional Archaeologist of the National Park Service, who, during my first period of research at the Library of the Saint Augustine Historical Society, introduced me to the wealth of local material and let me read his unpublished notes on New Smyrna's sites; to the Administrative Historian of the Saint Augustine Historical Society, Mrs. Doris C. Wiles, who during the summer months of two years placed at my disposal all the archival material of the Society and extended to me every courtesy thus making my work there most fruitful; to the Historian of the Castillo de San Marcos, National Park Service, Mr. Albert C. Manucy, who kindly let me work on the microfilm collection of documents at the Castillo; to Mr. J. Carver Harris, editor of *El Escribano*, who supplied me with a number of rare photographs; and to Mrs. Eleanor Philips Barnes, who graciously rendered to me genealogical information on descendants of New Smyrna colonists.

VII

Acknowledgments

Directors and staff of several libraries and archives in this country and abroad generously offered me their expert help and advice, without which my visits to these faraway places might have produced poor results. I should like especially to express my appreciation to the personnel of the Manuscripts Division of the Library of Congress and also of the National Archives; to Dr. William S. Ewing, Curator of Manuscripts of the Clements Library, University of Michigan; to Father Juan Gutierrez, Director of the Historical Archives, Museum, and Public Education of Mahón, Minorca; to Pierre Lamotte, Archivist of the Prefecture of Corsica and Director of the Public Archives at Ajaccio, Corsica; to Dr. Renato Orlandini, Director of Public Education, and Mr. Francesco Ferrero, of the Public Library of Livorno, Italy; to Dr. Peter W. Topping, former Director of the Gennadius Library, of Athens, and to Miss Euridice Demetracopoulou of the same Library; to the staff of the French National Archives of Foreign Affairs and the Bibliothèque Nationale in Paris; to the Archivo General de Indias in Seville; to the Library of the British Museum and the Public Record Office, whose archivist, Mr. E. Kenneth Timings, helped to make my work there most rewarding.

A number of scholars provided me with invaluable material. In Paris, the distinguished historian of modern Greek history, Nicholas G. Svoronos, introduced me to the documents related to New Smyrna found in the French National Archives, and he also made available to me a copy of his monograph, *The Greek Colony of Menorca*. Professor Gerard H. Blanken, of the University of Amsterdam, provided me with his study *Les Grecs de Cargèse* (*Corse*). Miss Maria Antonia de Olives Mercadal, a fellow historian of Minorca, expertly translated for me documents from the Mahonese dialect and during my visit there gave me an insight into Minorca's economic and cultural history. Mr. Juan Hernandez Mora, of Mahón, supplied me with an out-of-print study by his father, Francisco Hernandez Sanz, on *The Greek Colony Founded in Mahón during the Eighteenth Century*. Dr. Nelly J. M. Kerling, in London, clarified for me several questions connected with obscure documents, and Miss Smaragda O. Mostratou, of Athens, kindly offered me a copy of her informative book, *Kargeze, the Greek Village of Corsica*. To them I wish to express my indebtedness.

To the geographer, Mr. Nathan Hale Meleen, who expertly transferred the original plats of the New Smyrna land grants into contemporary scale on recent Florida maps; and to my colleagues, Dr. O.

Acknowledgments

Clinton Williams, Dr. David P. Edgell, Dr. Robert C. Gordon, and particularly to Mrs. Julie Rogers, who read chapters of this book, suggested corrections, and became greatly responsible for its improvement, I extend my warmest thanks. My deepest gratitude, however, is deserved by the great historian of the American frontier, Professor Ray Allen Billington, who read the entire manuscript and whose criticism was used by me as a Lydian Stone. But for all the shortcomings, whatever errors a reader may find, and other limitations of this book, I alone am responsible.

Finally, the writing of this study could never have been the gratifying experience it became for me without the constant encouragement and unfailing interest of my wife, Beata Maria.

E.P.P.

Contents

XI

Contents

REAR ENDLEAVES
(*1855 engraving by John S. Horton
showing the Gaspar Pappy house* (20)
(THE SAINT AUGUSTINE HISTORICAL SOCIETY)

The St. Photios Shrine

The need for the second edition of this book, *New Smyrna, An Eighteenth Century Greek Odyssey* by Professor E. P. Panagopoulos, gives witness to the deep interest in the historic presence of our Greek Orthodox heritage in America. The tragic story of the nearly 500 settlers from Greece who two hundred years ago helped carve out of the wilderness the future state of Florida is an important chapter in American colonial history.

It was in the early 1960's that authentic information concerning this early Greek presence in Florida was brought to the attention of the Archdiocese by Greek Orthodox residents living in St. Augustine. Under the leadership of His Eminence Archbishop Iakovos the property known as "Avero House" in the historic section of St. Augustine was purchased by the Archdiocese in 1965. It was in this two-story stone edifice on St. George Street that the remaining Greeks who had been enslaved in the New Smyrna colony for ten years and had struggled north to St. Augustine met and held worship services until eventually absorbed into the larger community of St. Augustine.

Since the acquisition of the Avero House property the Archdiocese has developed a series of plans and goals toward transforming it into a national shrine commemorating the arrival of these first Greeks in the New World. In 1971 the property was sanctified in a public ceremony by His Eminence Archbishop Iakovos, His Grace Bishop Aimilianos and Greek Orthodox Priests from the State of Florida. Civil officials from St. Augustine and the State were also present, led by the then Lt. Governor of the State of Florida, the Honorable Tom Adams, and Secretary of the State, Richard Stone. A large banquet and program followed the outdoor ceremonies with over 400 in attendance, and on this day the shrine was officially named after one of the most illustrious leaders in Orthodox history, the Ecumenical Patriarch, St. Photios the Great. St. Photios was selected as Patron Saint of the shrine because of his great missionary zeal resulting in the conversion of the Slavic lands to Orthodoxy under the missionaries SS. Cyril and Methodios. Indeed, these early Greek settlers in the Florida territory were forerunners of the hundreds of Greek Orthodox communities now located throughout North and South America.

The plans to construct a Greek Orthodox chapel representing the Greek Orthodox faith of these early settlers were first approved and later rejected by St. Augustine authorities. This reversal of a previous decision cost the shrine program valuable time and resulted in postponing the goal of its dedication set for the year of the American Bicentennial, and on the Feastday of St. Photios, February 7, 1976. That goal is now scheduled to be met in the near future. Meanwhile, efforts to have Avero House and the site of the shrine approved as an official project of the U.S. National Park Service were successful, thus making the project eligible for some assistance from federal matching funds.

The St. Photios Shrine will be the first National Greek Orthodox Shrine in America. It will honor the memory of this first colony of early Greek settlers who migrated to the New World in 1768 and will also honor the memory of all Greek pioneers who followed them to establish the Greek Orthodox communities that now dot the landscape of America from coast to coast.

Although the colonists of 1768 came to these shores seeking freedom, they found slavery. Yet, out of their slavery the timeless legacy of our Greek Orthodox heritage was implanted in the New World, and today that legacy shines brighter than ever as a beacon and testimony of the innate freedom instilled by God Almighty in the souls of all men. As future generations pause to light a candle and offer a prayer at the Shrine of St. Photios, may they be inspired by the spirit that guided these early pioneers as forerunners of the great nation that was then soon to be born, the United States of America.

Greek Orthodox Archdiocese
New York, N.Y.
August, 1977

XIV

Prologue

ONE WINTER DAY IN 1950 the author of this book and his wife by good chance found themselves in a charming little town in Florida. They were delighted with their discovery and happy in the prospect of spending a leisurely holiday on that semitropical coast. But instead, they plunged into a research adventure which carried them to faraway places and kept the author active for the next several years. It all started when they heard that the name of the little town was New Smyrna, and their excited curiosity made them forget their plans for a restful stay by the ocean.

What they knew about the place was a confusing, legendary account of its eighteenth-century past, which had particularly attracted their attention, because there, almost two centuries ago, took place the first mass migration from Greece. Their desire to know more about this incident carried them from the sites of New Smyrna to the archives of the Saint Augustine Historical Society, where the author became aware of the great attraction of the New Smyrna story.

It soon became clear that this story concerned more than a migration of Greeks. It was the moving chronicle of Greeks and Italians and Minorcans and Corsicans who, together with the amazing Dr. Andrew Turnbull, their colonizer, wrote a page of American frontier history; it was a British colonial enterprise of great magnitude, which was projected against a background of international mercantilistic rivalry; it was an affair of harsh colonial politics, with all its violence

and clashes; it was an exciting occurrence on the periphery of re-
belling America, which felt all the impact of and was developed
within the vibration of the American Revolution; it was a circumstance that brought together people of different languages and reli-
gions and backgrounds and caused, there in the swampy wilderness,
an amazing fusion of cultures; it was more than anything else a
struggle of courageous people who left their old countries in a quest
for freedom and in this process met frustration, suffering, oppression,
revolt, death, but who (at least those who survived) did create their
life anew in the New World.

There were several accounts of the New Smyrna Colony. Most
of them, written during the era of Jacksonian liberalism, expressed
a traditional version transmitted from generation to generation
among the descendants of the New Smyrna colonists. They emphasized the sufferings of the original settlers and condemned Dr. Andrew Turnbull, the founder of the colony. The best of these accounts,
despite their errors and omissions, offered valuable information; but
even these were narrow in scope, dealing with only one aspect of
the New Smyrna venture.

By far the most significant was the study by Carita Doggett
Corse, *Dr. Andrew Turnbull and the New Smyrna Colony in Florida* (Florida, 1919). This was the first book to emphasize the importance of the documents at the British Colonial Office for
the appreciation of the New Smyrna Colony and, more than this, for
an understanding of the personality and activities of its principal
founder. The main purpose of this book was to erase the unsavory
reputation created for Dr. Andrew Turnbull by almost all authors
who wrote about New Smyrna; and Dr. Corse was the logical person
to undertake this task, since she was a direct descendant of the remarkable doctor. The merit of her book was that it placed the New
Smyrna story in a historical frame and that it offered a warm narrative because of the author's involvement and the tender affection
that she felt toward her ancestor.

But for the contemporary reader the book has many limitations.
These do not stem from Dr. Corse's filiopietistic attitude, as one might
imagine, or even from the several inaccuracies which the book includes, but from the fact that since 1919, when her book was published, many more collections of British documents pertaining to the
subject have been studied; the Spanish Archives in Seville, as well
as those of Minorca, Corsica, Greece, France, and Italy, have been

better explored; abundant and significant material has been discovered in Florida and systematically preserved by the Saint Augustine Historical Society; and the work of competent scholars, such as W. H. Siebert, C. L. Mowat, M. J. Curley, J. B. Lockey, and others who wrote on related topics lying on the periphery of the New Smyrna story, greatly illuminated the background of the colony.

Moreover, the ambition of Dr. Corse to tell the story of New Smyrna through the activities of its founder constitutes one of her book's most serious shortcomings. All other persons except Dr. Turnbull appear in her narrative incidentally. Even the settlers who came from abroad fade away or, when they do happen to come to the proscenium, are described as at best "a community of violent and unprincipled men," "unruly," and "wild tribesmen from the mountains in the southernmost part of Peloponnesus." It takes, however, more than one man to make a colony, and, in this case at least, the activities, relationships, and the lives of all, colonizers and colonists, constitute what one may term the story of New Smyrna.

To the author of this volume it became clear quite early that in order to uncover this story from the beginning, he needed to visit and explore some of the greatest depositories of human experience. And thus the search started in the Manuscripts Division of the Library of Congress, where the East Florida Papers and other collections were located, and in the National Archives in Washington, D.C., where the unpublished and rather poor outcome of the Works Progress Administration study on the Greeks of Florida could be found; and from there it was continued in the hospitable library of the Saint Augustine Historical Society, where the author spent the summer months of four years studying the specialized collections of documents and the rich local material which the society had diligently gathered.

But as the story started to unfold, the author felt that certain questions on the puzzling personality of Turnbull and on the background of his colonists needed to be clarified. Since the answers to many of them could not be found in this country, he soon traveled abroad searching for material in the celebrated Library of the British Museum and the treasure-keeping Public Record Office in London; in the orderly Archives of Mahón, Minorca, and the imposing Archivo General de Indias in Seville; in the friendly Public Archives of Ajaccio, Corsica, and the historic Archives Nationales de France in Paris; in cities like Athens and Livorno and in places which a little

3

earlier he could not have imagined as related to a remote page of Florida's history. The result was the unearthing of a wealth of material, which placed the story in its proper setting and showed its profoundly moving quality.

Such a story could not but make one think how worldwide "local" history can be when it is set in its proper milieu. For here was an incident that took place in a little locality on the shores of Florida and yet was connected with the colonial activities of an empire, with international rivalries, with the birth of the American nation, and with the development of a state—an affair whose sources lay in places thousands of miles apart and in many countries.

The time came when the author wondered in what manner he should tell the New Smyrna story. If this topic had belonged to a field such as international relations, intellectual or economic history, or to another area of historic investigation, the task might have been easier. In these cases the trained historian, completely detached from his subject, could inquire, analyze, reconstruct, evaluate his material, grind it through his methodological apparatus, and then, with an anatomical precision, present the outcome in the form of a scientific report.

But the New Smyrna story was different. It was a warming tale of human endeavor, where hope and pain, and desperate struggle, anticipations, frustrations, and eventual success were all saliently projected against a plot in which the fate of people was interwoven. And these people did not appear as numbers, categories, species, or abstract factors; they were actual persons whose names and lives and plans had become known and who were directly involved in the whole affair. The author of this book soon realized that the New Smyrna story could not be told in the discursive way of the trained historian.

The answer to his problem came partially from the nature of the collected material. This was exceptionally colorful, vivid, and descriptive, despite the fact that it was mostly of an official character: reports from royal governors to Whitehall, court depositions, semi-official correspondence between the founder and important men in England, and the like. This material was not only informative, but also expressive of feelings, other psychological conditions, and designs; it mentioned trivial but very indicative details; it drew subtle inferences; and offered elements which are often lost in sources used by a historian for the reconstruction of an incident.

4

For instance, the optimism of an eighteenth-century *philosophe* is clearly reflected in Abbé Raynal's statement about New Smyrna. In his opening lines he asked: "Why should not Athens and Lacedaemon be one day revived in North America? Why should not the city of Turnbull become in a few centuries the residence of politeness, of the fine arts, and of elegance?"

The anxiety of Florida's Governor Grant is evident when in his official report to his government in 1768 he explained the enormous difficulties of the New Smyrna Colony: "I cannot help considering the dreadful situation which the Doctor and his Greeks would be reduced to, if such a misfortune was to happen, a single Bill being returned, my Lord, would be a total stop to his Credit, and the people in that case must unavoidably perish for want if I do not support them; . . . This affair my Lord, has hung heavy upon my mind since the Landing of so great a number of people at a time, without any previous provision being made for them."

The ingenuity of a cosmopolitan mind was expressed in Turnbull's description to Lord Shelburne of his innovation to apply in Florida "the Egyptians' mode of watering. This is new to American planters," he explained, "and is talked of as Chimerical; but as I have seen the utility of such modes of culture, and am convinced of the necessity of them in this Climate, I go on, being certain of succeeding." And his confidence in the future is indicated, when after he had overcome all the obstacles, he thought that he had created the conditions for success and wrote: "I have a certainty before me of succeeding in a very large way for which I have now laid a solid foundation." Turnbull's pride in being a British subject, his distress at being persecuted, his temperamental reactions, and his antagonism and contempt for Florida's Governor Patrick Tonyn are all included in his official statement to Lord Germain, then Principal Secretary of State: "If I had not been well affected to the British Constitution and to my Country, the Injuries and Wrongs I have suffered from Gov.ʳ Tonyn, added to Your Lordship's total Neglect of my Complaints, would long ago have irritated me into Disaffection, or goaded me into Rebellion and drove me among the Americans, where the Injuries mentioned might have provoked me to propose and execute Plans for them far beyond the Conceptions of a Tonyn, or even the Reach of Ministerial Abilities to prevent; and it is probable that Gov.ʳ Tonyn flatters himself of being able to drive me, thro' Despair, to such a Step, but he will find himself grossly mistaken, for the

Amor Patriae and of the British Constitution, while it lasts, will always hold me fast as a British Subject." Who can fail to note the pathos of Turnbull's appeal to Lord Shelburne for the removal of Governor Tonyn, when he pleaded: "My Lord, I have troubled you with a detail of some of the many injuries I have suffered from this Man of Morocco [Governor Tonyn], and I beg for the sake of humanity, if ever honest men are at the Head of Administration again, Your Lordship will please to influence a removal of such a Tyrant and Oppressor from this Government." Or, in the few lines Turnbull wrote in 1783, who can fail to detect a fatalistic acceptance of the fact that he might not see his beloved England again and that he would die in America: "It is now probable that I shall end my days here."

It is also difficult to find another description more alive than an official court deposition, which told of the sea of troubles of the Greek colonist, Anthony Stephanopoli, who saw "the rest of the People being Starved, they began to die, ten or eleven a day & some days fifteen; That He being very much Starved, agreed with some others, to run away again, and thought it better to die in the Woods, than live in such a miserable Condition; that this Dep.ᵗ was pursued, catched, brought back again, & received one hundred and ten lashes on his bare Back & was chained by the leg with a chain of fifteen Pounds weight, for six months and, . . ." after several torturous years, his time of service having expired, "he went to Doctor Turnbull & asked for his discharge & Dr. Turnbull told him he would not give it him, upon which this Dep.ᵗ answered 'Good sir, let me know how long I must serve you'; That Doctor Turnbull answered he could not tell him that he must pay for the Mischief he did at the time the People rebelled."

No other narrative can more movingly describe the despair of a woman colonist from Minorca, Paola Lurance by name, than a court deposition which related that one day when Paola was working in the fields "the said Simon one of Dr. Turnbull's drivers or Overseers came to the said Paola Lurance and asked her if she would sleep with him, she answered she would not, he then told her he would remember her. That about two or three days after, the said Paola Lurance being at her work the said Simon came on there, & immediately found fault with her work & began to beat her severely with a stick. That the said Paola Lurance answered & said to the said Simon 'Do for God's sake Corporal don't beat me, for I am big with

Child & you will kill my child.' The said Simon then answered 'I don't care for you nor your Child, I don't care if you both go to Hell.' That the said Paola Lurance then went home and about three days after was delivered of a dead Child."

A few words concluding in an unorthodox way Tonyn's report to his superiors in London suggested all his exhaustion on that June night of 1775, when the American Revolution was still young and Tonyn tried to keep it out of Florida's borders: "It is now very late at night, or rather early in the morning. I am so much fatigued I can scarcely prevent myself from falling asleep."

To the eyes of this author, suddenly the collected material gave to the New Smyrna story the form of a Greek tragedy. As the *dramatis personae* moved to their destiny, their voices, revealing their minds and hearts, came clearly through an abundance of powerful documents. As they talked, they used words that expressed their feelings and re-created the lost atmosphere in which the plot developed. It was for this reason that the protagonists were left in this book to tell by themselves as much of the story as possible. The task of the historian was thus limited to the role of the ancient chorus: Bring forth a time-honored experience, set the stage, point out meaningful relationships, and draw conclusions.

As a whole the New Smyrna story must have been for its time, and especially for the people involved, a remarkable affair. It was, as Florida's Governor James Grant said in 1768, "the largest Importation of White Inhabitants that was ever brought into America at a time." But after almost two hundred years, viewed in comparison with other important eighteenth-century events, such as great revolutions that changed the fate of large segments of humanity, devastating wars that decided who would rule enormous parts of the world, dynamic regimes established by powerful monarchs, currents of thought and periods in art that shaped generations of the western man, the New Smyrna story is a humble incident. The several interesting aspects of the colony's life, the deeply human quality of its story, its noteworthy local contributions, the few material remnants, and the several descendants of the original colonists are not enough to make New Smyrna "a turning point of the century," "a milestone of an era."

Perhaps this is so. But writing the story of New Smyrna was, at least for this author, a unique experience. Becoming aware of so many situations and problems related to the subject, studying in depth a limited period of time, having the opportunity to talk with men of great wisdom, becoming acquainted with new sources of historical evidence, hunting material in some of the most enchanting places of the world, and reliving during the reconstruction of the story the soul-stirring drama of the New Smyrna people was for him what Plato would call "megiston mathema," a "very great lesson," indeed.

ONE

The Birth of New Smyrna

THERE WAS GREAT EXCITEMENT in the little town of Coron on that September day of 1767.[1]* Men and women, children and old folks clustered at the water's edge, bidding their last joyous but anxious good-byes to several hundred compatriots leaving for an unknown land in the New World.[2]

The skies were true Aegean blue, the sea glassy clear. The hillside town was studded with sun-bathed little houses and crowned by the ancient Venetian castle overlooking the harbor. A mild landscape all around, silvered by the olive trees, rolled down to the lacy shoreline. Far to the east rose the splendor of historic Taygetus, its everlasting snowcap contrasted by its dark deep ravines.

However, this beauty and magnificence of nature failed to detain the several hundred Greeks, gathered ready to depart for a faraway land. Their excitement was great and so were their anticipations for brighter days. In the snug harbor of Coron, the little schooners tugged petulantly at anchor lines. The owner, Dr. Andrew Turnbull, had sailed from port to port in a tiresome search for adventurers willing to begin a new life in Florida. Here in this southernmost port of Greece his patience had been rewarded; here that Odyssean spirit of the seafaring Achaeans still survived.[3]

It had been several years since Florida had first captivated Dr. Turnbull's imagination and plunged him into an adventure destined to change his whole life.

Textual notes will be found at the end of each section.

NEW SMYRNA

It all started when England, by the Peace of Paris in 1763, decided to exchange the newly captured Havana for Florida. This was not an easy decision to make. An old royal decree of Spain, in 1634, had proclaimed Havana the "Key to the New World and the Bulwark of the West Indies." And one year of British occupation, since 1762, was enough to show how true that was. Havana was wealthy, a center of the lucrative slave trade, commercially important, with a unique strategic location, whereas Florida was almost unknown. And yet, the statesmen at Whitehall stubbornly clung to their decision. Reflecting the spirit of a rising class of manufacturers, they now decided to establish a solid, thickly populated, continental North America, designed to become a profitable market for England's ever increasing factory output. To this end, Havana could be sacrificed; one more sugar colony in the New World could add very little to the postwar growth of Great Britain.

Even from a military point of view, the exchange was considered desirable; the experience of the past had shown what a constant threat to the British trade in America was Florida's fortified port of St. Augustine in the hands of Spain. Since such strategic considerations weighted their judgment, the British government managed to overcome strong opposition; Havana was forfeited, Florida was gained.[4]

When the British took over, however, they found Florida completely depopulated.[5] More than 3,000 Spanish had departed, mainly for Cuba, leaving only eight persons who remained behind to arrange for the selling of Spanish property to the English. Without colonists all expectations and plans connected with this new acquisition were doomed to failure, so immediately the British government commenced a vigorous plan for the repeopling of this area.

By the Proclamation of 1763, easy terms had already been offered to prospective settlers who desired land grants. Then in the fall of the same year, a notice published by the British government in the London *Gazette* and immediately reprinted in several other periodicals broadcast the news of Florida's rich agricultural potentialities. The notice also gave instructions on how extensive land grants could be obtained. In addition, the proclamation of James Grant, the first Governor of East Florida, was also designed to stimulate interest. Grant described the mildness of the Floridian climate, the fertility of the soil, the variety of the produce; he told how each man, as head of his family, could claim 100 acres for himself and 50 acres for every other member of the family by applying directly to the colony's council at St. Augustine.[6]

Although at this time nobody in England had a completely clear picture of Florida, a few books and several articles appeared extolling the natural resources and beauties of this attractive land. Other less enthusiastic publications, written primarily by people who did not approve of surrendering Havana to Spain, included Florida in an area "being little more than *pine barrens,* or *sandy deserts.*"[7]

Such pessimistic reports, however, had not dissuaded Dr. Turnbull. While the majority of the British were phlegmatic in their attitude toward this controversy, and the government's effort to attract colonists was bringing very poor results, he had seen great possibilities in the development of this southern corner of the North American provinces. He began to dream of a large estate which would produce cotton, silk, indigo, and other valuable commodities, giving him and his large family the joy of a gay and sunny environment. This dream had soon grown into a resolute plan. He agreed with all those advocating the quick peopling of Florida—like William Knox who later served from 1770 to 1782 as the Undersecretary of State for American Affairs, and like Archibald Menzies, the Scottish pamphleteer.

Knox, with his great experience as a planter and government official in Georgia, had suggested to Whitehall that:

The nature of the soil and climate & the sort of Products which are best adapted to both point out your kind of settlers who ought to be encouraged to sit down in Florida. These are Greeks or any other of the Inhabitants of the Archipelago who profess the Christian Religion. I am well assured that great numbers of these People might be induced to become our Subjects if their Mode of worship was tolerated & the expence of their Transportation defrayed, their Priests who are the proper persons to employ might be easily brought to persuade them to emigrate & our Island of Minorca would be a convenient Place for them to rendezvous at.[8]

A similar idea was expressed by Menzies, who had recently returned from a trip in the Levant, where he had "an occasion to acquire some knowledge of the characters, the manners, and the present situation of the people" in these areas. He thought of "the peopling of *Florida* and the rest of his Majesty's Southern colonies on the continent of *America,* with inhabitants fit for the cultivating of the natural produce of that country, whose religion will be a bar to their forming connections with the *French* or *Spaniards;* and who will readily intermarry and mix with our own people settled there."⁹

Menzies had made his idea clear:

*The people I mean, are the Greeks of the Levant, accustomed to a hot climate and bred to the culture of the vine, olive, cotton, tobacco, madder, &c. &c. as also to the raising of silk; and who could supply our markets with all the commodities which at present we have from Turky, and other parts. These people are in general, sober and industrious; and being reduced, by their severe masters, to the greatest misery, would be easily persuaded to fly from slavery, to the protection of a free government. The Greeks of the islands would be the most useful, and the easiest to bring away, as they are more oppressed than any others, having the same taxes to pay as the Greeks of the Continent; with the addition of an annual visit from the Capitan Pacha, or Turkish High Admiral. The sums arising from their exportation of vast quantities of silk, wine, oil, wheat, tobacco, mastick, cotton, hardly suffice to satisfy their greedy tyrants, who fleece them upon all occasions. It may be observed, that they are excellent rowers, and might be of great service in the inland navigation of America.*¹⁰

Further in his pamphlet Menzies suggested that the Armenians of the Levant could also constitute a fine stock for settlers in Florida and that both Greeks and Armenians might be induced to this venture by their priests. He had concluded his remark with a quite persuasive argument, "The Greek and Armenian women are remarkably handsome. This circumstance would naturally prompt inter-marriages between our people and them, and soon put an end to all distinctions: Most of our merchants in Turky are married to Christian women of that country."¹¹

Menzies had believed that as it happened with the Venetians and Neapolitans who had taken to their countries great numbers of Greeks without provoking any protest by the Ottoman Porte, so could it happen with the British. He also had reported that, "There are great numbers of *Greeks* settled in *Minorca;* by their means many of their countrymen might be procured, as they well know how much happier they would be under his Majesty's government, than under any other whatsoever. I have been informed that almost all the *Greeks* settled at *Minorca,* left their Island on its being taken by the *French,* in the late war."¹²

The Birth

What Knox and Menzies proposed was nothing new for Dr. Turnbull.[13] He had been in several parts of the Levant, especially in Smyrna[14] where his first son, Nicholas, was born.[15] He had travelled through the whole area extensively, and he knew the Greeks, their industry and skill, and how fit they were for the Floridian climate and production.[16] As for the "remarkably handsome" Greek women, he probably could speak with more authority than could both Knox and Menzies. He had married Maria Gracia Dura Bin, the beautiful daughter of a Greek merchant from Smyrna.[17]

Turnbull had talked with some of his distinguished friends in London about his plans and had found great encouragement. One of them, Sir William Duncan, Baronet, was willing to join him in this venture; and in the spring of 1766 they both had submitted applications to His Majesty the King for land grants in East Florida. A little later, on June 18, 1766, they both obtained separate orders from the King in Council granting to each of them 20,000 acres of land and ordering the Governor of East Florida to survey any unoccupied tract in this province which they might choose.[18]

His Majesty's Lords, however, had placed several conditions on these grants. Both Dr. Turnbull and Sir William were required to people their lands within ten years in the proportion of one person for every hundred acres; and if one-third of the land should not have been settled within three years in this proportion, the whole grant would be forfeited "to His Majesty, His Heirs and Successors." Moreover, the settlers could be only white Protestants, and every year on the day of the Feast of St. Michael, both Turnbull and Duncan would have to pay a quitrent of one penny and a half per acre.[19]

As soon as he had obtained this grant and before making any effort to find settlers, Dr. Turnbull decided to go to East Florida in order to see conditions there with his own eyes. He wanted to survey his land and prepare it for the coming of his Greeks. He was anxious to determine the fertility of the soil, the climate, and the healthfulness of Florida, as well as the possibilities of cultivating crops and fruits the way it was done in the Levant. He wanted to meet the Governor and the other officials of the province and to secure their help in his grandiose scheme.

Accordingly, a few weeks later he sailed for Florida, taking his family with him. The journey was long and the ocean wild during those autumn months of 1766. The strong winds and the swollen

13

waters, the sounds of the struggling ship, and the fear of the elements of nature had made those long days on board a formidable ordeal for his wife and children. When, however, in November, they finally entered the little port of St. Augustine, what delight they must all have felt![20]

Here, built on the banks of the Matanzas River, was one of the most enchanting little towns they had ever seen, full of light and color. As they passed through the sand bars and entered the calm little harbor, to their starboard stood the old Spanish fort, the Castillo de San Marcos, with its deep moat and drawbridge—its big cannons protruding protectively through the battlements. To the east on their portside was Anastasia Island, a tropical landscape of clean sand and sweeping palms. What a pleasant change from the gloomy and misty atmosphere of London! Here was a land of lush fertility beneath a genial sun. Huge live oaks, palms, pines, and all kinds of fruit trees seemed to protect as well as shade the flamboyant flowering shrubs; the air was balmy and fragrant yet invigorating.

The family was soon happily established in St. Augustine, and then an extremely busy period began for Dr. Turnbull. His first duty was to meet Governor Grant and present the Orders from His Majesty in Council for both his and Sir William Duncan's tracts of land.

James Grant was a seasoned soldier, forty-six years of age at that time, who had made strenuous efforts to develop the newly acquired Florida. He was a Scotsman from Ballindalloch, Banffshire, and though originally he had studied law at Edinburgh, in 1741 he was commissioned in the army. In those troubled years, when old empires were struggling for their existence and new vigorous ones were determined to prevail, Grant's military career had been a tale of exciting adventure. He fought first in several European campaigns, and in 1757 he came to America as a major of the 77th Regiment, the Montgomery Highlanders. Soon, during the 1758 expedition against Fort Duquesne, close to the site of the present-day Pittsburgh, he was captured by the French and stayed as their prisoner for a whole year. When he was exchanged and returned to his command, he was transferred to Canada where it was thought that his recent acquaintance with the French *mentalité* could be of a practical military use. He remained there for some time, but when the Cherokee war started he was sent to South Carolina, and from there in 1762 he was sent to one of the most important fronts of the war, the Caribbean Islands. There he saw days of success and glory. He participated in the expedition against Martinique and in the successful siege of Havana. In 1763, upon his return to London, he was appointed the first British Governor of East Florida as a recognition of his extraordinary services in the army.[21]

When Turnbull came to Florida, he found Grant deeply involved in the problem of how to make the area a self-supporting province. Despite the many difficulties, Governor Grant maintained a glowing optimism, writing to his friend Robert Grant of Tammore, "This province which was a desert when I came into it tho' inhabited by Spaniards at least two hundred years will soon be a fruitful and plentiful country."[22]

Turnbull could not have come at a better time. With his dynamic character, sweeping designs, and bold ideas, he impressed the Governor from the first moment they met. A mutual esteem and friendship sprang up between the two Scotsmen, destined to last for many years.

The Highlander Grant immediately realized that nothing could nourish his plans for Florida's development more than the proposed establishment of a vast settlement of Greeks. Moreover, it was evident that his compatriot had close relations in London with some of the most influential men of the day. It seems that this fact particularly impressed the ambitious Governor. He offered Turnbull his help and continued to aid him until 1771, when he left Florida for England.

The two tracts of land were immediately surveyed in a location about 75 miles south of St. Augustine.[23] There, on the Hillsborough River, a little south of Mosquito Inlet, in an area mostly covered by swamps, were some of the most fertile lands of East Florida. The inlet, off the mouth of the Hillsborough and Halifax rivers, formed a natural harbor where "a vessel at anchor is landlocked against all winds."[24] Two years previously Governor Grant had offered this location to a colony of poor families from Bermuda. Inasmuch as this colonization plan had failed,[25] he offered the same land to Dr. Turnbull, who immediately approved the site. A few months later, speaking of it in his "Narrative," Turnbull said: "My Enquiries were made agreeable by the Satisfactory Evidence I found everywhere of the healthiness of the climate and Strength of the Soil which is particularly favourable for the Cultivation of Cochineal Indigo Madder Rice Hemp and many other useful articles of commerce Especially Cotton which is produced in East Florida of such Excellent Quality that it induced me to Establish a Considerable Cotton Plantation before I left that Province."[26]

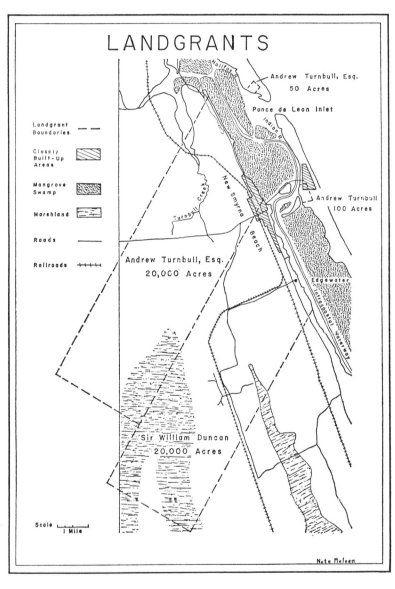

This twentieth-century map, made by Mr. Nate Meleen, geographer, on the basis of the 1767 plats deposited at the Colonial Office, shows the exact location of the original land grants to Dr. Andrew Turnbull and Sir William Duncan.

Without losing any time, he hired a skillful planter and settled him upon his estate and started forming a cotton plantation. He had purchased Negro slaves and ordered a number of cattle to be driven from Carolina and Georgia to the Mosquitoes and placed under the care of an overseer. He also employed a number of "artificers" and Negro slaves to clear the ground and build houses for about 500 Greeks whom he planned to bring to the New World.[27]

In the meantime, some of the most distinguished officials and planters of East Florida had become acquainted with Dr. Turnbull. His driving, forcible personality coupled with his great scheme of settling 500 Greeks at the Mosquitoes (only a fraction of the ultimate total to come); his dynamic talks envisioning roads, bridges, ferries, drained swamplands, and vast plantations; and, more than everything else, his volcanic energy, fired everyone he met with his own fervor. Governor Grant thought that Turnbull's conduct was "encouraging to every inhabitant of the colony"; that his "publik spirited measures have already been of utility to the country"; and that "if all the Gentlemen who have obtained Orders from his Majesty for Land in this Province act with the same spirit, East Florida will soon become an useful plantation to Great Britain."[28] Within three months in Florida he had accomplished many things, and on February 5, 1767, when he thought that things were on their way at his Mosquito estate, he left for England.[29]

A few days before his departure, however, the resignation of John Ainslie from the Council of East Florida gave Governor Grant the opportunity to ask the British government for the approval of Dr. Turnbull's appointment to Ainslie's place.[30] He wanted Dr. Turnbull to serve in the capacity of the Secretary of the Council as well as Clerk of the Crown and Clerk of Common Pleas. Dr. Turnbull was already in London when his appointment came through. While the Board of Trade had found him "well qualified" for this post and recommended him to the King on April 16 of that year,[31] Dr. Turnbull thought that all those new responsibilities were too much for him; he could not effectively carry his administrative duties, while residing 75 miles from the seat, occupied with the development of a newly established settlement. Thus, two weeks later, on May 1, 1767, in a letter he sent to Lord Shelburne, he resigned his post of Clerk of the Crown and Clerk of Common Pleas but retained his position of Secretary.[32] The final appointment as a member of the East Florida Council came to him by Order in Council on May 13, 1767.[33]

In London, Dr. Turnbull had many things to do before starting his Mediterranean voyage in search of settlers. First he saw his partner, Sir William Duncan, and to him and other distinguished members of the London Society he described East Florida with glowing colors, telling them about his personal experiences, the arrangements he had made, and his confidence in the success of his venture.

Turnbull's persuasive accounts brought immediate action. Lord Grenville himself, who had only recently served as Prime Minister of England, asked to join the partnership and soon a new company was formed. On April 2, 1767, the first indenture was signed by Dr. Turnbull, Sir William Duncan, and also Sir Richard Temple, Commander of the Navy,[34] whose signature represented that of George Grenville, who did not want to appear personally in such a partnership. Thus, Sir Richard Temple, as a trustee of George Grenville and his heirs, agreed with the other parties that they would apply for additional land grants which "when obtained were intended to be laid out as near each other as might be, and cultivated worked and improved together at a joint expence not exceeding £9,000 sterling for seven years."[35] It was furthermore agreed that after the seventh year of operation there would be a division in three equal parts of all buildings, improved lands, Negroes, and stock.

This agreement was most important for the success of the designed colony. Subsequent grants could immediately increase the area of the settlement, and Grenville's participation in the company had given great prestige to the scheme and secured the help of the British government. Moreover, it was implied, though not explicitly stated, that the financial burden of the enterprise would be carried by both Sir William and Lord Grenville, while Dr. Turnbull was to engineer the whole project, reside in Florida, and supervise it.

When this was arranged, Dr. Turnbull wanted to settle another matter. In order to encourage the production of cotton, indigo, and other produce in East Florida, Parliament had offered a bounty of £500 a year. For the past three years, however, no settler in the struggling colony had been so successful as to claim such a reward. While still in Florida, Dr. Turnbull had talked about the bounty to his friend Governor Grant, who obligingly wrote immediately to Lord Shelburne about it.[36] Turnbull wanted not only the £500 for the year 1767, but also the unapplied £1,500 of the previous years. He could not, of course, show a successful production, since he had not even started the cultivation of his land; and he hated to appear in the eyes of so many celebrated lords of the British government as if instigated by pecuniary motives. Under the unusual circumstances, he had to be very careful how he should present the whole question. Governor Grant expressed Turnbull's spirit when in his letter to Lord Shelburne he emphasized the great expenses involved in carrying so many settlers from the Levant adding that "the Doctor dos [sic] not expect an allowance from Government, for the freight of these settlers, but as a premium is given in other provinces upon the importation of white inhabitants he flatters himself that some allowance will be made by the publick for the Greeks who are actually landed, not to indemnify himself from the Expense of the Embarkation but to lessen the Expense of subsisting these people till they are able to raise provisions for themselves."[37] Grant furthermore recalled the successful peopling of South Carolina as a result of offering £4 to every white inhabitant who had settled there.[38] With this letter Governor Grant had prepared the ground for the petition of Dr. Turnbull.

The latter, while in London, presented a memorial to the First Lord of Trade and Plantations[39] asking not only for the unapplied £1,500 sterling as a bounty of £3 per head for the first 500 Greeks, but also the continuation of the payment of £500 for the years to come. He maintained in his memorial that while a bounty for the coming white settlers, in the manner of South Carolina, would be "expedient to put this Province in a capacity of supporting itself instead of being a Load on the Mother Country," the £500 of the following years should be applied in this manner: "£400 should be laid out yearly in making Roads & establishing fferies for opening a Communication with Georgia, West fflorida and the southern ports of the Province and that the remaining £100 of the annual bounty should be given as a Salary or stipend to the Pastor and Schoolmaster who accompanys the first 500 Greek Settlers."[40]

Turnbull had also solicited the loan of one of the laid-up sloops of war, which he offered to man, victual, and navigate at his own expense and which would be "continually employed in carrying Greek ffamilies to East Florida from Minorca where [he intended] to appoint a Rendezvous."[41]

Explaining his petition for the bounty to Lord Shelburne, Dr. Turnbull had stated that he did not propose it as a condition or step necessary to the execution of his scheme, but he meant it "as an encouragement for others to continue" what he hoped to begin.[42]

To this letter to Lord Shelburne, Dr. Turnbull had attached a long

"Narrative" where for the first time he had an opportunity to explain in detail the background and prospectives of his plan. There Dr. Turnbull, like Archibald Menzies earlier, said:

During my residence in Turkey and in Travelling thro' Greece I observed that the Christian Subjects in that Empire were in General disposed to fly from the calamities which they groaned under in that despotic Government. On which it Occurred to me that the Greeks would be a very proper people for Settling in his Majesty's Southern Provinces of North America. They being bred to the making of Silk and to the Culture of the vine, Cotton, Madder &c. And many of them Declared to me that they would Embrace the first Opportunity of Flying from that Country of Slavery and Oppression where their Lives and properties were at the Will of their hard Masters. These repeated Declarations from Thousands of that people Engaged me to Petition His Majesty's Order in Council for a Tract of Land in East Florida on which I might settle a small Colony of Greeks.[43]

Turnbull further along explained his initial activities and his plans, expressing his faith in the colony's bright future and believing that "very great advantages must accrue to this nation from the acquisition of so many useful subjects who will be employed in the Culture of Articles now purchased from foreign nations."

All these steps were taken by Dr. Turnbull as soon as he returned to London. His petition for the sloop of war was introduced to the Board of Trade by Lord Shelburne on March 31, 1767;[44] in a few days there followed his petition for the bounty.[45] The Board of Trade discussed these petitions immediately and on April 16, 1767, informed Lord Shelburne of its decision to pay "forty shillings per Head to the first five hundred Greeks (children excepted) that shall be imported and actually settled in that Province."[46] As for the £100 allowance to the first priest of the Greek church, that was left to Lord Shelburne to decide. One sloop of war of those not on active duty was also placed at the disposal of Dr. Turnbull.

The remainder of the preparations for the great journey took only a few weeks. Dr. Turnbull speeded up the complicated arrangements for the shipping of his settlers, he bought tools and other implements, and by June, when everything was ready, he sailed again for the Levant.

NOTES — Chapter One

1. Governor James Grant, in a letter to the Earl of Shelburne sent from St. Augustine on Mar. 12, 1768, stated: "I have received a letter from Mr. Turnbull on the 24th of September from Melo, in his way to a port of the Peloponnese where he was to embark his Greeks." Colonial Office, Class 5, Vol. 549, hereafter indicated as C.O. 5/549. The original letter of Andrew Turnbull to James Grant of Sept. 24, 1767, which could possibly contain more details, has not been found. Since, however, it is approximately 160 British miles from the Aegean island of Melos to the Peloponnesos port of Coron, and Dr. Turnbull was "in his way" there, it is almost certain that he arrived in Coron one of the last days of Sept., 1767, a date that is in agreement with the rest of the evidence on his itinerary.

2. The description of the departure of the Greek colonists from Coron is given by F. C. H. L. Pouqueville, *Voyage de la Grèce*, 2d ed., IV (Paris, 1826), 331-33; it appears also, almost identically, in E. d'Eschavannes, *Histoire de Corinth, relation des principaux événements de la Morée* (Paris, 1854), p. 266; Constantine N. Sathas, in his *Tourkokratoumene Hellas* [*Greece under Turkish Rule*, A Historical Essay on the Revolutions made against the Ottoman Yoke, 1453-1821] (Athens, 1869), p. 474, fn. 2, mentions d'Eschavannes' description; Sathas also knew the following statement made earlier by Kyriakos Melirrytos: "1767. Dr. Turnbull leads a colony of Peloponnesians to Florida of America. The colonists joined by Corsicans cultivate as tenants 60,000 stremmata [about 20,000 acres]. They inhabit New Smyrna, neighboring to St. Augustine." Kyriakos Melirrytos, *Chronologia Historike* [*Historical Chronology*] (Odessa, Russia, 1836), p. 245. However, Sathas, not knowing Pouqueville's account of the colonists' departure, doubted the accuracy of d'Eschavannes' data. See also, Michael B. Sakellariou, *He Peloponnesos kata ten Defteran Tourkokratian, 1715-1821* [*Peloponnesos Under the Second Period of Turkish Rule, 1715-1821*] (Athens, Byzantinisch-Neugriechische Yahrbücher, 1939) p. 119, fn. 6; and Take Ch. Kandeloros, *Ho Harmatolismos tes Peloponnesou* [*The "Harmatolism" of Peloponnesos, 1500-1821*] (Athens, 1924), p. 68.

3. In his letter to Shelburne from Minorca, on February 27, 1768, Lansdowne MSS, Vol. 88, f. 147, Dr. Turnbull speaks about "ships then with" him, and implies that there were at least three ships with him in his trip to the Levant. Both Pouqueville, *op. cit.*, and d'Eschavannes, *op. cit.*, speak about "ships" and not "ship."

4. George L. Beer, *British Colonial Policy, 1754-1765* (New York, 1907) pp. 132 f. and pp. 155-59; Charles Loch Mowat, *East Florida as a British Province, 1763-1784* (Berkeley, 1943), pp. 5-7.

5. Wilbur H. Siebert, "The Departure of the Spaniards and other Groups from East Florida, 1763-1764," *Florida Historical Quarterly*, XIX (Oct., 1940), 145-54.

6. Governor Grant's Proclamation of Oct. 31, 1764, in C. O. 5/540, p. 255. This Proclamation was destined for the inhabitants of the North American provinces primarily, but it also became well known in England; see *The Gentlemen's Magazine*, XXXVII (London, 1767), 21-22. Also, Charles Loch Mowat, "The First Campaign of Publicity for Florida," *Mississippi Valley Historical Review*, XXX (Dec., 1943) 359-76.

7. *Mowat*, "First Campaign," p. 364.

8. "Hints Respecting the Settlement of Florida," Knox MSS (William L. Clements Library, University of Michigan, Ann Arbor), IX, 3.

9. Archibald Menzies, *Proposal for Peopling his Majesty's Southern Colonies on the Continent of America* (Megerby Castle, Perthshire, October 23, 1763), p. 1. An original copy of this small and rare pamphlet is deposited in the John Carter Brown Library. A photostatic copy of it can be found in the Library of the St. Augustine Historical Society.

10. *Ibid.*, p. 2.

11. *Ibid.*, p. 3.

12. *Ibid.*, pp. 3-4.

13. Whether or not Dr. Turnbull had seen William Knox's proposal or other memorials on the same topic, such as Maurice Morgann's and John Pownall's (see Mowat, *East Florida*, pp. 10-11), is unknown. There is a possibility that he had their content in mind, since they were in the hands of the Earl of Shelburne, who had so much encouraged and protected Turnbull in his Florida scheme. Turnbull also could have read Menzies' pamphlet.

14. In several accounts (the most recent being "Minorcans of Saint Augustine," a paper read before the St. Augustine Historical Society on Dec. 14, 1948, by the late Edward W. Lawson) Turnbull appeared as having served as a British Consul in Smyrna. The names of all British consuls and other consular employees who served in any part of the Ottoman Empire can be found in the Public Record Office and especially in the volumes *State Papers Turkey* 97/32-42 which cover the period 1745-65. There is no evidence, however, supporting the fact that Turnbull ever served in any consular capacity in the Near East. The reasons for his stay in Turkey remain obscure.

15. The Spanish census of St. Augustine for the year 1783 states: "Don Nichol Turnbull; Native of Smyrna in the Levant although both son and parents are English." [See Siebert's footnote on Nichol Turnbull.]

16. "Narrative of Dr. Turnbull" in Lansdowne MSS, Vol. 88, p. 133.

17. Carita Doggett Corse, *Dr. Andrew Turnbull and the New Smyrna Colony of Florida* (Florida, 1919), p. 16 f.

18. Order of his Majesty in Council granting 20,000 acres of land in East Florida to Andrew Turnbull, Esq., and 20,000 acres to Sir William Duncan, Baronet. C. O. 5/548, p. 23.

19. *Ibid.*

20. Grant to Shelburne, St. Augustine, Jan. 20, 1767. C. O. 5/548, p. 285. Andrew Turnbull with his family arrived first in Charleston, S. C., in the ship *Mary*, on Wed., Nov. 5, 1766, and from there they sailed immediately to St. Augustine. *South Carolina and American Gazette*, Nov. 10, 1776.

21. For biographical data on Governor James Grant, see Alastair MacPherson Grant, *General James Grant of Ballindalloch, 1720-1806* (London, 1930); Philip C. Tucker, "Notes on the life of James Grant prior and subsequent to his Governorship of East Florida," The *Florida Historical Society Quarterly* ,VIII, 2 (Oct., 1929), 112-19; "Journal of Lieutenant Colonel James Grant, Commanding an Expedition against the Cherokee Indians, June-July, 1761," in *ibid.*, XII, 1 (July, 1933), 25-36; also Wilbur Henry Siebert, *Loyalists in East Florida, 1774 to 1785* (The Florida Historical Society, 1929), II, 309-10; Mowat, *East Florida*, pp. 12-13; Henry Manners Chicester, "Grant, James," in *D. N. B.* VIII, 388-89.

22. St. Augustine, Jan. 8, 1768, in A. M. Grant, *op. cit.*, p. 77.

23. James Grant to Shelburne, St. Augustine, Jan. 20, 1767, C. O. 5/548, p. 285.

24. William Gerard de Brahm, *History of the Three Provinces, South Carolina, Georgia and East Florida* (around 1772), unpublished, the manuscript of which is in Harvard College Library. The survey and the plan of the Mosquito Inlet area was made, according to de Brahm's statement, during the years 1765 to 1767. The plan of the area is found on p. 295. Also, *South Carolina and American General Gazette,* Mar. 2, 1765.

25. James Grant to Board of Trade, November 22, 1764, C. O. 5/540, pp. 231, 293-94, etc. Mowat in *East Florida,* p. 63, mentions the information given by the *Scots Magazine,* XXVIII (May, 1766), 271, that about 40 families from Bermuda did settle this site in 1766. This information seems most improbable, since it is not given by any of the several contemporary sources, nor have traces of this settlement ever been found.

26. "Narrative of Dr. Turnbull," *op. cit.* ,

27. Grant to Shelburne, St. Augustine, Jan. 20, 1767. C. O. 5/548, p. 285.

28. *Ibid.*

29. *South Carolina and American General Gazette,* Feb. 6, 1767.

30. Grant to Shelburne, Jan. 17, 1767, Lansdowne MSS, Vol. 52, p. 294.

31. C. O. 5/563, p. 229; *South Carolina and American General Gazette,* Aug. 10, 1767.

32. Turnbull to Shelburne, London, May 1, 1767, Lansdowne MSS, Vol. 88, f. 139.

33. Privy Council Register, Vol. 112, May 13, 1767.

34. Treasury 77/7, Mar. 9, 1781.

35. *Ibid.* Indenture of Apr. 2, 1767.

36. St. Augustine, Jan. 20, 1767. C. O. 5/548, p. 285.

37. *Ibid.*

38. *Ibid.*

39. C. O. 5/541, p. 211.

40. *Ibid.,* and "Narrative of Dr. Turnbull," *op. cit.*

41. "Narrative of Dr. Turnbull," *op. cit.*

42. *Ibid.*

43. *Ibid.*

44. C. O. 5/541, p. 211.

45. Memorial of Andrew Turnbull to the Lords of Trade, C. O. 5/548, p. 309.

46. C. O. 5/548, pp. 305, 313. Lord Shelburne on May 14, 1767, informed Governor Grant about the granting of forty shillings to each imported settler by Dr. Turnbull and asked him to give them "when they arrive every suitable encouragement." C. O. 5/548, p. 317.

TWO

Greeks Forsake the Blue Aegean

I NSTEAD OF GOING DIRECTLY to the islands of the Archipelago, Turnbull decided to go first to Minorca and make all the necessary arrangements for the use of Mahón as the place of rendezvous for his prospective settlers. He arrived there at the beginning of June, 1767; the openhearted Minorcans, their island with its convenient location, the port facilities, and the excellent protection by the British fleet that was stationed there, all met with his approval.

He visited, of course, Governor James Johnston to whom he gave an introductory letter from Lord Shelburne and explained the purpose of his trip. Johnston's response was more than encouraging. In a letter to Lord Shelburne he wrote: "I shall with the greatest pleasure punctually obey His Majesty's commands in giving all the assistance in my power to that Gentleman towards prosecuting his plan."[1]

And he gave it. He had, of course, good reason to do so. He had gone to Minorca for the first time in 1763 when the second British occupation of the island had started. Soon, however, he and his wife, Lady Cecil, managed to become the most undesirable persons on the island. Unfriendly and indifferent toward the Minorcans, selfish and arrogant, Johnston became involved in several financial scandals. The *jurados,* the local magistrates who represented the people of Minorca, protested to the British government for his onerous taxation on the islanders and for other financial irregularities, and they caused his temporary recall to London. He was, however, restored to his position,

24

and while his attitude toward the Minorcans remained the same after his return, he became very careful to please his superiors at White-hall.[2]

The arrival of Turnbull offered Johnston an opportunity to demonstrate his worth to his country. A former Prime Minister of England was a partner of this company and other important personalities were involved in it. The powerful Lord Shelburne, who since the previous year as Secretary of State for the Southern Department had undertaken a radical reorganization of the colonial administration, bringing all colonial governors under his personal jurisdiction, appeared to be a friend of Dr. Turnbull and displayed an unusual personal interest in this affair. And, last but not least, Turnbull himself, a master in personal relations, introduced himself as "Secretary of His Britannic Majesty in East Florida."[3] This was the time Johnston was waiting for to prove to His Majesty's government that he was an efficient and trustworthy governor. And so he helped Turnbull wholeheartedly.

It was during this first visit to Minorca that Turnbull heard that the migration of many husbandmen was possible in the Italian town of Leghorn. His trip to the islands of Greece was postponed again, and when he found an opportunity he left for Leghorn.[4] He arrived about the middle of June, 1767, soon finding several strangers in town willing to follow him. Turnbull thought of Leghorn as another convenient gathering place for colonists and he immediately made arrangements with people from southern France and various parts of Italy to come there to join him.[5]

Before the actual embarkation of those already gathered to leave Leghorn, Turnbull visited the Governor of the town, Count Bourbondel Monte,[6] seeking aid and approval of his plans. At first the Governor did not object to the departure of strangers, many of whom were already under deportation, as long as Dr. Turnbull did not lure away any of the silk manufacturers or other recent arrivals from Genoa.[7]

However, when the Governor saw the number of people ready to set sail for the New World, he changed his mind. He began to fear a mass exodus from Leghorn which would depopulate the town once again, and he therefore tried to prevent the recruits' departure by sending them threatening messages. This was an unexpected complication. Dr. Turnbull thought of requesting help from the British Minister in Florence, Sir Horace Mann; however, when his people expressed their fear that in such a case the Governor of Leghorn would resort to reprisals, Turnbull abandoned this plan. Instead he managed, with the help of the British Proconsul in Leghorn, a Mr. Burnaby, to ship on June 27th, 110 persons from Leghorn and sail with them to Mahón in Minorca, where he arrived on July 5, 1767.[8]

From there he wrote to Lord Shelburne explaining the difficulties caused by the Governor and asking that Sir Horace Mann be instructed about similar cases which might occur in the future. Upon leaving Leghorn, Turnbull had ordered his agent there, Edward Pumell, to send to Minorca within three months (by October, 1767) a ship loaded with Italians and Greeks. It was possible that the Governor could deter this order. The Scottish Andrew Turnbull also pointed out to Lord Shelburne that such obstacles created by the Governor of Leghorn, "a violent man," could: "deprive the Colonies of making an acquisition of a sober and industrious People fit for settling the Southern Parts of North America, and who offer their labour of half the Price usually given to British Subjects carried to the Colonies. This would undoubtedly engage the Proprietor of Land in the Southern Province to look for such cheap labourers instead of taking People from Great Britain and Ireland."[9] The Italians were left to wait in Mahón, and on July 11, 1767, Turnbull departed for the Levant. So far the Italians were the first numerous group he had recruited for Florida.

What Turnbull expected to be an easy and fruitful trip, however, came to be an adventure with great disappointments. The most persistent reaction against his efforts came from the Levant Company, which had a monopoly of the British trade in the Near East and therefore was afraid that Turnbull's company in East Florida, dealing with products similar to those of the Mediterranean, would soon become too highly competitive and damage their interests. The heads of the Levant Company decided to throw every possible obstruction in the path of Turnbull's plans, and for this purpose they sought the cooperation of the British diplomatic representatives in the Levant. A number of the Company's agents already had consular assignments in the area, and in some cases it was quite difficult to distinguish whether it was a representative of the Levant Company performing consular duties or a regular consul carrying on the work of the Company. The problem now was to persuade the higher diplomatic echelon that Turnbull's trip could be harmful to British interests. Accordingly, the Deputy Governor of the Company, William Cooper, in a long letter from London to John Murray, the British Ambassador at Constantinople, explained Turnbull's plans and pointed out that "the clandestine removal of Subjects from any state is often attended with most dangerous consequences"; that the Ottoman Empire would not like this departure of taxpaying subjects; and that the Turkish officials might resort to reprisals against the Levant Company.[10] Cooper sent a similar letter to the British Consul at Smyrna, Anthony Hayes.[11]

Ambassador Murray, however, did not heed the Levant Company's warning, for he had long before investigated Turnbull's purposes for himself and had been convinced of their merit. Even before Turnbull's departure for the Levant, he had followed with rising apprehension the preliminary activities of Turnbull's agents in the Levant, and in a confidential communication to Lord Shelburne, he stated that:

"... *there is a man arrived at Smirna, who calls himself a British subject, and goes by the name of Constantine Warwick, and pretends that he was a Lieutenant of Foot in the English Service last war in Germany, but is originally a Greek, Native of the island of Nio in the Archipelago and who is employed by one Doctor Turnbull, to engage as many Greek Families as possible, to withdraw from this country to East Florida, to carry on a scheme he has undertaken of clearing certain tracts, which have been granted him. I am told he has already engaged forty Greek families, with two Greek priests at Tripoliz in the Morea, to leave that place on certain promises; he ... is now gone to his island to engage as many as possible. He is to return in June, where he is to wait Dr. Turnbull's arrival.*"[12]

Furthermore, Murray called the attention of Lord Shelburne to the consequence of "this schemer's" acts, which might injure the Grand Seignior's public revenue, "which in a despotick country like this may occasion a good deal of trouble, if not expense, to pacify matters."

When Murray wrote this letter, he was not aware of the background of the East Florida venture. For him, this "one Doctor Turnbull" was simply a "schemer" who might engage the British in "disagreeable broils" with the Sultan. Soon, however, Lord Shelburne clarified the situation for him: in a letter on June 5, he explained to Murray that Turnbull's conduct "is so far meritorious as he can promote the peopling of his Majesty's colonies," and he added, "I am persuaded from his Character, with which I am perfectly well acquainted, that he will willingly hearken to any advice, or Directions you will favour him with, to avoid giving offence to the Porte."[13]

27

The interest of the government in this affair was obvious and the personal relationship of Turnbull with Shelburne was to Ambassador Murray a very strong argument, strong enough to make him answer in a rather apologetic way about his previous report, "Otherwise, my Lord, I very sincerely wish him [Turnbull] success," he added; Turnbull was, after all, not a stranger "and as I have the pleasure of knowing him personally, any Advice or Directions from me are needless as his Agent seems to be acting with great circumspection, I not having hither to heard of any Surmises of his design."[14]

With the change in Ambassador Murray's attitude, the Levant Company could not expect any significant reaction from the British side against Turnbull's plans. However, they still had their agents in the Near East, who promptly notified the Turkish authorities in their areas about the coming of this doctor from England, the purpose of his trip, and the subsequent revenue losses of the Ottoman Empire on account of the removal of so many people. Consequently, in every harbor he anchored, in every place he passed by, Dr. Turnbull found the Turks on guard, not allowing him to recruit colonists.[15]

It seems, however, that the agents of the Levant Company were not the only ones who were anxious to notify the Turks. The French consular authorities watchfully followed Turnbull's trip and, very possibly, snatched at the opportunity to inform on a Britisher. It is true that the Treaty of Paris, in 1763, ended the war; that Britain was undoubtedly the "mistress of the seas" and by that time the predominant imperialistic power of the world; but the economic war was still going on. France, with bitterness and persistence, was anxious to deal every possible blow against the economic expansion of England. The East Florida development had attracted the attention of France, and Turnbull's journey in the Aegean Islands became a frequent topic in the governmental reports of Peyssonnel, the experienced French Consul in Smyrna.

For weeks Turnbull wandered in the Aegean with very little success. On September 15, Ambassador Murray reported his arrival at Smyrna.[16] From there, the birthplace of both his wife and his son Nicholas, Turnbull took with him at least one person, a Gasper Papi, a lad then seventeen years of age.[17]

After Smyrna he went to the island of Melos picking up another settler, Anastassios Mavromatis by name,[18] and from there he wrote to Governor Grant on September 24 that he was on his way to a port of the Peloponnesos, where he was to embark his Greeks.[19]

28

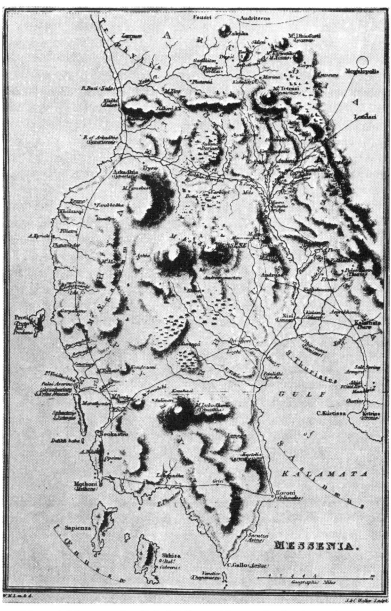

Map of Messenia by Col. William Martin Leake (1830). On the west side of the Gulf of Kalamata is the port of embarkation of the settlers from Mani, Koroni (Coron). On the southwestern corner of the peninsula is the port of Methoni (Modon) where the incident between Dr. Turnbull and the Turkish authorities occurred.

This trip was not included in Turnbull's first plan.[20] He had heard, however, about those few hundred villages of Mani, built like eagles' nests high on the cliffs of a rocky peninsula that reaches from the peak of Mount Taygetus southward for about 50 miles. He had been told about the sufferings of the people who had managed to defy the strength of the Ottoman Empire and about the heavy price they had paid for freedom, losing great numbers of men and women in these continuous fights. He had also learned about the frequent migrations during the last hundred years from Mani to the Ionian Islands, Italy, and Corsica, where the Maniotes preferred to go rather than to live in slavery.

When Turnbull reached the port of Coron, only 30 miles from Mani, he could hardly believe that life was possible on this steep rocky arm that protruded into the sea, the famed *Brazzo di Maina*. Up there on the cliffs, however, life persisted. It surely was not an easy life; especially during those days the atmosphere was grave, full of anxiety and despair. Plagues had lasted for several years until recently,[21] family feuds had taken a heavy toll in human lives,[22] and a meager living on the barren mountains had aggravated the natural hostilities of these people. They could bear almost anything, including their peculiar local government, their ancient customs, some of which came down since Homeric times, their hardships—content that their villages were an island of freedom surrounded by a world that sighed under the Ottoman despotism.

However, the recent terrorism incited by the Turks in Peloponnesos had made their hearts heavy. They knew that this was the beginning of more calamities; they had already endured too many.

The story behind this new situation had started in Russia rather than in Greece. It began when the ambitious Tzarina Catherine the Great conceived her plan to incite the Greek Orthodox population of the Balkans to revolt against the Ottoman Empire. For the Greek part of her plan she relied greatly on the services of George Papazolis, a Greek artillery captain in the Russian army.

Papazolis was bold and ingenious, tireless, and devoted to his empress; moreover, he hated the Turks. So he was sent as the chief Russian agent to prepare the uprising of the Balkan people. He passed through Trieste, and in 1763, having at his disposal great sums of money, he established his headquarters in Venice. From there he directed his agents in Yugoslavia and Greece. In 1765, his activities were intensified, and Papazolis himself went to Mani to persuade the people there to head the revolt in Peloponnesos. He promised them great help with a Russian army and navy, and he stressed to them the certain success of such an enterprise. The leaders of Mani were careful and reserved, having had bitter experiences of promises from the west. However, meetings of notables had taken place, protocols and agreements had been signed, secret preparations had started, and a restlessness was in the air.[23]

The Turks had sensed the atmosphere, and though they could not find out exactly what was happening, they knew what to expect. They decided to act before it was too late and their first action was to intimidate the people of Mani. Three years earlier, in 1764, they had executed five of the most important leaders of Peloponnesos.[24] Now they found that that was not enough. Especially, because as long as the Bishop of Lacedaemon, Ananias Theophilis, was alive, the people of this part of Greece could always derive new strength and hope.

A passionate lover of freedom and a defender of his faith, this Bishop Ananias was the real soul of the whole movement. He had built powder mills, he was in contact with all armed chieftains of the area, and he was continuously preparing Mani for the great upheaval. Then, just before Turnbull's arrival, the Turks decided to put an end to all these activities. In the medieval town of Mystra, on the slopes of Mount Taygetus, they arrested Ananias and without delay beheaded him.[25]

Sorrow and grief filled the hearts of the people. But while they were still stunned by the sudden loss of their leader, another tragedy occurred. A great number of men, women, and children were returning to Mani from a pilgrimage to the town of Patras where religious festivities had taken place. As they were approaching their village, ready to cross the limit of Mani, they were attacked by the Turks. The surprised crowds were unaware of the abrupt change in the Turkish policy and were caught without the protection of their warriors. They were all mercilessly slaughtered—and so close to Mani.

While every family, deep in mourning, was lamenting the death of so many people, there came the news from down below, from the port of Coron, that there had arrived an English doctor who wanted to take people with him far away to a new world. The doctor talked about a new life that everybody could begin, free from tyranny and oppression, about a sunny country with mild coasts and orange groves, where everybody could live in peace, have his own religion, and possess, in time, a piece of fertile land. He had also promised that if

31

anybody did not like the new place, he could return to his own country, and all expenses would be paid by the doctor.

The people of Mani loved freedom and, more than everything else, their own country. They were warriors, knowing how to use arms since early childhood. The birth of a boy in their village was saluted by firing arms, celebrating the birth of one more fighter. The censuses of Mani mentioned only the number of "rifles," the arms-bearing men only; though women, too, frequently fought beside their men. They were not afraid of the Turks, whom they resisted successfully for many years. But sometimes, even the most brave and fearless men long for a quiet and joyful life, without bloodshed and agony. Many of them, therefore, decided to leave their rugged mountains as their forefathers had done under similar circumstances several times before. Now, they were ready on the shore awaiting the signal for their embarkation, saying good-bye to their loved ones.

How much had happened before Dr. Turnbull had reached this happy moment of having this second group of settlers with him! Petitions, agreements, two crossings of the Atlantic, troubles with foreign authorities, and endless frustrations. Here, however, he had finally found a few hundred of the people he wanted; these were seasoned in hardships and accustomed to surviving on the cultivation of the few products of Mani: lima beans, lentils, and olive oil. Dr. Turnbull wrote to his friend Lord Shelburne:

Those now with me are from among a people who inhabit a chain of mountains which makes the southernmost proximity of the Peloponnese. That people submitted to the Turks when they conquered the Morea in the beginning of this century, but finding themselves hardly used, they shook off their fetters, and continue free to this day. The Turks have often attempted to bring them under subjection, but have always failed from the impracticability of attacking them in their mountains. These Greeks are ruled by Chiefs called Captains, to whom they pay a small tribute yearly, to enable him to provide warlike ammunition to defend them against the Turks. This, however, is frequently consumed in Civil Wars among themselves. Several mountains in the Turkish Empire are inhabited by people who maintain their liberty in this manner & who rather chose to work hard in cultivating the little pieces of ground they find among the mountains than live under tyranny in the fertile and extensive plains under them.[26]

And later, speaking of them on another occasion and of himself in the third person, he added that he had found: "a retreat for them, and their families, being reduced to the most wretched condition of indigence by the oppression and galling yoke of the Turkish government; they declared to him [Dr. Turnbull] when travelling in their country, that it was cruel tyranny and the most pinching poverty that made them wish to fly from such complicated distress; otherwise they would not have emigrated, for there is not a nation on earth more prejudiced in favour of their own country than the Greeks, and indeed with reason."[27]

Finally, the moment had arrived and the signal for departure was given by the Greek priests who stayed ashore. The boats took the emigrants aboard, and soon this human cargo set out on its great journey to freedom.

Leaving Coron, Turnbull continued his trip among the Aegean Islands.[28] He visited Crete, and it seems that he managed to take a few persons from there. Among them was Demetrios Fundulakis from Candia, about twenty years of age at that time.[29]

Turnbull also stopped at the volcanic island of Santorin, wherefrom came the only Greek woman known to embark, Maria Parta, or Ambross, the second name being her mother's maiden name. Years later, in Florida, after the death of her first husband, Domingo Costa (Kyriakos Costas), a Greek from Corsica, Maria married Demetrios Fundulakis, twelve years her junior.[30]

Turnbull then visited Smyrna for the second time.[31] With loaded ships, he sailed for months from port to port on the winter seas of Greece. His search for more settlers, however, was thwarted by the reaction of the Levant Company, which continued its harassments. The last and most disturbing of all was the incident at Modon, when Turnbull and his weary men were ready to return to Mahón.

Modon is a little town of southern Peloponnesos, on the west coast of the same peninsula where Coron lies. Built on a location that makes easy the control of ships coming in or leaving the Aegean, and being heavily fortified with castles of many periods, Modon had become, since ancient times, one of the most important ports of southern Greece. Turnbull, narrating the incident that evidently happened when he was ready to leave the Greek waters, said, referring to the Levant Company:

Ill grounded apprehensions or jealousy had influenced them to make it [the purpose of Turnbull's trip] public in all places, of which I felt the effects at Modon in the Morea, for on being obliged to put in there for refreshments for my people, after keeping at sea as long as I could in the worst weather I ever saw, on sending a boat with ten men ashore for water they were taken into custody, on pretext of my having some of the Grand Seignior's subjects on board the ships then with me; but they were released the next day in consideration of a present made privately to the commanding officer of the garrison, who desired me not to permit the people to appear on Deck for fear of complaints against him for letting me carry away Greeks, which he thought he had a right to detain as rebels.[32]

The French Consul at Smyrna, Peyssonnel, reporting the same incident to his government on January 28, 1768, stated that two of Turnbull's ships transporting settlers to Florida approached Peloponnesos on their way to Mahón, and that some of the men aboard changed their minds and escaped to the coast. It was they, according to Peyssonnel, who notified the Turkish authorities about the abduction of the Grand Seignior's subjects by the British, but Turnbull settled the issue by bribing the Turks with 2,000 talers.[33]

After six months of wanderings among the islands of Greece, meeting disheartening obstacles and rough seas, Turnbull finally had with him a number of Greeks and sailed with them to Mahón to join his Italian recruits who were waiting for him there.

Contemporary authors who followed his efforts to people Florida with Greeks became enthusiastic; and the celebrated Abbé Raynal, narrating the event with all the optimism of the enlightened men of the eighteenth century, exclaimed:

Why should not Athens and Lacedaemon be one day revived in North America? Why should not the city of Turnbull become in a few centuries the residence of politeness, of the fine arts, and of elegance? The new colony is less distant from this flourishing state than were the barbarous Pelasgians from the fellow citizens of Pericles. What difference is there between a settlement conceived and founded by a wise and pacific man, and the conquests of a long series of avaricious, extravagant, and sanguinary men; between the present state of South America and what it might have been, had those who discovered it, took possession of it and laid it waste been animated with the same spirit as the worthy Turnbull? Will not nations learn by his example, that the foundation of a colony requires more wisdom than expense? The universe hath been peopled by one man and one woman only.[34]

NOTES — Chapter Two

1. Mahón, June 6, 1767, C. O. 174/4, p. 147.

2. On Governor Johnston's policies in Minorca, see Mario Verdaquar, *La Dominación Britanica en Menorca* (Palma, 1952), pp. 13-16; also, the Spanish translation by Maria Rosa Lafuente Vanrell y Pons, *Relación de Deplorable Estado de la Isla de Menorca y de las muchas Injurias Inferidas a sus Habitantes bajo el mando del teniente Gobernador Johnston*, originally published anonymously in English under the title *Account of the Deplorable State of the Island of Minorca and the many injuries inflicted on its inhabitants under the Command of Deputy Governor Johnston* (London, 1766). Also C. O. 174/4, where the whole volume contains petitions, complaints, and protests, especially pp. 63-66, where the Agents of Minorca, John Pons and Andrea, on Aug. 6, 1766, complained to Lord Shelburne against Governor Johnston.

3. It seems that Turnbull liked to use this newly acquired title, which he did not omit in official papers signed by him in Minorca. See in Municipal Archives of Mahón, Files of Notary Antonio Flaquer, Book 363, fo. 27.

4. C. O. 174/4, p. 147.

5. Turnbull to Shelburne, Leghorn, June 15, 1767, Lansdowne MSS, Vol. 88, p. 141.

6. Andrew Turnbull, "The Refutation of Late Account of New Smyrna," *The Columbian Magazine* (Nov., 1788), p. 684.

7. The late Count Sforza, in a statement made to Mrs. Carita Doggett Corse, a copy of which is found in the archives of the St. Augustine Historical Society, asserted that he had read in the records of the City of Leghorn that the reason the Governor allowed Turnbull's recruits to depart was that they were mainly the overflow of a number of strangers who had been invited to come to Leghorn to occupy houses made vacant by a plague. M. Malafouris in his *Greeks in America, 1529-1948* (New York, 1948) p. 33—in Greek—gives the same information and suggests that perhaps several among Turnbull's recruits in Leghorn were Greeks. There are no grounds, however, to substantiate such an opinion. This author did not manage to find any records of Leghorn related to this migration from there, despite his strenuous efforts and the kind assistance he received from Dr. Renato Orlandini, of the Office of Public Instruction of the Municipality of Livorno, and from Mr. Francisco Ferrero, the local historian of Livorno.

8. Turnbull to Shelburne, Mahón, July 10, 1767, Lansdowne MSS, Vol. 88, p. 135.   9. *Ibid.*

10. London, July 31, 1767, State Papers, Class 105, Vol. 119, hereafter indicated as: S. P. 105/119, pp. 228-29.

11. London, July 31, 1767, S. P. 105/119, p. 230.

12. Constantinople, Apr. 15, 1767 [in secret code—every letter represented by a number], S. P. 97/43, doc. 140-42.

13. Whitehall, June 5, 1767, S. P. 97/43, doc. 144.

14. Constantinople, Aug. 17, 1767, S. P. 97/43, doc. 174.

15. Turnbull to Shelburne, Minorca, Feb. 27, 1768; Lansdowne MSS, Vol. 88, f. 147.

16. Murray to Shelburne, Constantinople, Sept. 15, 1767, S. P. 97/43, doc. 184.

17. Smyrna of Asia Minor is given as the birthplace of Gaspar Papi or Pape by every census or other contemporary record; see Hassett, also census of 1783, census of 1787 (on Father Hassett's, as well as on all Spanish censuses of this period, see fn. 30). In the census of 1793 it is mentioned that

he was the son of Miguel [Michael] Papi and Catalina [Catherina] whose maiden name was Auas. The same maiden name of his mother is given by Father Pedro Camps' Register. The census of 1793 also states that Gaspar Papi was during that year 42 years old, implying the year 1751 as the year of his birth; see, also, Historical Records Survey, Division of Community Service Programs, Works Progress Administration, *Translation and Transcription of Church Archives in Florida, Roman Catholic Records, St. Augustine, Parish, White Baptisms, 1784-1792* (Tallahassee, Florida, 1941) Vol. 1, entries 171, 285, 443, and Vol. II [White Baptisms, 1792-1799] entry 12; hereafter these volumes will be respectively designated as "WPA I" and "WPA II." Papi's descendants carried his name down to the middle of the twentieth century.

18. WPA I, entries 20, 117, 306.

19. Grant to Shelburne, St. Augustine, Mar. 12, 1768, C. O. 5/549, p. 77.

20. Turnbull to Shelburne, Minorca, Feb. 27, 1768, Landsdowne MSS, Vol. 88, f. 147.

21. On the chronology of the various plagues from which area suffered during the eighteenth century, see Sakellariou, *op. cit.*, p. 119.

22. Several authors have described the sensitivity of the people of Mani in matters of honor which became the cause of feuds among local families. *Vendetta* has been practiced for centuries in Mani and exists elsewhere in this area only in Corsica. See Anastasios Goudas, *Bioi Paralleloi ton Andron tes Epanastaseos [Parallel Lives of the Men of the Revolution]* (Athens, 1875), VIII, d, ff.; Also, for the customs and life in Mani, the almost contemporary description by Col. William Martin Leake, *Travels in the Morea* (London, 1830), I, 200, 209, 241-43, 318, 332-39. For a more recent description of the native people and their customs, see Pat Leigh Fremor, *Mani* (Harpers, 1960).

23. This revolt finally took place in 1770, two years after the departure of Turnbull's settlers. Few Russian warships and about 1,000 inexperienced Russian soldiers arrived in Mani during that year under the leadership of the brothers Alexis and Theodore Orlov. They represented the "colossal forces" promised by the Russians. Greeks and Russians were successful at the beginning. However, when the Turks recovered from their surprise and saw how insignificant the Russian aid was, they attacked the revolutionists with superior forces and defeated them utterly. The Russians retreated and left with their ships for their country, abandoning the people they had incited to revolt. An unprecedented slaughtering of the people of Mani followed. About this revolt of 1770, and its preparation by Papazolis, see Apostolos V. Daskalakis, *E. Mane Kai e Othomanike Aftokratoria, 1453-1821 [Mani and the Ottoman Empire, 1453-1821]* (Athens, 1923), pp. 168-91; Sakellariou, *op. cit.*, pp. 148 ff. Constantine Paparregopoulos, *Istoria tou Ellenikou Ethnous [History of the Greek Nation]* (Athens, 1925), V part II 196-206; L. S. Stavrianos, *The Balkans since 1453* (New York, N. Y., Rinehart & Co., 1958), pp. 189-90.

24. Sakellariou, *op. cit.*, p. 154.

25. *Ibid.*, Kandeloros, *op. cit.*, pp. 56-57, 67.

26. Minorca, Feb. 27, 1768, Lansdowne MSS, Vol. 88, f. 147.

27. Originally published by Turnbull in the *Columbian Magazine*, Nov., 1788, pp. 683-88, found in P. Lee Phillips, *Notes on the Life and Works of Bernard Romans* (The Florida State Historical Society, 1924) p. 107.

NOTES — Chapter Two

28. Turnbull's itinerary after Coron is extremely obscure. What is described here is based on the documents of the British Colonial Office, of the Archives National of France, and on the birthplaces of some of the settlers. Nothing, however, excludes the possibility that some of the settlers joined Turnbull's company while residing in another place.

29. As it happens with most of the Greek names of the colonists, his name appears in the various records and censuses in a great variety of spellings: Fudelache, Tudelache, Pedulach, etc. All records state that he was "a native of Candia" or "of the Island of Candia in the Levant." The Spanish census of East Florida of 1783 states that "he is of the Greek Church," which constitutes a unique exception among the known compatriots of his who were converted Roman Catholics by that time. The Spanish census of East Florida of 1793 states that in that year Fundulakis was 45 years of age, implying that 1748 was the year of his birth.

30. Census of Father Thomas Hassett of 1786 [hereafter cited as "Hassett"]; also the Spanish census of East Florida of 1793. A brief but informative analysis of Father Hassett's census can be found in Joseph B. Lockey, "Public Education in Spanish St. Augustine," in *The Florida Historical Quarterly,* XV, 3 (Jan., 1937) 152-54. East Florida, especially the Saint Augustine area, possesses the oldest and most complete census of any part of the country now included in the United States. They are all of the Second Spanish Period destined to serve the colonial and financial policies of Spain, and their wealth of information is due to the Spanish passion for bureaucratic perfection. Copies of the following censuses of East Florida used in this study can be found in the East Florida Papers, box marked "Census Returns 1784-1814," of the Manuscripts Division of the Library of Congress, as well as in the archives of the St. Augustine Historical Society, where they have been also translated into English by the late Edward Lawson, sometime member of the Society; Spanish Census of 1784; the above mentioned Father Hassett's census of 1786; Spanish census of about January, 1790; Spanish census of 1793; Spanish census of 1813-14. All references hereafter to the above censuses, with the exception of Father Hassett's, will be designated by the year in which they were taken, preceded by the letter "c," i.e. "c. 1783."

31. Though no details can be found on this second trip to Smyrna, there is no doubt about it as it is evident especially from the records of the Levant Company. See letters of the Governors of the Levant Company to the British Consul at Smyrna, Anthony Hayes, London, Feb. 5, 1768, and May 17, 1768, in S. P. 105/119, pp. 244, 256.

32. Turnbull to Shelburne, Minorca, Feb. 27, 1768, Lansdowne MSS, Vol. 88, f. 147. In 1951 a controversy arose in Greece whether Modon or Coron was the port of embarkation of the Greek settlers and whether they came from the areas of Mani and Messenia or only from Messenia. N. I. Rozakos in "Unemployment in Mani and Migration," *Nea Estia,* L, 578 (Aug., 1951) supported the fact that the settlers came from both Mani and Messenia and that they had embarked at Coron; Takes E. Politopoulos in "Maniates in America," *Nea Estia,* L, 580, (Sept., 1951) maintained that the settlers came from Messenia and left for Florida from the port of Modon. It is evident that both authors have derived their information from secondary sources.

In connection with the question of the settlers' place of origin, Turnbull has stated (*supra*) explicitly that those with him were "from among a people who inhabit a chain of mountains which makes the southernmost promontory of the Peloponnese," and he excluded Messenia by stating that these people prefer to cultivate the little pieces of ground they find among the mountains to living "under Tyranny in the fertile and extensive plains under them." Moreover, Turnbull has described the mode of life of these people, their struggles, government, customs, internal feuds, all unique characteristics of the area of Mani only. On the other hand, in all records and censuses of East Florida there is not a single case of a settler coming from Messenia; on the contrary, there are settlers whose birthplace is stated either as Mayne or Manya or Brazzo di Mayna. See, for instance, the records on Ioannis or Juan Giannopoulos, or Joannopoly, or Goannoply, or Janopli, or Chanaply, or Genopoli as his name appeared corrupted and Hispanized, in, c. 1787, c. 1793, Hassett. In entry 12 of the year 1778 in Marriages, Father Camps' Register, as well as in entries of Jan. 13, 1790, and Dec. 2, 1793, of White Marriages, 1784-1801, Book A, translated from Records at the Catholic Bishops' Residence, St. Augustine [described in the archives of the St. Augustine Historical Society], Giannopoulos is stated as coming from the village of Skoutari of Mani, being the son of George Giannopoulos and of Maria, whose maiden name was Canelas or Caneli. The same can be observed about Kyriakos or Domingo Exarhopoulos, or Hedzarcopoly, or Estarcopoly, or Sercopoly whose birthplace has been indicated as "Brazo di Mayna di Levante"; see Hassett, also WPA II, entries 110 and 510. It is rather improbable that settlers from Messenia, if any, could have died without leaving the slightest trace behind them. It is true that both Pouqueville, *op. cit.*, and d'Eschavannes, *op. cit.*, narrating in an identical way the departure of the Greek settlers for Florida, speak about "Messenians." It was, however, a custom of eighteenth- and nineteenth-century historians to refer to the whole southeastern section of Peloponnesos in a general way as "Messenia," and Col. Leake in his map of Messenia has included the whole section of Mani.

As for the port of embarkation, it is clear from Turnbull's letter to Lord Shelburne of Feb. 27, 1768, that Turnbull had his settlers already with him when he approached Modon; that he sent ashore a boat with ten men only who were detained by the Turkish authorities, as Turnbull says "on pretext of my having some of the Grand Seignior's subjects on board the ships then with me." Coron, moreover, has been mentioned by both Pouqueville, *op. cit.*, and d'Eschavannes, *op. cit.*, as the port of embarkation. This is the closest port to Mani and a logical place of departure for people coming from this area. Also, all records agree that the recruiting of settlers from Mani took place in Sept., 1767, while the incident at Modon took place sometime at the beginning of Jan., 1768. However, Abbé Raynal, in his *A Philosophical and Political History of the Settlements and Trade of the Europeans in the East and West Indies* (London, 1790), VI, 76, gives Modon as the port of embarkation, and this information has been repeated by others; see John Lee Williams, *The Territory of Florida* (New York: A. T. Goodrich, 1837) p. 188. The manner employed by Abbé Raynal in writing his history is well known: he used to ask various persons familiar with certain topics to write on them and then Raynal incorporated their contribution in his history without even acknowledging the authors. It is not known who wrote the section on New Smyrna for Abbé Raynal. Whoever the original author was, however, it seems that he had heard about Turnbull's incident at Modon and confused it with the place of embarkation. Turnbull's account, however, leaves no doubt that Modon was approached when he already had the Greek colonists aboard his ships.

The "present" offered by Turnbull to the Turkish commander of the garrison brings forth another question of a similar present made by him earlier. Both Pouqueville, *op. cit.,* and d'Eschavannes, *op. cit.,* mention that Turnbull bribed the Turkish commander at Coron, giving him 1,200 piastres in order to obtain permission for taking his settlers. This information has been repeated by several authors; Bernard Romans asserts that Turnbull had paid £400, in Philips, *op. cit.,* p. 42; the same sum is repeated by John Lee Williams, *op. cit.,* p. 188. Abbé Raynal, *op. cit.,* affirms that the sum given was 100 guineas. This information is very probable, since bribing was a safe and traditional way of persuading a Turkish authority.

33. French National Archives of Foreign Affairs, B¹ 1058. See also Nicholas G. Svoronos, *E Ellenike Paroikia tes Minorkas* [*The Greek Colony of Minorca. A Contribution to the History of the Greek Merchant Marine during the 18th Century*], Mélanges offers à Octave et Melpo Merlier (Athens, 1953), pp. 19 f.

34. *Op. cit.,* pp. 77-78.

THREE

Visions of the "New Atlantis"

O N FEBRUARY 1, 1768, Turnbull again entered the deep waters of the port of Mahon.[1] No one ever crosses the mouth of this natural harbor without a feeling of relief and security. This is perhaps what Turnbull and his men felt when they started to sail the three-mile length of this narrow tongue of sea that cuts into the rocky coast of the island. The water there is still and transparent, untrammeled by the north winds that whip the island during the winter. The rolling hills to the right offer a welcoming protection. And far in the harbor there are the hospitable stony houses of Mahón, tightly built on the sunny slopes.

Turnbull passed the castle of San Felipe, the formidable guardian of the port in older times, that lay high on the cliffs to the left, and then he continued toward the little island of Lazareto where he and his men were placed under quarantine.[2]

When he finally came ashore, he was delighted to find that his affairs had developed in a very satisfactory way. In the long quay of the port, among the ships moored side by side, he recognized one of his own that had arrived before him loaded with passengers for Florida. And there was another one coming with 200 Greeks aboard.[3]

Among the new arrivals, many came from Corsica.[4] Surprisingly enough, however, the names of most of them were Greek, such as Nicholas Stefanopoli,[5] Georgios Stefanopoli,[6] Antonios Stefanopoli,[7] Petros Drimarachis,[8] Petros Cosifachis,[9] and Michael Costas.[10] Their unexpected presence in Corsica was but a small part of those dramatic movements of people who are uprooted by war and conquest and are tossed to a foreign land.

The tragedy of these Greeks from Corsica, who comprised the third major group of Turnbull's recruits, began in 1669, when the island of Crete fell into the hands of the Turks, and thus ended a twenty-year war between the Venetians and the Ottoman Empire. It was then that the people of Mani on the mainland of Greece, had found themselves in a very precarious position. They had previously allied themselves with the Venetians in order to stop the westward expansion of the Turks. They were determined to stay free and they had fought desperately all these years. As soon as Crete fell and their Venetian allies were defeated, Mani felt the whole pressure of the Ottoman Empire. Promises and threats, reprisals, campaigns, and the building of Turkish castles at the outskirts of their area had made the life of the people of Mani unbearable.

During this time one of the most prominent families in Mani, the Medici, decided to migrate to Tuscany, Italy, the place of origin of their progenitors. They were descendants of Pedro de Medici, of the celebrated family of Florence, who in 1385 established himself in Athens. There, his relative Nerio Acciaioli had become the Duke of Athens. Pedro de Medici married an Athenian young lady, and his many descendants lived in that city until 1456 when Athens was conquered by the Turks. Then most of the Medici went to Mani where they became one of the first families.[11] Some of them had kept the name Medici, and some had translated it into the Greek *Iatros* or *Yatrakos*.

For more than two centuries the Medici of Mani had kept their contacts with their contemporary and distant relatives of Florence, and in 1663 they had decided to migrate to Italy. This plan, however, had not materialized then. In 1670, when the Turkish pressure over Mani had been alarmingly increased, once again they decided to leave Greece. They came in contact with the Grand Duke of Tuscany, Cosimo III de Medici, and they signed with him contracts providing for land grants, arrangements of their religious status, and various other aspects of their future life in Italy. Then, early in 1671, three hundred families, including about fifteen hundred men, women, and children related to the Medici, left Mani for Italy and settled in various places of Tuscany.[12]

Five years later, in 1675, the second mass migration from Mani

41

took place when the whole clan of Stefanopoli, for almost the same reasons as those of the Medici, decided to leave and go to Corsica. They had sent a representative of their family, John Koutsikalis, to scout Italy and find a proper place for their colony. Koutsikalis had visited the Pope in Rome and for some time had wandered in the courts of Italian princes without being able to find favorable terms for the planned colonization. Finally, he had approached the Genoese Republic, where his efforts met with success.[13]

Immediately providing land and protection, the Genoese, who dominated Corsica, were glad to aid the settlers from Mani. But actually the Genoese themselves were in need of help. The whole island of Corsica had been restless for some time; the Corsicans wanted their independence. Revolutions (destined to continue for more than a century) disturbed and exhausted the Genoese government. With settlers coming from Mani, trained in arms, experienced in war, the Genoese could very well form a bulwark against the revolutionists, so they were more than happy to help this colonization.

In 1676, 730 men, women, and children, of whom 430 were members of the Stefanopoli family, having with them their bishop, Parthenios Kalkandes, and their priests, arrived in Genoa. They signed an agreement with the Genoese Republic on January 18, 1676, the main terms of which were the following: the colonists were to recognize the supremacy of the Pope in every religious matter, though their rites would continue to be according to the Greek Orthodox Church in the same manner as the rest of the Uniates of Italy; after the death of their bishop and priests, their clergymen were to be appointed by the Vatican; they were to build houses and churches at their own expense; the Republic was to give them the land for three villages; the settlers were to be considered subjects of the Republic, serve her in land and sea, and pay the regular taxes; the settlers might organize campaigns against the Turks and might use the flag of the Genoese Republic; the Republic was to carry the settlers to Corsica at its own expense.[14]

In March 14, 1676, the Stefanopoli and the other settlers left Genoa and established themselves in three Corsican villages of Paomia, Revinda, and Salongo. With their industry and determination to make a new life, they prospered, introducing new agricultural methods and developing the trade of this area.

This was the largest Greek migration to Corsica since 560 B.C., when some other Greeks, the Phocaeans of Ionia, built Aleria and established a numerous colony there. As it happened, however, with the ancient Phocaeans, who continously had troubles with the native islanders, so it happened with the settlers from Mani this time.

The Corsicans did not like these Greeks. They did not fail to realize why their Genoese oppressors brought them there. They considered these foreigners as people who grabbed Corsican lands and who were willing to fight against the cause of Corsican freedom. Consequently, the settlers were attacked at every opportunity. When, in 1730, the Corsicans started a large-scale revolution, protesting against the heavy Genoese taxation, they asked the help of the Greek villages. The latter, however, honoring their agreement with the Genoese and faithful to them, refused to cooperate with the revolutionists and therefore became a major target. Only long war experience and boldness saved them from complete destruction. In 1737, however, after a bloody battle between the Greeks and the Corsicans, the former, despite their victory, abandoned their villages and came to Ajaccio, the capital of the island. There they joined the Genoese gendarmerie and were used for the suppression of the revolution.[15]

What a fate for them! They had left their country to escape bloodshed, war, and troubles and had come to Corsica to find a peaceful life; instead, they found themselves involved in everything they wanted to avoid: they had considerably changed their Christian dogma, placing themselves under the auspices of the Roman Pope; they had lost again their lands and their homes; and they had been transformed into mercenaries fighting against a patriot like Pasquale Paoli, and his revolutionists, who strived to gain independence.

By 1767, the Genoese were convinced that they could not keep the island any longer and they initiated negotiations to cede Corsica to France. The treaty was signed in 1768 and France took over, but it was just before the conclusion of this treaty that Turnbull's scheme came into the picture.

During that time, uncertainty and confusion disquieted the Greeks of Corsica. Their numbers had been considerably decreased because of the continuous fights against the revolutionists.[16] In the past they had tied their fate with the Genoese, but now these were leaving, transferring the Greeks to Corsica's new masters, the French. Nobody knew what would happen under the new regime. Any sense of security had been seriously disturbed. They considered for some time attempting another mass migration, to Spain, but after long negotiations their plans had been frustrated.[17] Some, however, left for

Minorca, for Leghorn, and especially for Sardinia, where they were massacred by the Sardinians.[18] In troubled days like those, Turnbull's invitation for Florida settlers was very appealing; it is not strange that so many of them decided to join Turnbull and escape to the New World.[19]

With his Greeks, Italians, and Corsicans, Turnbull had gathered the 500 settlers whom he originally planned to take with him.[20] Their number, however, was augmented every day. First, several of the Italians made their contributions. During the leisurely eight months of waiting at Mahón for Turnbull's return, these Italian men, sensitive to beauty and unable to resist the charms of the Mahonese young ladies, married these local girls. When Turnbull returned, he not only approved of, but encouraged, such unions.[21]

Over three years previous to this time famine had spread all over Minorca, bringing despair to the poor islanders. For several consecutive years there was a failure of crops.[22] Few fields in the world had seen so much human care as the scattered patches of land over this rocky and barren island. The Minorcans had cleared these fields, afterward using the rocks to build long dry-stone walls to protect the crops from the violent winds that blow hard over the island from time to time. Under continual cultivation the exhausted soil had yielded somewhat less than daily bread. Fruits and vegetables came from the several *barrancos,* old ravines covered with rich deposits brought down from the hills by torrents and floods. Fish was not enough, and meat and fowl scarce. A failure of crops meant starvation for the island; and this is what had happened during the three years previous to Turnbull's arrival.[23]

Then, in the summer of 1767, Turnbull left his Italians at Mahón. Their stories about a migration to the land of promise reached every islander and excited their imagination. When Turnbull returned the next February, people from Cuidadela—the ancient capital of the island with the milk-white houses—from Mercadal, from Fornells, from the adjacent little island of Colon, from San Felipe, from San Cristóbal, and from all over Minorca came to Mahón and pleaded with Turnbull to take them along to Florida. It was a desperate movement of a people who for centuries had experienced some of the most terrible disasters and calamities.

The great sin of Minorca was its location, so conveniently close to France, Spain, Italy, and Africa, and the fact that it possessed the best natural port of the Mediterranean area, able to shelter a whole fleet—an ideal naval base; and for this sin its inhabitants, since the very olden times, had had to experience bloody wars and ruthless oppression, poverty and exploitation, and plunders and raids.[24]

This time, however, it was nature that forced these people to leave their homes and seek a place in the crowded ships that were leaving for Florida, becoming the fourth and the most numerous group of Turnbull's men. With the other Minorcans who decided to leave the island were some members of the Greek colony of Mahón, like John Grammatos,[25] the one mentioned in Archibald Menzies' memorial.[26] They had been established there since 1745 when the British, in a period of strong Anglo-French rivalry, allowed them to found their colony and escape the Ottoman yoke. They were mostly sea captains and merchants, and soon their community prospered and augmented its numbers, reaching, sometime by the middle of the eighteenth century, 2,000 members. They had their own church and cemetery, and part of their wealth was the result of their privateering activities under the British flag. Their main target was the French merchant marine against which their fast, well-armed ships dealt serious blows. The French were gravely concerned with these "Angligrecs" as they used to call the Greeks from Mahón; and, of course, as soon as they captured Minorca in 1756, they ousted them. The Greek families were pushed to adjacent locations, mainly to Gibraltar and Leghorn. When Minorca became British again in 1763, they came back. This time they were the people who had suffered on account of their struggles for the British Empire. The latter, in recognition, bestowed upon them many favors, not merely the old privileges such as the monopoly of salt-making and various fishing privileges, but now new offers of fields and coastal property, tax exemptions, and government contracts. These very favors, however, became the cause of animosity which the local population felt against the Greeks, who were not only Greek Orthodox in a solidly Roman Catholic island, but were foreigners, brought there by the British who dominated the island. In their official complaints to the British government the islanders never failed to protest the favors the Governor granted the Greeks. It seems that life in Mahón became very unpleasant for a great number of Greeks. When the lure of the New World was added to this, Turnbull's venture to Florida was very appealing and several Greeks joined him.

Turnbull was delighted. After George Grenville became a partner of his company, the area of land comprising New Smyrna increased constantly and it was soon destined to reach 101,400 acres.[27] New settlers would be needed to people this extensive area and it was better to take them now than to try to find them later when this golden opportunity might have gone. All around him were poor islanders desiring to join him. If he had only known the situation of the island earlier, he might have stayed there, taking all the settlers he wanted from Minorca and avoiding the adventures of his Archipelago journey that had cost him so much time, trouble, and money.

By March 28, 1768, about 1,200 men, women, and children were on board Turnbull's ships and ready to leave.[28] All the preparations had been finished. The notaries public of Mahón had never before seen such a rush as the one during the last days of March of that year. Powers of attorney had been signed; houses, vineyards, and other property had been sold; dowries had been granted; inheritance rights were transferred. The islanders wanted to leave everything in order before starting what they thought of as a journey of no return.[29]

Turnbull during the same time had much to do, too. The main problem was to feed and maintain so many people in a place where, as he soon found, there was such a great scarcity.[30] Fortunately, his new friend, Governor Johnston, was most helpful; as he later confessed, he could never have surmounted the various obstacles he encountered in Minorca without Johnston's aid.[31]

Another important task of Turnbull's was the signing of contracts and the completion of the agreements with his settlers. Many years later, speaking on this subject, Turnbull asserted that he had signed contracts with all his colonists.[32] But it is very clear that he could not possibly have done so with all of them. How could he have found the time to sign such documents with settlers whom he tried to smuggle out of the Ottoman Empire under the vigilant eyes of the Turkish authorities? Or with the almost 200 Minorcan stowaways whom he discovered in his ships when ready to sail from Mahón? However, he could have made agreements, not necessarily written—and this is what had happened. In these, the terms and conditions varied, depending on the case of the settler and the circumstances of his recruitment.[33]

The terms of the contract which Turnbull seems to have signed in certain cases, were very clearly stated.[34] Turnbull was obliged to transport his men, who were "to work on the cultivation of the lands as countrymen and farmers," at his own expense and provide and maintain them with what was necessary for living "until the productive lands may be delivered to them. And they will be assigned the piece of land which they themselves judge them able and capable of power to cultivate."

When the lands would start producing, the farmers would take what would "be sufficient and enough for their nourishment," and then from the harvest of produce the payments were to be taken to reimburse Turnbull for his expenses made for them. When this would take place, "the products will be one half Mr. Turnbull's and the other half in equal proportion will belong to the countrymen and farmers who cultivate the lands in equal portion of what the lands produce."

Then it was made clear that "Mr. Turnbull, within the time of ten years, can neither discharge nor take from his service any of the below signed contractors, and equally none of them can separate from his service before having completed the ten years." Finally it was added that "when the contract with Mr. Turnbull is finished, each head of a family will have one hundred English quarters of land for himself, and fifty for each person of his family, and it will be as his property, and as land established in ownership forever, being a royal grant." There was, also, the following explanation added: "N.B. One hundred and sixty quarters of land have a perimeter of two English miles."[35]

Much later Turnbull himself explained the terms of the contracts quite lengthily. Speaking of himself in the third person, he stated:

The doctor offered them leases for ninety nine years, wishing to fix them and their children, though the terms were more advantageous to them than to the doctor; the agreement of farming lease (signed by him and them in Europe) being that the whole of the expense after their landing in East Florida should be paid out of the first produce; that they were to cultivate the same lands for ten years more on shares with the proprietor; that is, they were to share the net produce equally, the proprietor's share being to reimburse the expences of bringing them to America, the whole, however, of the expence of maintaining the farmer and his family was first to be taken from the gross produce, before the division mentioned was made, so that the farmer's share, for the most part, could not be less than two-thirds, even from good crops, but in a bad season, these expences would take the whole, which actually happened to the lazy and indolent; by this agreement the farmer was always certain of a living, for even in a total failure of a crop, the proprietor could not suffer the farmer to starve.[36]

As a whole, then, the settlers agreed to come to Florida as tenants who should divide the products of their land equally with Turnbull, letting him first withdraw the expenses he had incurred for their maintenance since their arrival in Florida but not for their transportation. They also agreed to serve him for several years, the majority of the settlers between five to eight years, before they would acquire, either as lessees or as full owners, a certain amount of land.[37]

On March 28, Turnbull thought that he was entirely ready. He put his 1,200 men in six ships and wrote a letter to Lord Shelburne that the next day, on March 29, he planned to leave for Gibraltar.[38]

Just before his departure, however, fearing that about a hundred of his recruits had deserted him and needing to know the accurate number in order to buy refreshments and provisions at Gibraltar, he decided to count his men again. To his great surprise, and a very pleasant one indeed, he found his people "being upwards of fourteen hundred men." The "intruders" were "able husbandmen who found means to get on to ships with the others."[39]

This new development caused a new delay. Fortunately, a Danish ship was found which could transport the surplus crowd as far as Gibraltar. On March 31, Turnbull and his men finally left hospitable Mahón.[40]

The wind was favorable and within four days they arrived at the Rock.[41] The cruising of the Mediterranean in April can be very pleasant and relaxing, but it was not so in this case. The Barbary pirates were active in these waters and only recently an Algerian cruiser had attacked Dutch and French ships. Among the men in Turnbull's ships anxiety and agony reigned; with foreboding they all anticipated possible troubles with the pirates who had struck terror in the hearts of so many people. But Turnbull had secured the protection of the British frigate *Carysfort* whose skipper, Captain Vandeput, took "the greatest care imaginable" to safeguard his ships from Minorca to Gibraltar.

Otherwise the trip was pleasant and to Turnbull's delight his crowd had "increased five by births since [they] left Mahón."[42] In Gibraltar, Turnbull finished his preparations for the long voyage. He was lucky to find there two English ships, smaller than the Danish one, but large enough to carry the load of the latter. Commodore Spry ordered the *Carysfort* to continue escorting the small fleet as far as the Madeiras. When everything was ready, all eight ships sailed from Gibraltar for the open seas on April 17, 1768. They were carrying 1,403 colonists: *Charming Betsy* carried 232 persons; *Henry and Carolina*, 142; *Elizabeth*, 190; *Friendship*, 198; *New Fortune*, 226;

Hope, 150; *American Soldier,* 145; *Betsey,* 120.[43] Some of these people, like the Minorcans, were escaping to the New World to secure freedom from starvation; some, like the Corsicans, because they longed for freedom from bloodshed and war; some, like the Italians, because they wanted freedom from persecution, uncertainty, and misery; and some, like the Greeks, because they desired freedom from tyranny and oppression. Among them perhaps several were seeking adventure, but all the ships were loaded with dreams and hopes and plans for a new life.

The British officials anxiously followed the departure of these settlers. As soon as Lord Hillsborough heard about it, he immediately wrote to Governor Grant that there were on their way to Florida "upwards of a thousand colonists Greeks and others" and that "this will be a noble addition to your Infant Settlement and I shall be very glad to hear of their safe arrival."[44]

Turnbull also, looking at the eight vessels scattered at a distance one from another in the wide sea, rolling on the choppy waters with their sails swollen and their bows cutting the ocean in the direction of the New World, must have had a feeling of deep satisfaction. He had with him almost three times the number of colonists he had wanted to find when he started his wanderings. This was a veritable achievement, because no one before had ever managed to bring so many people in one trip to colonize an American area. This task had been accomplished thanks to his own courageous persistence, to the support of the British government, to the financial backing of his partners, and to the paternal protection offered him by his powerful friend, Lord Shelburne.

Turnbull was not one of those guilty of ingratitude, especially toward the services rendered to him by Lord Shelburne. He searched for an appropriate gift, something that his Lordship would really like. In a period when neoclassicism was so much *en vogue* and Renaissance revivals adorned so many mansions, Turnbull had a brilliant idea. Somewhere in Greece he divested a temple of Venus of several sculptures and sent them directly to the home of Lord Shelburne. Later, after Turnbull arrived in Florida, being anxious to learn if they had arrived at their destination, he wrote to his protector:

My friend Mr. Humphreys has taken them under his care, and promises to see them carried to your house. I left some other Marbles in Mr. Davis's hands to be forwarded to your Lordship. I shall be sorry if they have not been forwarded as there was an Alt Relief of a Venus

49

NEW SMYRNA

at her Toilet, among them, not a despicable piece; others were worth little. I meant them as a Testimony of my Endeavors to execute your Commands.[45]

NOTES — Chapter Three

1. Johnston to Shelburne, Mahón, Feb. 3, 1768, C.O. 174/5, p. 22. Turnbull in his letter to Lord Shelburne from Minorca of Feb. 27, *op. cit.,* said that he arrived there on the 3d. He evidently means that he landed there on the 3d, after being under quarantine for two days.   2. *Ibid.*
3. Turnbull to Shelburne, Minorca, Feb. 27, 1768, *op. cit.*
4. Though Turnbull in his letter to Lord Shelburne from Leghorn on June 15, 1767, Lansdowne MSS Vol. 88, f. 141, stated that he had taken measures to recruit settlers "from the South of France and from several parts of Italy," there is not the slightest evidence that he himself had visited Corsica. It is most probable that those who came from there were recruited by Turnbull's agent Edward Pumell and dispatched to Minorca via Leghorn.
5. C. 1783; Hassett; c. 1787; c. 1793 states that he was the son of Charles and Martha Stefanopoli, and that he was 45 years of age, implying the year 1748 as his birth date; c. 1813, however, gives his age as 60, indicating 1753 as the year of his birth. See, also Father Camps' Register, entry 22 of the year 1775, entry 1 of the year 1777, entry 11 of the year 1778, entry 25 of the year 1780, entry 14 of the year 1783. Also, WPA I, entries 34, 84, 207, and WPA II, entry 51. The name Stefanopoli, hispanicised, had suffered many corruptions in Florida, and in the various records and censuses is found as Stephanopoly, Estefanople, Estepanopoli, Estefanoply, Estefanobili, Estanople.
6. C. 1783; c. 1784.
7. C. 1783; also, Father Camps' Register, entry 19 of the year 1771, entry 2 of the year 1772, and entry 7 of the year 1778.
8. C. 1783; Hassett; c. 1787. Also, in Father Camps' Register, entry 19 of the year 1774, entry 12 of the year 1776, entry 7 of the year 1778, entry 16 of the year 1780. His name appears as Drimarachi, Drimarari, Drimarere, Madrari, Madraxi.
9. C. 1783; Hassett; c. 1787; c. 1793 states that he was that year 41 years of age, implying that he was born in 1752. Also that he was the son of Theodore and Martha whose name was "Noxachisa." See, also, Father Camps' Register, entry 2 of the year 1779, entry 6 of the year 1779, entry 14 of the year 1781, entry 9 of the year 1781, entry 6 of the year 1782, entry 22 of the year 1783, WPA I, entry 109; also, in Marriages, Father Camps' Register, entry 4, 1778. His name appears as Cosifacho, Cocifacio, Cosifaxi, Cosifachi.
10. C. 1783; c. 1787. His name appears as Costs, Acosta, Costas.
11. On the history of the Medici branch in Athens and Mani, see Ferdinand Gregorovius, *Istoria tes Poleos Athenon kata tous Mesous Aionas* [*History of the City of Athens during the Middle Ages*] translated into Greek by Spyridon P. Lambros (Athens, 1904), II, 232, fn. 2; also, pp. 670 ff., pp. 738 ff., pp. 741 ff. Jean A. Buchon, *Nouvelles recherches historique sur la Principauté française de Morée et ses hautes baronies* (Paris, 1845) I, 131, 276. [Fr.] Miclosich-Muller, *Acta et diplomata Graeca medii aevi* (Vindobonae, 1865) III, 248-53. Constantine Sathas, *Monumenta Hellenicae historiae* (Paris, 1880-90) VIII, 370, 407. See, also, Daskalakis, *op. cit.,* p. 61, fn. 1.
12. The relative documents including the correspondence of the Medici of Mani with the Grand Dukes of Tuscany, Fernandino Medici 2d and Cosimo Medici 3d, their decrees and contracts, have been located by the late Professor Spyridon P. Lambros in both the Public Archives of Venice and those of Flor-

NOTES — *Chapter Three*

ence and they are now found in the latter in *Real Archivio di stato, Miscellanea Medicea Doc. di Corredo filza XXVI, No. 11*, and they are labelled *Trattati e Capitoli corsi tra il Ser^mo Gran Duca Ferdinando 2⁰: et i Greci de Braccio di Maina nel 1663 rinovati poi da medesimi con Cosimo 3: nel 1670 per transferirsi molte delle loro Famiglie nel Dominio di Toscana;* they are published in their original Italian and Greek forms by Lambros in "The Migration of Maniates to Tuscany during the Seventeenth Century," *Neos Hellenomnemon*, II (1905) 396-434. The fate of this colony in Tuscany has been written by A. Moustoxydis, in *Hellenomnemon* (Athens, 1846), pp. 265 ff.

13. G. G. Papadopoulos, *Chronographia peri tes Katagoges ton en Mane Stefanopoulon, tes aftothen eis Korsiken Apoikeseos* &c. [*Chronography on the Origin of the Stefanopoli of Mani and their Migration from there to Corsica*] (Athens, 1845), p. 19. Papadopoulos included in this study a unique chronicle written by a priest, Nicholas Stefanopoli, of Corsica, in Aug. 26, 1738, narrating the early adventures of the colony until 1738. Although the material related to the colony of Mani in Corsica and deposited in the archives of Genoa and Ajaccio has not as yet been fully explored, there is a great deal of literature dealing with this incident. Besides the description of this Greek colony found in almost every history of Corsica, the following monographs are the most significant. Nicholas B. Fardys, *Yle kai Skarifema Istorias tes en Korsike Ellenikes Paroikias* [*Material and Draft of a History of the Greek Colony in Corsica*] (Athens, 1888). During the years 1886-87, Dr. Fardys was the teacher of the Greek school of the village of Cargese, Corsica, where most of the descendants of the early colonists live. Using the archives of the Prefecture of·Ajaccio, the documents collection of the Stefanopoli who live in Corsica, and the baptismal, marriage, and death records of Cargese, he wrote an informative history of that colony. To this he had added a collection of songs, proverbs, vocabulary, and other Greek folk-lore material found among the Greeks of Corsica by the end of the nineteenth century; Papadopoulos, *op. cit.*; Nicolas Stephanopoli, *Histoire de la colonie grèque établie en Corse* (Paris, 1826); P. Stephanopoli, *Histoire de la colonie grèque établie en Corse* (Pise, 1836); Demetrios Gr. Kambouroglou, "Peri tes apo tes Manes eis ten Neson Kyrnon Ellenikes Apoikias" ["About the Greek Colony from Mani in the Island of Corsica"], *Hebdomas* II, 61 (April 1885), 179-92; G. G. Papadopoulos, "Asmata Demotika ton en Korsike Ellenon," ["Folk-songs of the Greeks in Corsica"], *Pandora*, XV, 353 (Dec. 1864) 413-20, including a few marriage records since 1724; Smaragda D. Mostratou, *Kargeze, To Elleniko Horio tes Korsikes* [*Cargese, the Greek Village of Corsica*] (Athens, 1963). The most complete study, however, is Dr. Gerard Blanken's *Les Grècs de Cargése (Corse), Recherches sur leur langue et sur leur histoire* (Leyden, Holland, 1951).

14. Fardys, *op. cit.*, pp. 39-41; Daskalakis, *op. cit.*, pp. 128-29.

15. Fardys, *op. cit.*, p. 71.

16. Daskalakis, *op. cit.*, pp. 143-44, comparing the censuses of Ajaccio, notes that according to the census of 1740 there were 812 Greeks, while in the census of 1773 there were only 428 left.　　　　　　　　　　17. *Ibid.*

18. See Blanken, *op. cit.*, I, 8.

19. The Florida censuses of the second Spanish period imply that the Greeks from Corsica were mostly of a very young age. It seems that the bulk of their families remained behind in Corsica and the names of the Stefanopoli, Drimarakis, Cosifachis, and others are found in records deposited in the Archives de la Corse, in Ajaccio, such as: 68/c 76; 69/c 77; 70/c 77; 71/c 77.

20. Though we know that the number of Italians was 110, and we have one statement about the Greeks from Corsica that they were 70, the exact number

NOTES — Chapter Three

of the Greeks who were recruited in Greece is unknown. The information, however, leading to an approximate estimate of their number is the following: Both Pouqueville and d'Eschavannes speak about Turnbull having "ships" and not one ship at Coron. The French Consul of Smyrna, Asia Minor, Peyssonnel, in his report of Jan. 28, 1768, says that Turnbull stopped in Peloponnesos with two ships. Turnbull, himself, narrating the Modon incident also speaks about "ships"; in his letter to Lord Shelburne from Minorca, on Feb. 27, 1768, he clearly indicates that there were three of them when he says: "I arrived in this island (Minorca) the third of this month [Feb., 1768] after a long passage from Turkey. One of my ships with passengers for Florida got in here before me, & I am in daily expectation of a third ship with 200 Greeks. These added to the men, women and children now with me will make nigh a thousand of them." Shipping during these days, as Turnbull himself stated in another letter to Lord Shelburne of Apr. 4, 1768, was not only expensive but also difficult to find. He, being a good Scotsman, would never hire another ship without needing it badly and before exhausting the shipping capacity with him. Thus it is evident that the ships with him were loaded with people. He stated that the third one was carrying 200 Greeks; the capacity of the other two is not known but his own would hardly be the smallest. The minimum number of settlers in each of the ships must have been 100. Thus, approximately 500 were recruited in Greece.

21. Turnbull to Shelburne, Minorca, Feb. 27, 1768; Lansdowne MSS, Vol. 88, f. 147.

22. Bishop of Minorca to the King of Spain, Palma, Feb. 5, 1771 in Annie Averette, trans., *The Unwritten History of Old St. Augustine* (St. Augustine, Fla.: Record Co., 1909), p. 202.   23. Corse, *op. cit.*, p. 32.

24. On the history of Minorca see Clements R. Markham, *The Story of Majorca and Minorca* (London, 1908); Frederick Chamberlain, *The Balearics and Their Peoples* (London, 1927); Juan Victory, *Guide of Minorca* (Mahón, 1948); Mario Verdaquer, *op. cit.*; J. Mascaro Pasarius, *Mapa de la Isla de Menorca* (Mahón, 1953).

25. John Grammatos' name appears in several documents concerning this Greek colony deposited in the Archives of Mahón. Later, in Father Camps' Register he is listed as a godfather of Franco J. A. Troti, whose baptism took place on Mar. 3, 1773, in New Smyrna; he was also godfather of Clara M. Segui by proxy on Mar. 4, 1779, at St. Augustine as his proxy served another Greek, Petros Cosifachis.

26. *Op. cit.*, p. 7. About this colony, see Nicholas G. Svoronos, *op. cit.*; Francisco Hernandez Sanz, "La Colonia Griega establecida en Mahón durante el siglo XVIII," in *Revista de Menorca*, XX (1925), 327-408. To this study 26 documents have been attached; F. H. Marshall, "A Greek Community in Minorca," *The Slavonic and East European Review*, XI (1932-33), 100-107. Most of the records covering this colony can be found among those of the Colonial Office and at the Municipal Archives of Mahón.

27. Treasury 77/7, Mar. 9, 1781.

28. Turnbull to Shelburne, Mahón, Mar. 28, 1768, Lansdowne MSS, Vol. 88, f. 151.

29. In the Municipal Archives of Mahón can be found several of these notarized deeds in the files of Notary Bartholomé Deyá, Book 3, f. 94, 103, 129; Notary Ramon Ballester, Book 86, f. 143, 147, 148, 149, 150, 152; Notary Andrés Vila, Book 265, f. 229, 231, 233, 246.

30. Turnbull to Shelburne, Minorca, Feb. 27, 1768, Lansdowne MSS, Vol. 88, f. 147.   31. *Ibid.*   32. Phillips, *op. cit.*, p. 108.

33. This is especially evident from a number of court depositions under oath

made later, in which the terms of the agreements are explained by numerous settlers. None, however, speaks about written contracts, but about "agreements." See C. O. 5/557, pp. 429-32, 435-36, 437-38, 439-40, 441-42, 443, 445-47, 449, 453, 457, 461, 463, 465, 467, 469, 471, 473, 475, 477, 479.

34. A copy of this contract dated Feb. 11, 1768, written in Spanish and signed by Turnbull only, has been found in the Municipal Archives of Mahón, and a copy of it has been deposited at the Archives of the St. Augustine Historical Society. An English translation of this contract has been published in the *St. Augustine Record*, Sept. 2, 1953.

35. Which is, of course, the size of an American quarter of a section and makes the size of one English quarter of land equivalent to one acre.

36. Phillips, *op. cit.*, pp. 107-8.

37. There is a great confusion in the various sources concerning the nature of the settlers' indenture, the length of their service, and the amount of land they would receive after their service. Melirrytos, *op. cit.*, wrote that the colonists came to Florida as "tenants," and later Governor Grant highly praised the principle of sharing the crops applied in New Smyrna. (C. O. 5/541, pp. 423,424.); Henry Siebert, in his *Loyalists in East Florida, 1774-1785* (Florida, 1929), II, 325, col. 2, asserted that they came as "indented servants." In connection with the length of their service, the several deponents, all of whom were settlers, in court depositions taken under oath at a later period, stated that they had to serve between five to eight years; Johann David Schoepf in his *Travels in the Confederation* (Philadelphia, 1911), p. 234, asserted that the period was between seven to eight years; and with him agreed Siebert, *Loyalists;* Williams, *op. cit.*, said that it was three years service only; the copy of contract at the Municipal Archives of Mahón and Turnbull himself give the time of service as ten years; Bernard Romans, who passionately disliked Turnbull, stated that the latter "granted them [the settlers] a pitiful portion of land for ten years, upon the plan of the feudal system: this being improved and just rendered fit for cultivation, at the end of that term it again reverts to the original grantor, and the grantee, may, if he chooses, begin a new cycle of vassalage for ten years more" (in Phillips, *op. cit.*, p. 104). As far as the size of the land is concerned which the settlers were to receive after the termination of their service, Schoepf, *op. cit.*, affirmed that "each family was to have the land, now worked and improved on lease"; Williams, *op. cit.*, maintained that Turnbull had promised "to give fifty acres of land to each head of families, and twenty five acres to each child." Siebert agreed with him, but he affirmed that there were only five acres for each child. The terms of the Mahón contract have been already explained, and Turnbull himself nowhere ever mentioned the granting of land to settlers in full ownership. The whole question is important in relation to a moral issue involved in the fulfillment of the terms of the agreement between Turnbull and settlers during and after the life of the colony.

38. Mahón, March 28, 1768, Lansdowne MSS, Vol. 88, f. 171.

39. Turnbull to Shelburne, Apr. 4, 1768, Lansdowne MSS, Vol. 88, f. 145.

40. Johnston to Shelburne, Mahón, Apr. 9, 1768, C. O. 174/5, p. 23. There Johnston reported that Turnbull's men were 1,348 "near 1,100 of which from this island." He evidently exaggerated the number of the Minorcans, perhaps in order to stress the good results of his help to Turnbull which he was asked to render by Lord Shelburne.

41. Turnbull to Shelburne, Gibraltar, Apr. 4, 1768, Lansdowne MSS, Vol. 88, f. 145.   42. *Ibid.*   43. C. O. 5/549, p. 257.

44. Whitehall, May 12, 1768, C. O. 5/549, p. 81.

45. Smyrna in E. Florida, Sept. 24, 1769, Lansdowne MSS, Vol. 88, f. 155.

FOUR

Disillusion & Revolt

This, My Lord I believe is the largest Importation of White Inhabitants that was ever brought into America at a time.—Governor Grant to Lord Hillsborough, July 20, 1768.

FOR MORE THAN THREE MONTHS, these men and women, newly born babies, and old folks were sailing on the high seas. Packed in their little ships, without comfort or ample supplies, beaten by strong winds and wild storms, they thought that the days between swollen waters and dark skies would never end. Down in the hulls of the vessels the moaning sick people and crying children with their mothers were lying on the slippery and soiled boards, feeble and impotent in the omnipresence of death.

Only a short time before, in Gibraltar, they had been happy and vigorous. Dr. Turnbull had reported from there to Lord Shelburne, "All the people are healthy and fit for a new colony."[1] Now sickness and scurvy were taking a heavy toll daily. By the time their long journey came to its end, of the 1,403 who had set out, only 1,255 survived. It is said that on one ship alone 28 persons lost their lives.[2] All in all, 148 had died during the trip and had been buried in the deep Atlantic.[3]

54

Their 700 passengers breathed with great relief when finally, on June 26, the first four of the ships arrived in St. Augustine.[4] Of the other four, two brigantines were carried by the Gulf Stream and the southerly winds to the north, and the brig *Hope* and the snow *Friendship* were blown off course and were forced on June 23 to put into Georgia temporarily.[5] Governor Grant was afraid that these seasonable winds would make them have "a tedious Navigation"; but all four found their way south and soon moored in the Matanzas River between Anastasia Island and the bayfront of St. Augustine. From the crowded decks, this polyglot human cargo, though tired and exhausted, looked with utmost delight at the extensive silver shores, the mild landscape, the thick unusual vegetation, and the gay houses of the town.

For all the ethnic groups on board, this was their first mass migration to the New World. Never before had Minorcans come to this country in so great numbers; and the same was true of the Italians, because from the time of Christopher Columbus up to that day, the party with Turnbull was by far the greatest number to come from Italy at one time.

As far as the Greeks were concerned, they may have thought that they were the first group that had ever come from Greece to this continent and that they were the first among their compatriots who ever set foot in Florida. But they did not know that long before them, 240 years to be exact, one of those restless Greeks had found his way unexpectedly to the same sandy coasts and there ended his days. This incident happened during the dramatic expedition of Alvar Nuñez Cabeza de Vaca. He related that on September 20, 1528, the expedition was in a difficult position somewhere in West Florida, possibly near the present location of Tampa or Clearwater. Since all the ships were destroyed by tempests, and the crews were not only starving but were also facing the continuous raids of near-by Indians, it was decided that they should leave that inhospitable coast as soon as possible. They built, consequently, five barges "coulked with palmetto oakum and tarred with pitch, which a Greek called Don Teodoro, made from certain pines."[6] This was a time-honored manner to tar boats, which has been continually practiced by the Greek fishermen down to the twentieth century. The name of this Greek was given by Cabeza de Vaca more fully in his next relation of the same expedition. When these barges were probably near the present Pensacola Bay, a canoe with Indians approached them. The Governor,

Pánfilo de Narváez, asked them for water. The Indians "offered to get some, provided we gave them something in which to carry it, and a Christian Greek, called Doroteo Teodoro (who has already been mentioned), said he would go with them. The Governor and others vainly tried to dissuade him, but he insisted upon going and went, taking along a Negro, while the Indians left two of their number as hostages. At night the Indians returned and brought back our vessels, but without water; neither did the Christians return with them. Those that had remained as hostages, when their people spoke to them, attempted to throw themselves into the water. But our men in the barge held them back, and so the other Indians forsook their canoe, leaving us very despondent and sad for the loss of those two Christians."[7] Thus, although they were not the first Greeks who ever landed in Florida, they were definitely the largest group that had ever come to this country.

As the passengers looked toward the welcoming little town of St. Augustine, their hopes revived, and their thoughts turned to their much-dreamed-of arrival in New Smyrna. An impatience now and a kind of anxiety possessed them. So, when all eight ships finally gathered at the port, they headed toward their new home. Some continued their trip by water; and some, who thought that they had had enough of sailing by that time, began the last 70 miles of their long journey on foot, still feeling the ground moving under them like the ocean's swollen waters.[8] The original plan of Governor Grant was to have them landed directly at the colony, where the provincial schooner and other vessels were sent to assist the disembarking of so many people. There, also, Governor Grant had some provisions stored ready for their reception.[9] But the stormy weather had changed these plans.

When the colonists arrived at the settlement they thought that it was formed on a beautiful site. On the east there were the calm Hillsborough River, the sandy shores, and the little islands of the inlet. It was such a strange sight, this Hillsborough River running northwards parallel with the ocean and meeting the Halifax River, which was flowing in the same manner southwards. At the point where they both met and emptied their waters into the Atlantic, they formed the very beautiful inlet and port of Mosquitoes.

Only three years previously, in 1765, the British had rediscovered this port. Governor Grant had read a Spanish report describing it, and immediately realizing its importance, he decided to locate it and

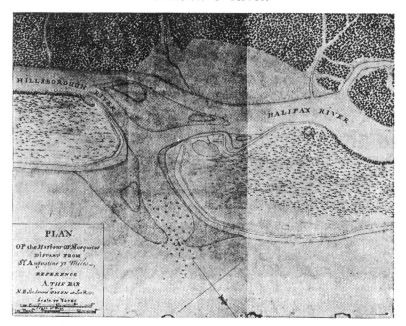

JAMES MONCRIEF'S PLAN OF THE HARBOR OF MOSQUITOES (1765)

for that purpose sent a boat with two men; but the boat sank in the rough waters off the coast and the two men drowned. Then he made another attempt, sending one party by sea and another by land with instructions to meet at the port; but both parties lost their way and barely managed to get back to town. Finally, two Spaniards came to St. Augustine from Havana. As they were talking to Governor Grant, he realized that they knew the area very well, so he asked them to help him locate the port. When he met their terms, they agreed to help and, together with the engineer-topographer James Moncrief, went to Mosquitoes. Moncrief made a beautiful map of the port and the coast from the Mosquitoes to St. Augustine, which Governor Grant forwarded to the Board of Trade together with a description of the area and the statement that this was "the best Harbor which has been found in the Province."[10]

Though the country around the inlet was low, the west bank of the Hillsborough was higher and had some excellent land. There, on a high shelly bluff, some shacks hastily erected to shelter the new-comers became the beginnings of New Smyrna, the colony that Dr.

Andrew Turnbull had named after Smyrna of Asia Minor, the birthplace of his Grecian wife, Maria Gracia, and his son Nicholas.

The lowlands were covered by palmetto forests, savanna, and salt marshes, with extensive areas of pine barrens, and the higher parts had an abundance of cabbage palms, papaw trees, and exotic tropical plants. To the west, about two miles from the coast and running parallel to it for almost forty miles, there was a famous orange grove, remnant of much older Spanish and Indian settlements. Its width was approximately half a mile, and with its palms and huge live oaks decorated with Spanish moss its beauty was unsurpassed.[11]

The preparations for the settlers, however, were insufficient. Instead of the 500 Greeks who were expected, there came at one time the largest number of white inhabitants that had ever migrated to America, as Governor Grant had reported to Lord Hillsborough.[12] The Governor was fearful and anxious. He prophetically wrote to his superiors at Whitehall that, despite the exceptional qualifications of the doctor, "if he is not supported, I doubt much of its turning out to good account."[13] In the meantime, a cargo of 500 Negro slaves destined for New Smyrna was wrecked off the Florida coast and all of them were lost.[14] And in the land of New Smyrna—truly a part of the American wilderness—there was not a cleared field.[15] It was now the duty of the new settlers to clear the swampy land, where alligators and cottonmouth moccasins were not rare, and to make out of it the indigo fields; it was for the settlers to clear the dry land full of palmettos, and to plant their corn, securing in this manner what was to become their steady diet for almost ten years, hominy grits; and they had to make gardens for their vegetables on the shelly bluff where their huts were built.

Life in New Smyrna certainly was not what the newcomers had expected. Nature was beautiful there, the land extensive, and some of it would become theirs in time; but at their arrival it was only a wilderness and they had to wait for a long time until, cultivated, it could eventually support them. In the meantime they had to work hard, and their overseers, former noncommissioned officers of the British army and some Italians, made the work even harder. Their families were suffering. Food was scarce and there was danger of death by starvation. The lagoons had plenty of fish and there were many good fishermen; but fishing required time, and time no one was permitted to have, because it was so badly needed for the establishment of a plantation.[16] This primitive life of deprivation and complete lack of elementary conveniences weighted the hearts and spirits of small children and sick men particularly.

The real menace, however, came from the mosquitoes. The whole area, since it was first discovered by the Spaniards, was called "the Mosquitoes," which legend claimed were more vicious and numerous there than in any other part of the southern colonies. Day and night, but especially after dark, clouds of the hungry insects swarmed by the millions over the palmetto huts, attacking the unfortunate settlers who longed for a night's sleep after a summer day's work in the fields under the strong semitropical sun. What no one knew, however, was that the mosquitoes were bringing malaria, which was soon added to their other adversities.[17]

There was no way to improve their lot, however, but by hard work. So, "they were obedient to their overseers, seemed pleased with the situation, went regularly to work," and in fact by August 10, only a few weeks after their arrival, they had done "a great deal of Clearing and Planting."[18] Some planters from Carolina who visited New Smyrna and stayed with Dr. Turnbull for a few days "were astonished at the progress which had been made, [and] they agreed that the same number of Negroes could not have done more." They did not hide their admiration and were sure "that it must turn out to be the best Settlement upon the Continent of America if they went on as they had begun." The planters stayed there until August 18 when they left New Smyrna accompanied by Dr. Turnbull, who was going to visit a neighboring plantation. Everything appeared to be normal, the men "in perfect good humor," and on the morning of the 19th, when "everything continued quiet," the men went as usual to their work.

Then, suddenly, a rapid succession of events occurred. At eleven o'clock the settlers abandoned their work and gathered in the center of the settlement, angry and desperate. They were convinced by that time that they were trapped and that death soon awaited them. They wanted to leave, and they agreed on Havana as the only possible destination. A ship that had just brought supplies for the colony from St. Augustine was immediately captured. In the midst of the revolt one of the overseers, Carlo Forni, seized the opportunity to become their leader. An accused rapist and probably one of the basest of men[19] he declared himself "Captain General and Commander in Chief," and in the middle of great excitement and wild enthusiasm, the storehouses were broken into; blankets, linen, and flour were taken and loaded on the ship; and a cow was killed to supply them with meat during their trip. The confusion was great and became even greater when "Rum was given in plenty, which is a prevailing argument in those Woods," while the casks of wine and oil which could not be put on board were shared. The overseers were seized; one of the cruelest and most hated, named Cutter, tried to stop them and had his ears and nose chopped off by the Italian Giuseppe Massiadoli. "The Rioters who at first did not consist of above twenty, soon increased to two or three hundred." Firearms, taken from the plundered storehouses, were distributed, and about 300 went aboard and sailed southward, following the waterway close to the beach.

In the meantime, "two Italians who continued faithful to their Master," managed to escape. They went to a near-by plantation, about four miles away, which also belonged to Turnbull. An overseer there dispatched a messenger to his master immediately. At midnight the doctor was located at the plantation of Mount Oswald, where he was on his way to St. Augustine. The messenger "according to custom expressed things to be in a worse state than they really were."

Turnbull was gravely alarmed. All the troubles and the expense, the incredible efforts and sacrifices were lost, and he envisioned the breakup of his settlement on which so many dreams and hopes were based. He dispatched the news to Governor Grant, asking for help, and he himself turned back to New Smyrna hoping to salvage the remnants before it was too late.

At eight o'clock the following night, Governor Grant received Turnbull's message. Realizing the seriousness of the situation he set aside every other duty in order to enforce immediate drastic measures. Within nine hours he had the provincial frigate *East Florida* and another vessel under sail "with Troops, Provisions, Ammunition and everything necessary to pursue the Greeks," in case the *East Florida* should not get to Mosquito Inlet in time to prevent the rebels' escape in Turnbull's vessel which they had seized. In the meantime he dispatched by land a detachment under the command of Major Whitmore, but despite the fact that "the Gentlemen under his Command were ready and willing to do everything," it was certain they could not reach New Smyrna in time on account of the bad roads and the great distance.

It was on August 22, at eleven o'clock in the morning, that the *East Florida* spotted the rebels' vessel. It had been caught by the low tide in the lagoon, off New Smyrna, and was waiting to sail as soon as the tide was high again. One cannon ball fired from the *East Florida* was enough to persuade the 300 settlers aboard to abandon their plans of escape. Thirty-five of them, however, jumped into a small boat and headed southwards. They followed the lagoons off the coast, landing only to hunt and find some food. Behind them were their pursuers, the little vessel that accompanied the *East Florida* to the Mosquito Inlet with a number of soldiers on it. The rebels, hungry and miserable, continued to flee for several weeks until, exhausted, they finally gave up in the Florida Keys, less than 100 miles from Havana.

They were brought to St. Augustine and put into prison to await trial. Governor Grant was positive that the immediate suppression of the rebellion had impressed the colonists and that "they will not be apt to attempt such a thing again." But he thought that a public trial would serve a definite purpose; some of the rebels should suffer as an example to others. The British government's attitude toward rebellion, a contagious affair, should be clarified; for there were several large plantations in East Florida and an increase in their number was soon expected. There was, of course, the question of the degree of guilt of these people and the technicality of finding the nature of their crime. Governor Grant did not worry about five of them at least: "the proof against them is said to be clear in that case they probably be made Examples of," he reported to England. Later, on October 20, while 20 of the rebels were in prison, Governor Grant still had not made up his mind about how many and who should be punished. For it was one thing to demonstrate the stern official attitude toward rebellion, by execution, and a different thing to deprive a colony of precious labor. The Governor, however, expressed his confidence that "circumstances will no doubt appear at the Tryal, to determine which of them should suffer as examples to the rest, two or three will be sufficient for they'l [not] make such another attempt, as not one of them has escaped."[20]

Finally, in January, 1769, the trial took place, East Florida's Chief Justice, William Drayton, presiding.[21] The outcome was as expected. Three were sentenced to death: Carlo Forni, the leader, for piracy; Giuseppe Massiadoli, alias Bresiano, for stabbing Turnbull's supervisor, Cutter; and the Greek from Corsica, Elia Medici, for killing a cow[22]—it was still the time when killing a cow in England merited capital punishment. The court spared the life of two more Greeks from Corsica, Georgi Stephanopoli and Clatha Corona, and, as Governor Grant reported, "several others were tryed & acquit for want of proper Evidence, which in fact was not Material as two Examples were quite sufficient."²³

Elia Medici, however, was lucky. According to a British practice, his life was spared under the condition that he should execute the other two. When the day of the execution came a tragic incident took place which was vividly described by the contemporary Dutch surveyor, Bernard Romans, who eyewitnessed the event:

On this occasion I saw one of the most moving scenes I ever experienced; long and obstinate was the struggle of this man's mind, who repeatedly called out, that he chose to die rather than to be executioner of his friends in distress: this not a little perplexed Mr. Woolridge, the sheriff, till at last the entreaties of the victims themselves, put an end to the conflict in his breast, by encouraging him to act. Now we beheld a man thus compelled to mount the ladder, take leave of his friends in the most moving manner, kissing them the moment before he committed them to an ignominious death.²⁴

Governor Grant had asked His Majesty's government to approve of a full pardon to the three condemned men (Medici, Stephanopoli, and Corona), but he forgot to mention their crimes. Lord Hillsborough was satisfied, of course, with the outcome of the trial and he was certain that "the rest of the Foreigners introduced by Doctor Turnbull will be persuaded by such Examples to become good Subjects and usefull members of Society." But in connection with the fate of the other three, he informed the Governor that "His Majesty has no objection to granting His full Pardon to the three Persons you have reprieved, but as you do not express the Crime of which they were convicted, I must wait for further information, before His Majesty's gracious intention can be executed in proper form."²⁵ With the mail being so slow between the colonies and the mother country, it was only on July 21 that finally Governor Grant informed Lord Hillsborough that "the three Greeks" were accused for the following crimes: Georgi Stephanopoli for forcibly taking and carrying away a boat belonged to Sir Charles Burdett, Baronet; Clatha Corona, for breaking open Dr. Turnbull's warehouse and stealing from thence linen, blankets, flour, etc.; and Elia Medici for killing a cow.²⁶ By the time the reply came from England and the question of their freedom had been settled, more than a year had passed. It was an era when awaiting an official act to "be executed in proper form" meant a delay of many months.

The revolt of New Smyrna brought forth the question of the protection of the area, not only from the Indians who were living near by, but from its own settlers too. As soon as the colony had been established, Governor Grant had expressed his anxiety and had said that he expected this great number of people, collected together from so many different parts of the world and imported into an infant country at the same time, might cause riots and give trouble at times; but he never expected these riots to reach such great dimensions.[27] What made him particularly anxious at this time was that the planters in Dr. Turnbull's neighborhood were alarmed, and nothing could ease their minds except the presence of the King's troops. In his report on the revolt, Governor Grant asked his government once again to take practical steps for the erection of a fort at the Mosquitoes.

This was an old proposal of Grant's made for the first time when a great migration was expected to take place, in 1765, from Bermuda to the Mosquitoes. Governor Grant had studied the area at that time and found the proper spot for the erection of the fort on the well-protected eastern bank of the Halifax River. On the map of the Mosquito Inlet drawn by James Moncrief, the Governor marked the place on which he proposed building the fort, and he explained to the Lords of the Board of Trade: "From the situation of the place which your Lordships will see is a Peninsula, No Indian Enemy, if we should unfortunately differ with them, could hurt the garrison, which can always be supplied with Provisions by water and that Circumstance removes the Objection which is made to many of the American Forts."[28] Governor Grant wanted it on this specific location and wanted it large enough to contain barracks for three officers and fifty men. Because stone, lime, and wood were found in that area, he had estimated its cost at only £400. He reasoned that from the fort he could dispatch small detachments of soldiers to the various plantations of the area, where they could stay in wooden posts built at no cost at all to the government.

The Governor sent proposals and plans to London only to find out two months later, in May, 1765, that the *Grenville Packet,* carrying this mail, was lost at sea. He immediately sent a duplicate letter and copies of the plans,[29] and when finally the Board of Trade discussed his proposal on July 4, 1776, it gave its approval wholeheartedly.

But the Bermudian migration had failed to materialize, and the desire to build this fort had evaporated. However, now New Smyrna was there with its settlers, threat of riots, and everything that could justify the building of his fort. Lord Hillsborough answered the Governor's new appeal immediately: "I entirely agree with the Board of Trade in the opinion they gave in 1766,"[30] and he asked the Governor to proceed to contact the Crown Agent and receive the already approved sum of money. It was destined, however, that this fort should never be erected—for reasons completely unknown, the building never was begun.[31]

When the tumult of the revolt settled down, Andrew Turnbull totaled his losses and reported to Governor Grant that they "amount to four or five hundred pounds at most."[32] Later, however, narrating the incident, Turnbull stated that the rebels originally looted the stores of goods amounting to £2,000 of which they loaded on the seized schooner £1,300 worth, later thrown into the water when the rebels found that the schooner was too heavy to sail over the very shallow water of the bar.

The colonists also counted their losses, only they had to continue counting for a long time since their losses continued to mount up. After the tempest of the rebellion, heartbroken and numb they returned to their "regular" life. The work continued hard, the food as little as before, the mosquitoes as many as ever; and death took the same heavy toll. "Some time after [the revolt]," Anthony Stephanopoli, one of the colonists, related, "the rest of the People being Starved, they began to die, ten or eleven a day & Some days fifteen."[33] On December 1, of that year, Governor Grant solemnly reported that since the colonists had come to New Smyrna—that is, within five months— "they had lost above three hundred, chiefly old people and Children."[34] And in a later official report recording the number of the dead among the settlers from the time they left Gibraltar to the end of December, one soberly reads:

*1768 — Men and women: 300. Children: 150.
Total dead for 1768: 450.*[35]

N O T E S — Chapter Four

1. Gibraltar, Apr. 4, 1768, Lansdowne MSS, Vol. 88, f. 145.
2. Corse, *op. cit.*, p. 42 f.
3. Tonyn to Germain, St. Augustine, Jan. 15, 1778, C. O. 5/558, p. 107.
4. Grant to Hillsborough, St. Augustine, July 2, 1768, C. O. 5/541, pp. 423-24.
5. *Ibid.* Also, *South Carolina Gazette*, July 4, 1768; *Boston Chronicle*, July 18, 1768.

NOTES — Chapter Four

6. *The Journey of Alvar Nuñez Cabeza de Vaca and his Companions, from Florida to the Pacific, 1528-1536* (New York, 1822), translated into English by F. Bandelier, p. 38.

7. *Ibid.*, p. 46.

8. Grant to Hillsborough, St. Augustine, Aug. 29, 1768, C. O. 5/549, pp. 281-85.

9. Grant to Shelburne, St. Augustine, Mar. 12, 1768, C. O. 5/549, p. 77.

10. St. Augustine, Mar. 1, 1765, C. O. 5/540, pp. 353-60.

11. The description of the area is given on the basis of contemporary descriptions by de Brahm, *op. cit.;* William Stork, *A Description of East Florida* (London, 1769), p. 10; William Bartram, *Travels Through North and South Carolina* (Philadelphia, 1791), pp. 142 f.

12. C. O. 5/541, p. 423.

13. *Ibid.*

14. Schoepf, *op. cit.*, p. 234. Schoepf, however, is the only source of this information.

15. Bartram, *op. cit.*, pp. 142 f.

16. In 1788, while in Charleston, S. C., Turnbull asserted that the colonists were encouraged to fish and that all families had quantities of dried fish in their houses. See Turnbull, *op. cit.*, p. 685. The settlers themselves, however, had stated under oath exactly the opposite, C. O. 5/557, pp. 459, 463.

17. Michael J. Curley, *Church and State in the Spanish Floridas, 1783-1822* (Washington, D.C.: The Catholic University of America Press, 1940) pp. 30, 35.

18. All the following unnumbered quotations come from Governor Grant's report to Lord Hillsborough of Aug. 29, 1786, in which he described the first revolt in New Smyrna. C. O. 5/549, pp. 281-85. When material relative to this incident comes from another source, this source has been indicated.

19. Bernard Romans, in Phillips, *op. cit.*, p. 105.

20. Grant to Hillsborough, St. Augustine, Oct. 20, 1768, C. O. 5/550, p. 2.

21. Turnbull, *op. cit.*, p. 637.

22. There is every reason to believe that since Elia Medici came from Corsica, he was from the Mani branch of the Medici that had immigrated there. Moreover, Governor Grant calls him, together with Stephanopoli and Corona, "Greek." C. O. 5/550, p. 129.

23. Grant to Hillsborough, St. Augustine, Jan. 14, 1769, C. O. 5/550, p. 55.

24. In Phillips, *op. cit.*, p. 106. Corse, *op. cit.*, p. 60 ff., completely rejects the account of New Smyrna by the "irresponsible youthful draughtsman" Bernard Romans, in which the above description of the execution had been included. It is true that the Dutch Romans, with an intense dislike of the British, gives a prejudiced version of New Smyrna; moreover, his account includes several inaccuracies, such as his date of this revolt as 1769, whereas it occurred in 1768. Such information, however, can be easily checked by an interested scholar. In relation to the description of the execution, however, there are many grounds to support its accuracy, the most important being that while for most of his information about New Smyrna Romans relied on other sources, for the scene of the execution, quoted above, he depended on himself, because he witnessed it.

25. Whitehall, Apr. 13, 1769, C. O. 5/550, p. 71.

26. St. Augustine, July 21, 1769, C. O. 5/550, p. 129.

27. C. O. 5/549, p. 283.

28. St. Augustine, Mar. 1, 1765, C. O. 5/540, pp. 353-60.
29. St. Augustine, May 8, 1765, C. O. 5/540, p. 393.
30. Whitehall, Dec. 10, 1768, C. O. 5/549, p. 339.
31. In the town of New Smyrna, north of Canal Street where once upon a time one of Turnbull's irrigation canals used to run, and on Riverside Drive there is a small park around what they call "Old Fort." Historical markers have been placed and articles in local newspapers have been published maintaining that it was either the fort planned by Governor Grant or an Old Spanish fort. It is very unfortunate that not only Mrs. Corse but also official organizations and societies with historical pursuits fell victims of fantastic amateur "historians," whose strong imagination gave birth to this opinion. This author made a persistent search at the Public Record Office and in every other possible source of information in London without being able to find anything supporting that this is the fort planned by James Grant. The location also of this "Old Fort" compared with the one indicated in Grant's map is alone enough to show that this is by no means Grant's fort. This author, leaving aside the amusing opinion that this is a sixteenth-century Spanish fort, agrees with John W. Griffin, Regional Archaeologist of the National Park Service, who, in an unpublished study, showed clearly that these ruins do not belong to a fort at all, but that they are foundations of a mansion. There is every reason to believe that this is the mansion started and never finished by A. Turnbull. After the revolt of 1768 and fears of an Indian attack, he wanted to build what the Spanish would call a *casa fuerta,* a kind of block-house, strong enough to resist an attack. Although internal arrangement of space clearly shows that a house was planned there, the exterior massive coquina wall could serve both for defense and for the support of a possible three-or-more-story-high stately mansion.
32. C. O. 5/549, p. 283.
33. C. O. 5/557, p. 430.
34. C. O. 5/550, p. 5.
35. C. O. 5/558, p. 107.

FIVE

Fruitful Bondage

N EW SMYRNA HAD NOT BEEN ESTABLISHED for philan-
thropic or religious purposes as had many contemporary
settlements in the English colonies of America. New
Smyrna's purpose had been repeatedly stated as being
"the Cultivation of Cochineal Indigo Madder Rice Hemp and many
other useful Articles of Commerce Especially Cotton," silk, wine, and
the "Culture of Articles now purchased from foreign nations."[1]
It was a financial enterprise, having as sole purpose the materializa-
tion of profit, which had attracted the interest of its distinguished
founders.

Also, that this colony would save some of the badly needed gold of
the Empire by producing goods previously purchased from other
countries greatly appealed to the mercantilistic minds of the statesmen
at Whitehall. New Smyrna fitted so well into the postwar plans for
the economic growth of Great Britain that it became, as the Board of
Trade declared, a matter "of publick utility."[2] This official attitude
was amply displayed by such statesmen as the Earl of Shelburne, the
Earl of Hillsborough, and Lord George Germain. They all outreached
themselves in rendering a helpful hand to the struggling colony, and
they never ceased urging the Governor of East Florida to do the same.

The assets of New Smyrna were the great amount of land which
its founders had received in East Florida, the capital invested in them,
the financial aid which the government extended to the company, the
profits made by selling the colony's products, and the great number

67

of settlers who were the labor force of the colony. The story of these assets constitutes to a great extent the story of New Smyrna.

The acquisition of such an extensive area of virgin land started with the first grants of 20,000 acres each given to Andrew Turnbull and Sir William Duncan in 1766.[3] When Lord Grenville became the new partner, he added 20,000 acres which he had received from the government.[4] To the company, Turnbull offered his land and the personal management of the colony in East Florida, whereas his two partners in London agreed to pay jointly an amount of money not exceeding £9,000 during the next seven years, which was to be spent for the settlement and improvement of these 60,000 acres. Another provision of the original indenture, which they signed on April 12, 1767, was that after seven years they would divide all the property of the company into three equal parts and each one of the three partners would receive by lot one part.[5] By 1769, however, the expenses were great and the London partners thought that they should reorganize the company.

In order to counterbalance their financial expenses, Duncan and Grenville asked Turnbull, in a new indenture of October 2, 1769, to contribute to the land property of the company 20,000 acres which he had recently obtained; and they agreed that should any of the parties receive any further grants, the lands should be added to the company's 80,000 acres. Unfortunate for Turnbull was the condition that after seven years, when the distribution of the company's property would take place, the division would be into five equal parts of which each of the London partners would take two and Andrew Turnbull the remaining one.[6] In the meantime, the latter's four children, Nicholas, Mary, Jane, and Margaret, had received by Order in Council, 5,000 acres each[7] and Turnbull himself sundry small lots amounting to 1,400 acres. Grenville and Duncan thought that this land "should be thrown into the mass with the former," so the new indenture stated that "since the date of the last indenture Andrew Turnbull and others in East Florida [his four children] have obtained another 21,400 acres or thereabouts for the benefit of the Settlement amounting in the whole to 101,400 acres."[8] It was a harsh condition for Turnbull, but the colony needed financial aid, credit, and backing; and he had to accept the terms of his partners. It was in this way that the colony had obtained this significant amount of land.

The truth is that since the recruiting of the settlers had started, both Grenville and Duncan had paid enormous sums of money, far exceeding the original £9,000 which they had agreed to pay jointly during the next seven years. A picture of this alarming situation was given in Governor Grant's report to Lord Hillsborough on December 1, 1768:

Twenty thousand pounds sterling at least, My Lord, have already been laid out for the Embarkation, Provision and Clothing of those people, so large a sum is not to be recovered but by perseverance and a further Expense, the settlers may do a little for themselves in the course of the Winter & Spring, but they must be subsisted for many Months, and Clothed at least for two years before Returns can reasonably be expected—tho' they are supplied with Oeconomy and good Management there is no trifling of Expense, where twelve hundred people are concerned, even Salt and Italian Corn exclusive of every other species of Provision run high.[9]

Governor Grant was very anxious about the fate of the colony. He was particularly afraid that "Mr. Turnbull will find great difficulty in carrying the projected plan into Execution—it is upon a larger Bottom than was concerted with his Friends at home, and has already far exceeded double the sum which they agreed to advance, for which reason, my Lord, I am under some uneasiness about the future Conduct of those Gentlemen, they may probably tire of paying the large and frequent Bills, which Mr. Turnbull is under an absolute necessity of drawing upon them, their affairs certainly could not be in better hands, the Doctor is active, intelligent and Aisiduous [*sic*]—but his friends tho' they have the highest opinion of Mr. Turnbull's Integrity and Ability, may possibly be alarmed at rising such large sums in a New World, without a more immediate prospect of returns for their Money."[10]

The London partners were really apprehensive of the colony's financial development, but it was too late to stop there. By July 21, 1769, the expenditures had been raised to £28,000;[11] as if this was not enough, Turnbull had drawn in advance on his London partners £24,000 more.[12] Duncan and Grenville decided to jointly pay this £24,000, the already drawn bills upon their credit, thus making their total investment in money £52,000.[13]

Along with the land and money invested by the members of the company should be mentioned also the financial assistance given to New Smyrna by the government, which most of the time came at very critical moments.

The first grant was the one which the Board of Trade decided to give Turnbull from the unapplied bounty offered by the Parliament for the encouragement of the culture of cotton, vines, silk, and other products. This amounted, by 1767, to £1,500, but of this sum the government approved only the "payment of 40 shillings per head to the first five hundred Greeks that shall be imported and actually settled in New Smyrna."[14] That made the sum of £1,000.

Turnbull had asked, however, for the continuation of the payment of this bounty every year, so that he could spend £400 for roads, ferries, and other improvements of the area and pay the remaining £100 as a salary to a pastor and schoolmaster."[15] The Board of Trade never gave a clear reply to this request. The fact that it left it up to Lord Shelburne to decide if "the remaining one hundred pounds should be allowed to the first Priest of the Greek church which shall be established in that colony,"[16] shows that the annual bounty payment continued until September 1, 1770, when Governor Grant emphasized "the necessity there was of continuing His Majesty's most gracious Bounty for the support of the Adventurers." He added that "last years Bounty had been laid out entirely for their subsistence and had actually saved them from starving for without that well timed help from the Government, there must have been an end of that numerous promising settlement." And further in the same report, once again the Governor asked this "Royal Bounty to be continued."[17]

During those dark days of December, 1768, Governor Grant, full of anxiety about the new settlement, confessed: "I cannot help considering the dreadful situation which the Doctor and his Greeks would be reduced to, if such a misfortune was to happen, a single Bill being returned, my Lord, would be a total stop to his Credit, and the people in that case must unavoidably perish for want if I do not support them." He then asked his government for the approval of a £2,000 relief grant. The official response came quickly. "I lost no time communicating to the Lords of the Treasury" the news about distressed New Smyrna, Lord Hillsborough replied, and now he was happy to announce the approval of the requested £2,000. At the same time he strongly exhorted Governor Grant as to which products were to be cultivated: silk, wine, raisins, corinths, flora-indigo, olives, figs, and honey[18]—all products that drained British gold into foreign countries. What Lord Hilllsborough omitted to mention then and mentioned only next June[19] was that the Lords of the Treasury desired that "it may be understood by Governor Grant that the Public are to be at no further expence upon that Account."[20] To all subsequent appeals of Governor Grant in 1770 and 1771 for the continuation of the bounty, the official refusal was given by quoting the above statement of the Lords of the Treasury.[21]

The payment of the bounty and the granting of the £2,000 relief were not the only ways in which the British government helped New Smyrna financially. From the day the man-of-war was lent to Turnbull for his Mediterranean trip, down to the last years of the colony's life, an inestimable number of services were offered.

The colony as a productive enterprise did not impress its contemporaries very much. And yet, after the first critical years there was an amazing economic recovery which, under other circumstances, could have made New Smyrna one of the most flourishing economic ventures of the times.

When the colonists arrived in St. Augustine from Europe, and while they were on their way to the Mosquitoes, Governor Grant reported that:

Most of them are to be fixed in Familys, and to have half the Produce, which is well judged on the Dr.'s part, as it is the surest, indeed the only method of making new Adventurers Industrious, for no Man in America can be prevailed upon to work for his Master in order to repay the Expense which the Master may have been put upon his account—on the Contrary if a Servant has not an immediate Prospect of profit to Himself, he takes care that his Labor shall not pay for his clothes, and Subsistence, Servants by that means tire out the patience of Their Masters, and get rid of Them upon easy terms."[22]

The very pertinent remarks of the Governor were based on Turnbull's plans for the future. What actually happened, however, was that the colonists never received half of the produce during the life of New Smyrna. Perhaps this fact was the chief cause of their hostility toward their master. They were, however, "fixed in families." By September of 1769, a year and a half after their arrival, they were established on farms on the western bank of the Hillsborough River, each tract having a river front of 210 feet and reaching several acres westwards toward the interior. All these farms, about 200 in number, one after another, extended for almost eight miles on the bank of the navigable river.[23] "The nearness of the Hutts to one another gives the whole a Resemblance of an Eastern or Chinese plantation" said Turnbull, explaining the aesthetics of his settlement to Lord Shelburne.[24]

NEW SMYRNA

There the settlers for the first time saw around their huts how vegetables could grow on the sandy land whose soil was nothing but shells crushed into dirt through the centuries. They needed these gardens badly to fight scurvy and to complete their diet. They had some seeds with them, but Governor Grant ordered additional ones from England because he did not trust the vegetable seeds coming from other parts of America. In order, however, to be sure that the newcomers would be able to start their gardens soon after their arrival, he "took care to save a considerable quantity for Mr. Turnbull, from [his] own Garden, of which a grain does not fail here."25

And indeed, after a few years, these small private gardens became very important for the survival of their owners. Sometimes, together with the poultry they raised, these vegetables became a source of a small income for them. In connection with the poultry, Turnbull narrated that his people used to sell the produce to St. Augustine merchants and that once a Captain Brown came there with his schooner and bought more than 1,200 poultry at one time and more than 800 at another.26 On the same shelly bluff the settlers could also cultivate corn and the indigo plant, both of a fine quality.27

For the advancement of New Smyrna, however, this subsistence agriculture of its settlers was not very important. It was mainly the production on the extensive fields of the colony that could determine its financial success. These fields were what was called high swamp. When they were cleared and drained they yielded a fine soil, rich enough for sugar cane.28 Indigo and corn were usually planted there.

When planning his plantation in Europe, Turnbull took care to bring gins for cleaning cotton, tools, and "several models of engines of agriculture," as well as grains, seeds, and plants which he hoped were right for the climate of Florida. He also carried with him grape vines for wine production, small olive trees which in time would produce enough olives for the making of olive oil, and mulberries whose leaves would feed his silkworms.29

As soon as the settlers arrived in New Smyrna, they immediately set to work clearing and planting the land. Clearing high swamps, full of palmettos and other semitropical trees and plants with running roots, draining the water, and preparing the soil was a tedious and time-consuming task, but the results were gratifying.

Everything they had brought from Europe was planted in a few months. Then came the long wait—at least two years until the first fruit would be produced—and in the meantime all these people must survive. Almost a year after their arrival, on March 4, 1769, Governor Grant wrote to London: "I shall never be easy in my mind about that Settlement 'till they raise Subsistence for themselves."[30] When this could be achieved, the whole situation would be changed. Grant added in another letter of the same period, "If they can only raise provisions for themselves next year My Lord every thing will be well, Produce must follow, and if Mr. Turnbull can once begin to send Rice, Indigo, Cotton, Silk, Wine or Sugar to Market he and his Friends may be re-imbursed the Expense they have been at, which is high indeed."[31]

Concern with the production of food for the colony did not mean a negligence of the production of staple products that would make New Smyrna stand on her own feet financially. They had been in their new homes only a year when Governor Grant reported to London that though grapevines had been planted by the Greeks and the Mahonese, wine was of slow progress. But, Grant added, Turnbull was busy in the production of barilla, the impure soda which was produced by the ashes of various plants of saline regions, and he expected to send some that year to the London market on board the same vessel on which Grant planned to send the whole produce of East Florida, consisting of indigo, cotton, and rice.[32] Barilla was in great demand in Europe at that time, because it was widely used for the making of glass, soap, paper, and many other products.

Wine was never produced in New Smyrna, at least for commercial purposes, nor was rice, cotton, or silk. The making of sugar, however, had begun,[33] and in a few years corn of an excellent quality was produced. It seems that during the last years of New Smyrna's life the production of corn was so satisfactory that in 1777 Dr. Turnbull sold about 5,000 bushels of it in St. Augustine and its environs.[34]

Another source of income for the colony was the production of naval stores, much in demand by the British navy and merchant marine during this time. The extensive forests of pine enabled the colony to produce tar, pitch, and especially turpentine, which was shipped directly from Mosquito Harbor from the convenient wharfs built with coquina stone by the settlers. A few years later, in a description of New Smyrna's assets, there were stressed "the peculiar advantages of its [New Smyrna's] situation in general and particularly of its large Wharf and Navigation for disposing of Naval Stores—Of the very large profits which the article of turpentine alone would have afforded them from the extensive tracts of pine land."[35]

Thus, the production of New Smyrna was mainly of cash products of a wide variety. The one plant, however, that absorbed most of the activities of the settlers and that contributed greatly to the income of the colony was indigo.[36]

When Turnbull, after his arrival, realized that indigo was at the center of life of almost every East Florida plantation and that a high quality of flora-indigo was a native plant of the area, he decided to plunge into its cultivation, hoping that he would have a fast and happy return. He knew very well how high indigo was priced in England. Dyers and painters used it, and housewives needed it to bleach their linen; a great amount of gold had escaped abroad for its purchase from Spanish, Dutch, and French colonies, where it was mainly produced. On March 25, 1749, the British government had taken drastic steps to restrict the importation of indigo to England and to encourage its cultivation. Thus, besides the prizes and bounties offered for this purpose, it was ordered that all persons who imported indigo to England and Scotland directly from the British colonies in America should be entitled to sixpence for every pound, to be paid immediately by the collector of the port of entrance. With all this in mind, Turnbull prepared his fields for cultivation.

Producing indigo, however, was a very difficult and delicate operation not only on land in the middle of the wilderness, but even on a smooth, well-cleared field. The ground needed to be levelled, and completely cleaned and "dressed"; seeds were planted about a foot apart sometime in the spring, between March and May. With favorable weather—that is, moist and rainy—in a few weeks the plant was about two feet high and its leaves ready to be cut. When the production of a fine quality indigo was desired, only the leaves were cut; but most of the time, the whole plant was cut before blossoming, bound into bundles, and thrown from one to another of three kinds of wooden vats filled with water. This was an important part of the process. Through a kind of churning of the leaves or plants in the second vat, the separation of the bluish dye residue from the liquid mass was possible, and this separation was completed in a third vat. After this, the residue was strained and dried in conical cloth bags, called "Hippocrate's sleeves," which were hung in a shady place. Before its complete hardening, it was cut into small square pieces and left then to dry entirely. In this form it was shipped to Europe.[37]

Turnbull went ahead with all the preparations and by September, 1769, he was very optimistic. "We have done good Work," he wrote to Lord Shelburne, "and intend to send indigo to Market next year."[38] But this had to wait for two more years. The cleaning of the ground continued, the various installations were speeded up, and the experience of the other planters was utilized. In October, 1770, Governor Grant, boasting slightly of his own progress, reported to Lord Hillsborough: "When he [Dr. Turnbull] came last from Smyrnea it was to pass some days at my Plantation to see the process of making Indigo, in which great Improvements have been made This Year by my Manufacturers."[39]

That spring a great area was planted with flora-indigo. It is not difficult to imagine the joy of Turnbull when a few weeks later his eyes rested on the extensive, neat indigo fields where, lined one after another, grew the small plants with the precious thick round leaves; their color was a peculiar green on the upper side, quite reddish toward the edges, and the underneath had an unusual silver tone. The stakes were so great on the success of this first harvest that when a little later the processing of the plant started, probably no one cared about the terrible smell of the vats, the swarms of the flies around the drying places, and the tedious work involved.

On April 26, 1771, the brigantine *George,* master Peter Regan, left St. Augustine directly for London carrying 2,420 pounds of New Smyrna's indigo. A few months later, on November 29, the schooner *Margaret,* Benjamin Barton master, carried to Charleston 9,138 pounds to be shipped from there to England.[40] Thus in the first year of production 11,558 pounds were sold, which is as much as any of the old and great plantations could produce. The income must have been over £13,500 and it came at the right time—when both the London partners and the government had stopped their financial support of the colony.

After this initial success, Turnbull continued developing his indigo plantation on a grand scale. By 1777 he had cleared more land, built, for £100, an indigo house for the drying and cutting of the dye residue, and constructed 22 double sets of indigo vats, for which he had paid £1,000.[41]

The production continued to be successful. When a British merchant bought the second harvest, that of the year 1772, he paid Turnbull £3,300.[42] It seems that the hazards of other plantations did not bother New Smyrna at all. The caterpillars, which were the nightmare of the West Indian indigo planters especially, did not harm the colony's plants; and the drought that ruined several East Florida

75

harvests left the colony almost untouched. This was due to an amazing irrigation system introduced by the much-travelled doctor which, as he explained to Lord Shelburne, was "the Egyptians' mode of watering. This is new to American planters and is talked of as Chimerical; but as I have seen the utility of such modes of culture, and am convinced of the necessity of them in this Climate, I go on, being certain of succeeding."[43]

And he did succeed. During the year of the drought he suffered a setback and his production fell to 1,633 pounds of indigo. Next year, 1775, the production was higher and in 1776 it reached 6,390 pounds. In 1777 the production fell again, but this was due to other circumstances and not to a failure of his irrigation system. More than a century and a half later, one could still see on the New Smyrna site the impressive canals, lined with coquina, the only kind of rock found in the area. This stone is made of small shells and corals cemented together in a process that has lasted thousands of years, and its beautiful texture makes the structure in which it is used very attractive. The canals were quite wide and several miles long. In case of a drought, they carried water to the fields from the swamps or from the many wells that Turnbull had opened; and they drained the surplus water of the swamps into the inlet.[44] Thanks to these canals, the agricultural production of the colony was much more assured.

From 1772 to 1777 ships carried the following quantities of indigo from New Smyrna to England, either directly or through Charleston:

December 19, 1772, on schooner *Sukey and Betsey,* for Charleston	9,065 lb.
December 24, 1773, on schooner *Harriet,* for Charleston	10,262 lb.
December 24, 1774, on brigantine *Betsey,* for London	1,633 lb.
October 23, 1775, on brigantine *Betsey,* for London	1,978 lb.
March 26, 1776, on snow *Elizabeth,* for London	3,209 lb.
November 11, 1776, on brigantine *Betsey,* for London	3,181 lb.
April 12, 1777, on brigantine *Nancy,* for London	2,397 lb.

All in all, from 1771 to 1777, Turnbull exported to England 42,283 pounds of indigo.[45]

Fruitful Bondage

After the first difficulties and the serious crisis in the company's finances, a recovery began slowly, but steadily. In 1773, when Lieutenant Governor Moultrie, an experienced planter himself, visited New Smyrna, he was pleased with the "Spirit of Improvement of Industry" he saw there. He thought that they were "beginning to recover the expences they have been at on their first settling in this New Colony."[46] This spirit was expressed by Turnbull himself, who confidently stated in 1774: "I have a certainty before me of succeeding in a very large way for which I have now laid a solid foundation."[47]

Indeed, nine years after its first settlers set foot in this part of the Florida wilderness, New Smyrna had wrought a tremendous change in that area. By 1777, a small village had been established. There were two larger stores for provisions and a smaller one, the construction of which had cost £600; a windmill and one using horsepower, worth £330; 145 other houses valued at £35 each; Dr. Turnbull's dwelling house, for which the carpenter's work alone had cost £270; roads and bridges, at least four of which had been made of cedar at £30 each,[48] the others being made of coquina. There were the indigo works and other constructions where the processing of various products took place; there were large wharfs, canals, wells, boats that belonged to the settlement, and a great many other structures that had changed the landscape. What was more important, however, was the fact that by 1777, not only a diversified economy had been well established, but a cash crop, the precious indigo, was successfully produced and profitably sold in the British markets.

New Smyrna definitely was not a failure as an economic enterprise.

NOTES — *Chapter Five*

1. Lansdowne MSS, Vol. 88, p. 133 ff.
2. C. O. 5/548, p. 305; Governor Grant also called New Smyrna a concern of "great public Utility," of "much Utility to the Public." C. O. 5/550, p. 51, and C. O. 5/552, p. 30. Lord Hillsborough: "I am very sensible of the Advantage which the Public may derive from the success of Dr. Turnbull's Settlement at New Smyrnea," C. O. 5/551, p. 157; and later Lord Germain was concerned with "the very great advantage which the public must derive from the valuable Settlement at Smyrna," C. O. 5/556, pp. 232 f.
3. C. O. 5/548, p. 23.
4. Treasury 77/7, Mar. 9, 1781.   5. *Ibid.*   6. *Ibid.*
7. Privy Council. Register, Vol. 112, May 13, 1767.
8. Treasury 77/7, Mar. 9, 1781.

NOTES — *Chapter Five*

9. C. O. 5/550, pp. 5, 6.
10. *Ibid.*
11. Grant to Hillsborough, July 21, 1769, C. O. 5/550, p. 129.
12. *Ibid.*
13. Indenture of Oct. 2, 1769, Treasury 77/7, Mar. 9, 1781.
14. C. O. 5/548, pp. 305, 309, 313, 317.
15. "Narrative of Dr. Turnbull," *op. cit.*
16. C. O. 5/548, p. 313. It seems that this statement caused the erroneous belief that a Greek Orthodox Church with a Greek priest was established in New Smyrna.
17. C. O. 5/551, p. 38.
18. Whitehall, Apr. 3, 1769, C. O. 5/550, p. 71.
19. Whitehall, June 7, 1769, C. O. 5/550, p. 93.
20. Thos. Bradshaw to John Pownall, Treasury Chambers, Mar. 3, 1769, C. O. 5/550, p. 67.
21. C. O. 5/551, p. 157; C. O. 5/552, pp. 25, 30, 38.
22. Grant to Hillsborough, July 2, 1768, C. O. 5/541, pp. 423-24.
23. New Smyrna, Sept. 24, 1769, Lansdowne MSS, Vol. 88, p. 155.
24. *Ibid.*
25. C. O. 5/550, p. 5.
26. Turnbull, *op. cit.*, p. 685.
27. *Ibid.*, p. 688.
28. *Ibid.*
29. Turnbull to Shelburne, Minorca, Feb. 27, 1768, Lansdowne MSS, Vol. 88, f 147.
30. C. O. 5/550, p. 85.
31. C. O. 5/550, p. 55.
32. C. O. 5/544, p. 205.
33. In his report to the Spanish government of Nov. 17, 1790, Luis Fatio, describing the commerce of East Florida, stated: "In the time of the English two or three [sugar] mills had been begun at the Mosquitos and on the Aip River which produced sugar that was very white and of the best quality." Further down, Luis Fatio, who was a resident of St. Augustine and knew East Florida well, proposed a resettlement of the New Smyrna area with the colony's refugees then in St. Augustine. His proposal is interesting as indicating implicitly some of the occupations at New Smyrna of its old settlers: "If it were permitted to settle in that region and post a detachment of twenty men in the former towns of the Mosquitos, it would soon begin to be peopled, for there are in St. Augustine, Florida, families from Mahón who are accustomed to living there and only await permission to go to cultivate the land, raise bees for their honey and wax, catch fish to salt and make oil to be sold on this island [i.e. Cuba]. There are enough fish on that coast to support a very large fishery of all Kinds of fish of very good quality, and that infant settlement would soon be the beginning of one of the most important in this country." Luis Fatio, "Description of the Commerce of East Florida, Havana, Nov. 17, 1790", in Arthur Preston Whitaker, *Documents Relating to the Commercial Policy of Spain in the Floridas* (Florida, 1931), pp. 130-33. Charles Vignoles, in his *The History of the Floridas with observations on the Climate, Soil and Productions* (Brooklyn, N. Y., 1824), p. 72, also asserts that sugar was produced in New Smyrna.
34. Turnbull, *op. cit.*, p. 688; also, Turnbull to Germain, St. Augustine, Dec. 8, 1777, Sackville Historical MSS, II, 82 ff.
35. "Memorials of Thomas and William Grenville and Lady Mary Duncan," Dec. 30, 1786, Treasury 77/7 in Siebert, *op. cit.*, II, 299.

36. Kenneth H. Beeson, Jr., in his thesis presented for the Degree of Master of Arts at the University of Florida, in Jan., 1959, emphasized New Smyrna's character as an indigo plantation and he gave an account of the process of making indigo in East Florida drawn primarily from contemporary sources.

37. *Ibid.*, pp. 87 ff. For indigo's cultivation and processing, as well as for the laws and policy of the British government related to its production, see Malachy Postlethwayt, *The Universal Dictionary of Trade and Commerce* (London, 1757), entry: "Indigo," I, 981 f.

38. New Smyrna, Sept. 24, 1769, Lansdowne MSS, Vol. 88, p. 155.

39. C. O. 5/551, pp. 172-75.

40. C. O. 5/558. Enclosure of St. Augustine Custom House's statement on New Smyrna's exportations of Jan. 24, 1778.

41. Enclosure on carpenter's work in New Smyrna, of 1777, in Treasury 77/7.

42. "Memorials of Thomas and William Grenville and Lady Mary Duncan," *op. cit.*, p. 299.

43. New Smyrna, Oct. 3, 1774, Lansdowne MSS, Vol. 88, f. 157.

44. In the contemporary town of New Smyrna, Canal Street is built on one of those canals.

45. Enclosures of St. Augustine Custom House in C. O. 5/558.

46. Moultrie to Dartmouth, C. O. 5/545, p. 289.

47. Turnbull to Shelburne, New Smyrna, Oct. 3, 1774, Lansdowne MSS, Vol. 88, f. 157.

48. The facts and the prices cited can be found in the 1777 enclosure of "Carpenter Work on the Smyrnea Settlement" in Treasury 77/7.

SIX

Misery & Death Ravage the Frontier Swamp

THE MOST IMPORTANT ASSET OF New Smyrna was its colonists. Hard-working, pious, experienced farmers, they had cut the ties with their past on the other side of the ocean and were now determined to build a new life in this New World.

These were the times of imperial expansion for England. Men were badly needed to people the new areas, but they were hard to find. In other colonies in America, planters had to advertise abroad or to resort to the services of sea captains, who frequently provided the worst stock of labor. But even this was scarce, since it was very difficult for anyone to bring from Europe a significant number of people, and even more difficult to bring them all at one time. In the light of this situation, the settlers of New Smyrna—all these hundreds of seasoned Mediterraneans—were definitely the most desirable labor force. Together with the invested capital, the paternalistic policy of the British government, and the ready market for the products of the colony, they had made the prospect of Turnbull's venture very bright.

But the Florida wilderness had received them in a harsh manner, and conditions in the colony made life a constant struggle for survival. When after almost ten years the story of New Smyrna came to an end, failure was due not to a decline in the finances of the settlement, but to the attitude of its settlers, the result of what these people had experienced since they arrived in this land of promise.

Misery & Death

Everything was different in East Florida. The climate, for instance, was a great change for all of them. Used to the invigorating mountainous air of Mani, or to the sweetness of the Aegean Islands, or to the dry atmosphere of Corsica and the Mediterranean mildness of Minorca, they found the country around the Mosquito Inlet humid and hot, with torrents of rain in August and strong winds in the fall in comparison to which the Minorcan *tramontana* was a gentle zephyr. They all had come from places lying at least ten parallels farther north, and the subtropical climate of Florida was very strange to them.

It was difficult for them to become accustomed not only to the novelty of the flora and fauna and the nature of the South, but even to small things, such as the lack of rocks. Mani was nothing other than huge rocks with small ones between. The houses there were stone built; the roads were stone paved; the paths were among rocks; the children had fights with rocks; and since Homeric times young men in the village square used to throw the *lithos* to measure their strength. Corsica was also renowned since ancient times as the "rocky" island; and to these rocks the rugged Corsican temperament was attributed. Minorca was the same; since the stone age, when with the *talayots* and *taulas* and other megalithic and stony structures the early Minorcans expressed their religious feelings, down to modern times, when they still continue the centuries-old cleaning of their limited land from the rocks with which they make the picturesque dry-stone fences of their fields, the stone was deeply rooted in their consciousness. Then, in Florida, all these people found themselves in an unbelievable place where they could not find a single stone, for coquina, to them, was not really a stone. These innumerable little shells cemented together with some sand by a natural calcareous substance were beautiful, curious, practical, but they were not what they knew to be a stone.

They came to New Smyrna weary and sick. Six months after their arrival, Governor Grant reported: "They have been sickly, a seasoning no doubt was to be expected upon their Landing, but it has been attended with worse consequences that I lookt for" and then he described in a more detailed manner that "the only Disorder remaining among them is a scurvy which brings in Gangrenes mostly in the mouth. When their Gardens are got into Order 'tis to be hoped vegetables will effectually remove the bad Effects of a long and tedious Voyage from the Mediterranean."[1] It was only recently that the British had discovered that lemon juice, fruits, and vegetables were the most effective remedy against scurvy; and the considerate Governor had placed great expectations in the newly planted gardens. The only problem was, of course, to have these plants grow—a stage toward which they were all looking forward six months after their arrival.

Governor Grant, however, did not know that the most pernicious menace to their health was malaria.[2] People like the Maniotes, who did not have the terrible disease on their mountains, had little resistance and suffered tremendous losses. By 1777 only a few of them were left. The Minorcans, however, who had malaria on their island, seemed to have developed a greater defense, as if they had become immune to it.[3] The same was true of the Italians and Corsicans. It seems that the settlers suffered from various other diseases too, in addition to the many accidents and unfortunate incidents which ravaged their health. And the recovery of their exhausted constitutions could not take place fast, because their housing was poor, food was scarce, and working conditions very difficult.

The most grave mistake of Andrew Turnbull was that he brought to Florida almost three times as many colonists as he had originally planned, without having the means to accommodate and feed them. When he found so many willing settlers in Minorca, he could not resist the temptation, so with an unjustifiable optimism he piled them on the few ships he managed to find, hoping that somehow in Florida the problem of their maintenance would be solved. This impetuous act had frightened a wiser man, Governor Grant. "This affair, my Lord," he wrote to Lord Hillsborough, "has hung heavy upon my mind since the Landing of so great a number of people at a time, without any previous provision being made for them and without the Consent of the other parties concerned."[4]

A few weeks after their arrival, Turnbull placed them in individual farms on which they constructed palmetto huts. These huts were cool on warm days, but could offer neither comfort nor protection. When the occasional storms came the strong winds could harass them, and the palmetto leaves could not keep the rain out. Into the innumerable openings came mosquitoes, ants, "palmetto bugs," and the great variety of small and large insects of this semitropical climate which were attracted by the advantages of human habitation. Utensils and other commodities were very rare, for these people, leaving their countries under irregular circumstances and travelling in small ships with just enough space for them, could carry nothing but their very few personal belongings. Furniture was nonexistent and the floor of their huts, only sandy ground, could scarcely improve the sanitary conditions of their abode. Under such conditions lived the families, with their sick and their old and their newly-born babies.

Having in mind the improving of this situation, a year after their arrival Turnbull stated: "Tho' my People are comfortably lodged in Palm Hutts at present, I hope to have all the Farm houses built in one year more."[5] One year later, on September 1, 1770, the condition of the huts was thus described by Governor Grant, who failed to be aesthetically impressed by their exotic appearance: "[The colonists] are obliged to live in small hutts put up in a hurry to shelter them from the weather upon their first arrival. Doctor Turnbull . . . has not the necessary Tools and Materials to build Houses for them, in that distressed condition."[6] It seems, however, that some construction had already started. In accordance with orders given by Governor Grant, there was among several shipments to New Smyrna made by a prominent businessman, a John Gordon of Charleston, a schooner, *Carren,* which, on August 31, 1769, carried to the colony about 250 pounds of nails, plus axes, saws, and tools needed for construction.[7] But the huts—and in them the settlers—remained for many years to come. At some time in 1777, there were about 145 houses in the settlement. Though no one knows how they were constructed, it seems that a great number of them were used by the settlers.

The main problem of New Smyrna for several years was the scarcity of food. Before the arrival of the colonists, no food had been stored, although so many people were certain to need enough to last at least until they would be able to raise their own gardens. They had to rely, therefore, on what they could find in the New Smyrna area, mainly fish and game. Turnbull affirmed that he encouraged them to fish and that "they became so dextrous and successful that many families had for the most part great quantities of dried fish in their houses; fish being so plenty in the river, on the banks, on which their houses were built, that one man could generally catch as much in one hour, as would serve his family twenty-four, almost all having small canoes for that purpose."[8] Yet it seems that this was not always the case: when time was needed for urgent tasks, fishing was not permitted. In his deposition under oath, Rafael Simenis stated that he and Clegora (Gregorios) Calamaras and Michael Grasias (Garcia) "were very weak with hunger & bad usage, and were not able to fetch much grass, for which reason Dr. Turnbull whipt them severely with the Horse Whip every Morning and if they happened to fetch some Oysters or fish, they were taken away so that this Deponent and many others were obliged to kill snakes & eat them, or any other Vermin, or otherwise starve."[9]

The first two years were pitifully arduous. On the one hand it was too early for the colony to support its people with its own production, and on the other the London partners had become reluctant to continue the financial backing of New Smyrna. In vain, Governor Grant recommended to Turnbull to keep at least six months' provisions constantly in store.[10] Turnbull's funds were limited and he used to renew his provisions only when they were nearly exhausted. He knew, of course, that the Governor was right when he said that "if he [Turnbull] at any time had [provisions for] less than four [months] he might from the disappointment of a Vessel run the risk of starving the settlement, by not following my advice and by persisting in too nice computation, which won't do when a thousand people living in a wilderness may be deprived of Subsistence by an error in Calculation."[11]

The day came, in March, 1769, when Turnbull found himself "much pinched for Provisions." He was left with Indian corn enough for only one month, and it was his good compatriot again, Governor Grant, who came to his rescue. Without telling him anything and leaving him uneasy and worrying, the Governor sent the provincial schooner *East Florida* to Charleston to be loaded with corn and then to go directly to New Smyrna.

He was afraid, however, that the people in St. Augustine would be alarmed by such news of starvation in New Smyrna; hearing about it, they might even justify the rebellion of the previous year for which only a few weeks earlier two men had been publicly executed. For this reason, Grant spread rumors in town that the vessel was going to Savannah "for lumber and other things which [were] wanted."[12] When the *East Florida* arrived at New Smyrna with her food cargo the crisis was over.

A few months later, in July, 1769, the food situation was serious again,[13] and Grant had again to send them new shipments of foodstuff. On August 1, the *East Florida* carried, directly from Charleston, 600 bushels of corn and, strange as it sounds, "a large Copper Still" worth £101 5s. 4d; on the same day the schooner *Industry* left St. Augustine with 587 bushels of Indian corn and other provisions for the colony; on August 31, another, 1,412 bushels of corn were sent on the schooner *Carren,* and a little later the schooner *Sally* brought to the settlement 464 bushels of red pease, 332 of black-eyed pease, 402 of Indian corn, 2,200 pounds of rice, and 90 bushels of pease in casks. Finally, on November 10, the schooner *Active* arrived at Mosquito Harbor with a most welcome cargo—a little over 36,000 pounds of flour and 796 gallons of rum.[14]

After September, 1770, a slow improvement was noticeable. Several individual gardens produced "Indian corn, pease, potatoes, . . . greens of all kinds,"[15] "cucambers and melons" (437).[16] It seems that a few people at least received some pork once a week (435), sometimes four ounces a week (457), sometimes eight (450), and sometimes, if the settler happened to be a specialized workman like the master blacksmith, Louis Margan, as much as one pound of pork per week (441). In general, however, the steady diet for all and for every meal during the colony's life was hominy grits. Though it sounds odd, the settlers considered themselves lucky to have grits, because starvation was endemic in New Smyrna, and in this manner they could survive. Of all the dreadful experiences there, it was the agony of those who starved to death that gripped the memories of the survivors. When Anthony Stephanopoli narrated his life in the colony, he recalled that in the agreement he had made with Turnbull he was supposed to receive two pounds of fresh bread a day, or in case there was no bread, eighteen or twenty ounces of biscuit; also one pound of fresh meat a day or in case there was no fresh meat, half a pound of salt pork, plus a pint of wine or of whatever liquor there was in the country. However, he received nothing of all these, and "sometime after [the rebellion of 1768] the rest of the People being Starved, they began to die, ten or eleven a day & some days fifteen; That He . . . being very much Starved, agreed with some others, to run away again, and thought it better to die in the Woods, than live in such a miserable condition" (430). Giosefa (Joseph) Marcatto also said that he "almost starved to death," and he repeated this statement twice as if he particularly wanted to stress it (435). Juan Partella remembered that "about seven years since [their arrival in Florida, he] & the other people being almost starved, he agreed to go to Dr. Turnbull in their name & Complain, that he did so," and that all during his stay in New Smyrna he was "much stinted in Victuals, as also his Wife & all the rest of the People" (449, 450). Similar stories are endless. In them one finds people suffering and acting the way hungry people have always acted throughout history—like Juan Partella, for instance, who together with his wife "being almost starved," ate a "turkey buzzard" killed by one of the overseers (449); or like the "numbers of People" whom Petros Cosifacis saw, "who were starving catch the Alligators and eat as also the Cow-hide that was given them by Dr. Turnbull to make Moccazines" (473).

The clothing of the colonists was also in a wretched state and their bedding very poor. The few clothes they had brought with them from Europe were soon worn out on account of the hard work in the fields and their outdoor life. The one blanket which almost every one of them brought from the old country was, after some time, in a very bad condition. A little over two years after they had settled, Governor Grant found them "destitute of every convenience they are ill Clothed, many of them almost naked."[17] It was a very fortunate circumstance that the climate was warm and not much clothing was needed. Turnbull, however, was concerned with this grave situation and it is certain that he was the author of the following "Indent of Clothing and Tools etc. wanted for the Distressed Greek Settlement at Smyrnea—Under the direction of Andrew Turnbull, Esquire," enclosed in Governor Grant's report to Lord Hillsborough of September 1, 1770:[18]

Best blue Plains—3000 yards at 1/4d per Yard		200
Best white Plains—5000 yards at 1/4d per Yard		33. 6. 8.
Check't Linnens—3000 yards at 1/ per yard		150
Strip't Cottons—5000 yards at 1/3d per Yard		31. 5.
Strip't Linnens—2000 yards at 1/ per yard		100
Scots Canagraggs—4000 yards at 6d per yard		100
Neger Blankets—600 at 5sh each		150
Men's shoes of different sizes 600 pr		
at 2/3d per pair		100
Indigo Sickles 60 Doz at 6/6d per Dozen		25. 10
Broad Hoes, Crowley's, of a Middling size		
60 Dozen at 20/ per Dozen		60
Building Nails the greatest part sixpenny		100
		£1,050. 1. 8.

It seems that this order was materialized and that the clothes they made with material lasted for several years, because, in 1777, the settlers complained about not having clothes except for only the previous two or four years. Among those "almost naked" were Anthony Stephanopoli, who stated in May of 1777 that he "had no Cloaths for the last two years, & one blanket for nine years", (432)[19] and others like Giosefa Marcatto (436), Juan Partella and his wife (450), Rafel Hernandes (455), Luigi Cappelli (459), who were exactly in the same condition; Giosefa Lurance "had no Cloaths for four years past & except a Jaccket" (455). Rafel Simenis "had no Cloaths for three years" (463); Babpina Poutchedebourga "had no Cloaths [for] two years and a half" (465); Juan Serra, "no Cloaths for Eighteen Months" (461); Pompey Posse "had no Cloaths for fourteen Months Past & a Blanket for Nine Years" (438).

Conditions of work were in general harsh. The days were long, the hours many, and in most cases the week had seven days of work with no rest at all. There were several of them like Giosefa Marcatto who were "working days & nights, not even Sunday excepted without any rest" (435), or Petro Cosifacis who "hath served Turnbull Sundays, Holidays and all times" (440). And as if conditions were not miserable enough, there were the overseers who made the life of these people quite unbearable. Former noncommissioned officers of the British army, overseers of plantations in the Carolinas, and a few of them from among the ranks of the Italians, all had applied what one of the colonists has called every "unchristian manner" (479) to extract from the settlers the maximum of their productivity, the most handy method being flogging and a variety of other corporal punishments.

Alas for the one who would refuse to work because of sickness! Overseers, like the ex-corporal Nichola Moveritte, or another ex-corporal Simon, or John Brace, or a "Mr." Watson, or Lewis Pouchintena could beat them to death rather than let them stay away from the fields. Such was the fate of Anthony Musquetto, who "was sick in his bed [and] the said Nichola Moveritte came there and beat him very Severely with a large Stick and . . . Anthony Musquetto died within two Hours after . . . the beating he received, together with being put on half Allowance was the cause of his Death" (457, 467). And of Anthony Row who "being sick in his Room Lewis Pouchintena Came to his Room, beat him & drove him out to work, & when the said Anthony Row got to the field he beat him very much until the said Anthony Row leaned himself against a tree & dropped down dead" (457). And of James Grunulons who "being very sick in his bed, so much that he was not able to get out of bed to ease himself, that the aforesaid Simon came to his room, and asked the said James Grunulons what was the Matter, he answered that he was almost dead Simon then said you lie you are lazy & began to beat him and broke a stick on him in the bed & then beat him with his fists till he was tired, & then left him. That in about two or three days after, the said James Grunulons died" (446-47). And of Petros Demalachis "who was then sick in his bed, & drove him out of his room & Corporal [Moveritte] beat him with a Stick, & made him go to work at all times. At some time after, the said Peter Demalache being very sick, the said Nichola Moveritte went to his room and ordered him to go to work," and then after inhuman torture he left him lying in the fields all night; "in the morning the people went to work in the field when they found the said Peter Demalache laying Dead with his body covered with Musquitoes, all full of Blood" (443). And this was the fate of many, many others who being sick could not go to work.

Those who were healthier also faced heavy punishment and even death if their work were not satisfactory. Of course, if one happened to be lucky he might save his life. One day, for instance, the overseer "Nichola Moveritte, the Corporal, was quarrelling with a colonist Joseph Spinata, who was standing close by the said Mathew Trei [Triay, a servant of Dr. Turnbull, who happened to work in the fields that day] and . . . Moveritte lift up an Ax, & threw at the said Josefa Spinata, but missed him & hit the said Trei in the head & killed him" (477). That is the way lucky Spinata survived.

It is true that in all these incidents which caused the loss of human life Turnbull was not directly involved. He could not have been, because he was careful in handling property, and he knew only too well how irreplaceable was the life of his laborers. His role was different. In a place where work had ceased being a joy and the lack of reward and remuneration made it indifferent to the settlers, where a great number of people of different languages and backgrounds had to live together and the many deprivations had made their relations difficult, there was a need for a kind of order and regulation. And in this case, Turnbull was the law, or, as he worded it, "he was a Justice himself" (432).

Unless there was a major incident like the revolt of 1768, when His Majesty's government of East Florida had to interfere, Turnbull was the sole disseminator of justice in New Smyrna. In this role he appeared as being preoccupied mainly with two concerns: how to exert the full capacity of his men's labor and how to extend the originally agreed time of his men's service, in case this time had expired. Also, in a few known instances he appeared as simply regulating relations among the colonists.

The nature of the punishments which Turnbull inflicted upon those who had committed what he judged as being a crime, was either restriction of their personal freedom by confining them in prison—indicated as "stocks," "stockades," or "gaol"—or the imposition of a corporal punishment such as flogging and beating in various manners, placement in "irons," "chaining," and sometimes attaching to the chains heavy iron balls. A very frequent and quite convenient punishment was the drastic reduction of the violator's share of food. In several instances both confinement and corporal punishment were applied.

For the enforcement of his decisions, Turnbull used mostly his overseers, who, acting in his spirit, often exceeded the master in severity. There is no doubt that he had instructed them to be rigid and ironhanded in executing his decrees. One of the colonists, Juan Partella, stated among these overseers there was one, Lewis Sauche by name, who happened to be human; and that "one Morning Dr. Turnbull came into the field, & told the said Louis Sauche to beat the People very hard, not to Mind Killing a Man, for that was nothing, the said Louis Sauche Answered if you want to kill a Man you may do it yourself, for I will not. Dr. Turnbull then said if you dont I will break you & put another in your place" (450). Turnbull's suggestion for such a cruel treatment of the colonists was also confirmed under oath by Sauche himself (479). Sauche did not follow Turnbull's instructions literally, but other overseers did. And they killed men. But no one of them was ever punished for such a killing. Others used by Turnbull for the execution of his orders were Negro slaves or even colonists who reluctantly performed this duty. Not very rarely, he personally carried out his own verdicts. The result was that in New Smyrna fear reigned over all.

There is no need to narrate the depressing stories of many colonists since a few examples will be enough to tell about crime and punishment in the colony. When Giosefa Marcatto attempted to run away because "he was very badly used and almost starved to death," he was caught and brought back and confined in the gaol, with his legs "ironed"; and after some time he "was taken out of Gaol, & the Irons taken off & a large Chain twenty four pounds weight put on him, & was tied to a tree, & received one hundred & thirteen lashes . . . then [he] was sent to work, with the Chain & Chained to a log. That sometime after Doctor Turnbull came into the field, upon which [Giosefa Marcatto] went to him, & begged him for Gods Sake to take the Chain off; But Dr. Turnbull said, get out you Scoundrell, It is not time yet and . . . he wore it Six Months (435)."

Giosefa Marcatto's troubles did not end there. When the six years of service, to which he had agreed, had expired and he went to Dr. Turnbull to ask him about his release, he was instantly placed in solitary confinement, with only grits and water for food, and when he asked Dr. Turnbull why he was imprisoned, Turnbull answered that he had "cursed the English Justice." When the pressure was increased on him, Giosefa Marcatto "for fear of being Chained by the leg & Starved, Signed a Paper to serve him four years longer" (436).

Pompey Posse had similar experiences. At some time in 1773 Turnbull came into the field and asked Posse why he had not done his task well; when Posse answered that he had done it as well as the rest, "Doctor Turnbull beat him on horse back, & afterwards dismounted & beat him again, & struck him on his private parts, which obliged him to lay in a Palmetto house in the field all night" (437). When the 1768 revolt took place, Pompey Posse was arrested and because he had stated that he did not know anything about it, he was put in irons and then carried out and tied to a tree, where he received "five and thirty lashes from a Negro by Dr. Turnbull's order, who was likewise present" (437).

Stories like the above are many, often one more gruesome than the other. Though there is no case recorded of Turnbull himself killing one of his colonists, there are many where the punishment he imposed on them was terribly harsh. In the criminal code he had established, it seems that after the crime of rebellion and that of running away the most serious crime of all was the settler's request to be freed when the agreed time of service had been terminated. When Anthony Stephanopoli asked for his release, he was put "in the stocks," was maltreated, and finally was forced to sign for four more years of service (431-32). Petros Cosifachis was also forced to prolong his service for six more years (440). Louis Margan, after he had served the agreed five years, asked for his release and instead received fifty lashes, was put in irons, confined in gaol without any subsistence except a little Indian corn and water, and asked to sign again for a new period of service; and so Margan, "seeing the miserable Condition his Wife and Child [being six months and four days old] and likewise himself was in, being almost starved he was forced to sign a paper to serve Dr. Turnbull five years longer" (441-42). Luigi Capelli had agreed to serve six years, and "after having faithfully served his time out he applied to the said Doctor Turnbull for his discharge [and] Turnbull answered he would not give him his discharge, & ordered

[him] into Confinement with a Chain to his leg, & ordered no person to see him or give him any Victuals, not even his Wife. Except a little Hominy that Dr. Turnbull saw & stirred with a spoon, to see if there was any Meat or fish under it. And on the Monday after ordered [him] to be taken out of Confinement & tied up to a tree & had twelve Lashes given by a Negro and ordered [him] in the Stocks for six days, at the Expiration of which he was Put to his work" (459). Luigi Capelli did not ask Turnbull again for his release. But Anthony Generina (459), Pedro Quashi (459), Juan Serra (461), Christopher Fleming (475), Lewis Sauche (479-80), and others did, and they were all treated in the same manner. Babpina Poutchedepourga, like the others, having served the agreed six years, "was afraid to ask for his discharge for fear of being flogged & put in Irons" (465).

There were, of course, many wrongdoers in a colony where misery produced frictions in human relations and invited violations of moral standards. Turnbull was always there, however, to administer justice and apply a convenient *lex talionis.* Such was the case of a woman in New Smyrna who "told Dr. Turnbull that Anthony Lavay's Wife had used her ill upon which he [Turnbull] ordered the said Lavay to be tied up & made the other Woman flog her" (469).

But these stories are many and one should repeat what an unfortunate Greek of New Smyrna, Petros Cosifachis, stated before the judge when he told him—in a biblical simplicity reminding one of the closing lines of Saint John's Gospel or of Dante's *Inferno*—that he "verily believes if he was to relate every thing that was done on the Plantation there would be no end to it."[20]

These stories sound horrible and unbelievable. And yet only if one takes into consideration the deprivation, diseases, and starvation in New Smyrna, the living and working conditions, the atmosphere of terror, and the desperate feeling of "no-way-out," can one realize why 24 months after the arrival of the 1,255 colonists only 628 were left. An almost equal number of them, 627 to be exact, had died within this short time.

The Governor's official report of deaths in New Smyrna for the first ten years, up to 1777, reads as follows:

1768—Men and Women:	300	Children:	150
1769—Men and Women:	155	Children:	22
1770—Men and Women:	34	Children:	6
1771—Men and Women:	10	Children:	6

NEW SMYRNA

1772—Men and Women:	8	Children:	3
1773—Men and Women:	11	Children:	13
1774—Men and Women:	5	Children:	19
1775—Men and Women:	30	Children:	21
1776—Men and Women:	45	Children:	8
1777—Men and Women:	72	Children:	12
	670		260

To these, the Governor added 34 more adult Greeks, so during the span of ten years, 704 adults and 260 children died in New Smyrna —a total of 964.[21]

N O T E S — Chapter Six

1. C. O. 5/550, p. 5.

2. Since no description of sicknesses exists and no death records, it is difficult to express an opinion on the extent of this endemic disease. When the sickness is indicated in the records in a clear way, like Pompey Posse's "pleurisy" (C. O. 5/557, p. 438), there is no question. When, however, it is vaguely described, there is a great possibility that this was malaria, in the way that malaria was called the "fever" (*thermos*) in Greece as well as in other places. Thus, when Anthony Blaw was "always sick" (C. O. 5/557, p. 438), Peter Demalaches "was sick" (C. O. 5/557, p. 446), Biel Venis, was "very sick in his bed" (C. O. 5/557, p. 467) there is a possibility that they were cases of malaria.

3. George Cleghorn, a "lecturer then in Anatomy in the University of Dublin and former Surgeon to the Twenty-Second Regiment of Foot," devoted to malaria in Minorca during the eighteenth century the whole third chapter, "Of Tertian Fevers," of his book *Observations of the Epidemical Diseases in Minorca, from the Year 1744 to 1749* (London, 1779) pp. 147 ff.

4. C. O. 5/550, p. 7.

5. Lansdowne MSS, Vol. 88, p. 155.

6. Grant to Hillsborough, St. Augustine, Sept. 1, 1770, C. O. 5/551, pp. 154 f.

7. Grant to Hillsborough, Feb. 15, 1771, enclosure, C. O. 5/552, p. 37.

8. Turnbull, *op. cit.,* p. 685.

9. In connection with the depositions of settlers made before the Justice of Peace in May, 1777, Corse, *op. cit.,* p. 161, tends to disregard them, as not representing the truth: "Beyond a doubt, if these charges were true, Turnbull was not the good man that he had always been considered." The point, however, is not to establish the goodness or not of the author's ancestor, but to endeavor a reconstruction of a certain historical situation. The depositions include names of many colonists not found in any other document; they inform about aspects of the colony's life which are not given by any other source; they illuminate relationships of the people who lived and died there, and all are told with a moving spontaneity which, in this case, constitutes an assertion of frankness. In connection with the veracity of their statements, it should be

remembered that these were made under oath; and the deponents were very God-fearing people. On the other hand, it is true that the settlers were biased. But so were Tonyn and Moultrie and Drayton and Turnbull himself and many others. Historical criticism, however, carefully applied, can help to a certain degree in clearing the prevailing obscurity through acts and records of the above men.

10. Grant to Hillsborough, St. Augustine, Mar. 4, 1769, C. O. 5/550, p. 85.
11. *Ibid.*
12. *Ibid.*
13. C. O. 5/550, p. 129 f.
14. Enclosures of accounts in C. O. 5/552, pp. 37 ff.
15. C. O. 5/551, pp. 154 f.
16. C. O. 5/557. Page numbers are cited in text.
17. C. O. 5/551, p. 155.
18. Enclosure in C. O. 5/551, p. 156.
19. C. O. 5/557. Page numbers are cited in text.
20. *Ibid.*, p. 473. St. John 21:25, "Which, if they should be written every one, I suppose that even the world itself could not contain the books that should be written." In a paraphrase Dante says: "How faint and frozen I then became, Reader, do not ask for I do not write it down, since all words would be inadequate." *Inferno,* Canto XXXIV, 22-24.
21. C. O. 5/558, p. 107.

SEVEN

The Indians

THEIR FIRST CONTACT WITH THE Indians was a strange and terrifying experience for the colonists. As they had not actually seen "redskins" before, they were informed only by the wild stories they had heard. But in May of 1771, a number of braves came to New Smyrna. These strange creatures, sulky, with painted faces and armed for war, frightened the white people desperately.

There were many Indian nations in Florida during this time, and a little over a hundred miles from New Smyrna lived the Lower and Upper Creeks. Their relations with the British of East Florida, contrary to their relations with those of West Florida, were peaceful and friendly. This was the result of the wise policy of Governor Grant who, as soon as he arrived at the province, assured the various tribes that he was a friend, that they should not be afraid for their hunting grounds and their lives, and that his purpose was the maintenance of peace in East Florida.

In November of 1765, a congress took place at Fort Picolata where the chiefs and headmen of Florida's Creeks, Governor Grant, and the Superintendent of Indian Affairs in the Southern Department of North America, John Stuart, all agreed on the boundaries of the Indian lands.[1] This was a good opportunity for Governor Grant to give new assurances of his friendly sentiments, which he accompanied with generous gifts and expressions of hospitality to the prolonged visiting of chiefs and their families. Grant continued pursuing this policy of Indian appeasement, which was the predominant philosophy behind the Proclamation of 1763.[2] His contacts with the neighboring tribes were frequent; and later, in November of 1767, another congress took place at Picolata like the one of 1763.[3]

By following such a policy, Governor Grant had maintained peace and allayed the fears of the people of East Florida, who could devote their activities to agricultural pursuits without living under the uncertainty and nervousness of an expected Indian attack. This was not true, however, in West Florida, where friction between the British government and the Indians provoked savage attacks resulting in tragic loss of lives and property.

East Florida had avoided all these dreaded experiences, with the exception of a few unfortunate incidents which resulted in Governor Grant's appearing in the eyes of the Indian population as a trustworthy and just man. When in the spring of 1768 Indian renegades killed two white men at St. Marys River and burned their houses, Grant asked the aid of all tribes for the arrest and punishment of the killers. Strangely enough, he received all possible Indian support.[4] Again Grant's attitude was apparent the next year in January, when a backwoodsman killed a young Indian near St. Johns River. Grant ordered the arrest of the backwoodsman, who confessed his crime but refused to state the motives for the murder and subsequent hiding of the corpse. In a trial that followed he was found guilty, and Grant ordered his hanging, which took place on January 9, 1769, in front of the father of the murdered, with many other Indians watching.[5]

This unheard-of policy of uniform justice for redskin and white was not only a matter of conformity to the postwar spirit of the British government, but it was also a matter of expediency. Grant knew very well that "these Indians could lay waste this Infant Colony in a week."[6] He therefore decided to sacrifice the sentiments of the white backwoodsmen for the tranquillity of his province. The Indians, of course, were completely satisfied. When the father of the slain Indian saw the woodsman dead, he was "so much pleased as if his murdered son had been brought to life again"[7]; and all the other Indians agreed that here was a man whom they could trust and respect.

Grant's Indian policy, which had been entirely approved by Whitehall,[8] was very beneficial for the New Smyrna Colony. Knowing the "mortal antipathy" the Florida Indians nourished toward the Spaniards, Governor Grant was afraid that the complexion and language of the colonists would probably make the Indians think of them as

Spanish. So, when the colonists arrived from Europe, Grant invited the chiefs of the neighboring Indian tribes and explained to them that the people at Mosquitoes were not "White People," that is, Englishmen, but nevertheless they were subjects of the Great King; that they came from a little island with a warm climate; that they had been oppressed by the Spaniards whom they hated; and that now they had come to help their brothers, the English, to cultivate the new lands.[9] And the Indians, who had every reason to believe the good Governor, did not bother the settlement at all for a long time.

In May of 1771, Governor Grant was in England and was replaced by Lieutenant Governor Moultrie. It was during this time that two Indians informed the Upper Creeks that at the Mosquitoes there was a village of Yamasee Indians, their once-upon-a-time deadly enemies. Another Creek had added that there was also a Spanish settlement.[10] Such news was enough to excite the whole tribe into putting a party on the warpath.

This information was, of course, completely inaccurate. By that time, the Yamasee did not exist any more as a tribe. Their warlike years, when they enjoyed a reputation as ferocious warriors and as the best Indian allies of the Spanish, had long since come to an end. In 1727, the British had destroyed their last settlement close to St. Augustine, and by 1764 there were left no more than 40 of them, men and women, living in Pocolalaca,[11] just outside the southwestern walls of St. Augustine. A few more lived in Pensacola and all of them soon became slaves of the Seminoles. The misunderstanding about the Spaniards was caused by the Spanish idiom spoken by the Minorcans. But the Creeks wanted to be sure. Seventy-two braves under an Upper Creek chief, the Cowkeeper, one more chief, the Long Warrior, and a third headman left for New Smyrna. In their fierce ill-humor, upon their arrival at the Cowpen, they beat the crew of one of Turnbull's boats.

Turnbull at that time was in St. Augustine, but as soon as he heard about what he thought to be an Indian raid, he rushed back to New Smyrna and was happy to see that the situation was not as horrible as the frightened people had described it. He invited the headmen and 20 warriors into the settlement, treating them generously with food and drink. He explained to them that their information was erroneous, and he repeated Governor Grant's talk. After two days the Indians broke camp and one party went around the head of St. Johns River, returning home, while the other passed through New Smyrna southwards to explore the area and verify Turnbull's assurances that there were no Yamasee in the area. An overseer, Langley Bryant, and a Negro, Sandy, accompanied them as far as the southern plantations of the Hillsborough River, but the warriors soon returned when they found it to be true that there were no Yamasee there.[12]

Turnbull had an opportunity to explain to the Cowkeeper, the Upper Creek chief, that Governor Grant had gone to England to visit the Great King, but that another governor was in St. Augustine who would welcome a visit from the chief. Whereupon, on May 23, the Cowkeeper and another chief, with a few braves, visited Lieutenant Governor Moultrie, who received them in a friendly way. Moultrie explained that he was pleased to see the young, unruly warriors kept well disciplined and asked the Indians to avoid visiting plantations in the future. The chiefs promised to do so.[13]

The incident was not a serious one. With the exception of the beating of a few men and the carrying away of some provisions, no other harm was done to New Smyrna. Chief Cowkeeper, who was described by Turnbull as "a Sober manly Indian . . . very watchful over the others for fear they should do anything wrong,"[14] managed to keep his men in line, especially when he saw them drunk after Turnbull's hospitable treats. He beat some warriors "very severely" for offering to kill a calf that belonged to Turnbull, and he did not leave the plantation until everyone else had gone. A few days later Chief Long Warrior went to Turnbull and asked for one calf for his hungry people. The request was promptly granted, to avoid the possibility of the Indians' taking any stock without permission.

But though the visit was not harmful, it was enough to frighten the settlement and to add to their worries the most usual one among people who lived in the American wilderness: the Indians.

There was a side story related to this incident, which revealed the new political climate in St. Augustine after Governor Grant's departure for England. It is a story of political antagonism and personal antipathies, which started during this time and which, building up like a snowball, exploded in 1777. Among other damages, it contributed to the destruction of New Smyrna.

When Turnbull reported the Indian threat to his settlement, despite the fact that he knew Governor Grant had departed, he addressed his letter to him, "or in his absence to the Lieutenant Governor &c. &c.," as if he did not want to report directly to Moultrie. The report did not give much importance to the incident, but stated that

Turnbull "should be glad of a Reinforcement" of the small army force which was posted there—one sergeant and eight men of the 31st Regiment. These men had been stationed in New Smyrna since the rebellion of 1768. Turnbull thought that this military aid was needed "not so much for the Protection a small number can give us as for the appearance of our being under the care of Government, which these Indians seemed at first to doubt."[15]

On the basis of this report Moultrie wrote to Lord Hillsborough that the whole affair was "a false alarm and [that Turnbull was] commending the good conduct of the Indians."[16] But after Moultrie had sent the letter to Hillsborough, Turnbull sent another to Sir William Duncan, his London partner, in which he described the incident in a grave tone. He stressed especially that his people were "much alarmed," and asked Sir William to let Lord Hillsborough read this letter. Such an act was as if Turnbull really reported to Whitehall directly, passing over the Lieutenant Governor. After some time Turnbull visited Moultrie, revealing the colonists' fear of a new Indian attack and the widespread distrust of these Indians who, no doubt, had come purposely to attack New Smyrna. Then Turnbull made a decent gesture; he told Moultrie that he had reported all these opinions and events directly to Hillsborough through Sir William.

Moultrie was dumbfounded. He felt exposed to his government and expressed his surprise to Turnbull for what he termed the "two diametrically opposite" reports written within such a short time. Then he wrote and apologized to Lord Hillsborough for the discrepancy, also enclosing a copy of Turnbull's first report to him. He added that all the information he had collected was in agreement with what he personally knew, since he had lived most of his life in these parts of America and had been in war and peace with Indians: everything was peaceful and the British subjects had no reason to be afraid.[17]

Moultrie, however, suffered one more blow when a decision taken in Council requested the commanding officer of the British troops in Florida, Major Alexander McKensie, to reinforce the New Smyrna detachment with 12 more men.[18] McKensie was a friend of Turnbull, and perhaps under other circumstances he would have obeyed the order immediately. But in his reply, after stating that "Doctor Turnbull is a Gentleman that I have the greatest regard and esteem for," he added that it was not in his power to quiet the apprehensions and fears of the settlers, because he could not send reinforcements.

The Indians

The detachment of the 31st already there is very sufficient in my humble Opinion to Answer the purpose they were sent for. That is to prevent Mutiny and insurrection among the Greek settlers on that Plantation. If any other accident sho'd happen to make it seriously necessary to have more Troops Sent to the Mosquitos, you'll be so good as to make Application to General Gage, the Commander in Chief, who no doubt will give me Orders relative thereto.[19]

This was the Major's answer, expressing a definite contempt toward the acting Governor of the province. Apparently, in this preliminary round of a long fight, Moultrie was defeated. It was not so, however, in the long run. Moultrie immediately informed his government about these developments and Lord Hillsborough's anger could hardly be concealed on account of "such contradictory Accounts from Dr. Turnbull [which] had no other foundation than the Irregularity of a few drunken Strangers." Moreover, in connection with Major McKensie's conduct, Lord Hillsborough added: "I think however there was Sufficient Ground for the Application you made to the commanding Officer for a small reinforcement to the Party posted at Smyrnea, and I shall not fail at a proper time to consider what measures it may be advisable to take in consequence of his Refusal to comply with Your requisition."[20] Moultrie also did not forget this humiliation; and when the "proper time" came, he took "measures" that made his revenge ferocious.

This rupture of the relations among the notables of East Florida and the tension that followed had broken out a few months earlier, when Governor Grant decided to leave for England. To all who knew him it was not a leave of absence, but a departure from the colony. Already, in July, 1770, Lord Hillsborough had written to Grant that Robert Grant, a relative, had explained that circumstances in the Governor's private affairs rendered his presence necessary in England. As a mark of regard and attention, His Majesty's government had decided to grant the Governor a leave of absence for fifteen months unless, of course, the situation in America was unfavorable and made this leave inexpedient.[21] Grant, on the other hand, did not decide on leaving for eight more months. Perhaps it was the question of his replacement that made him undecided.

By March, 1771, Grant had made up his mind. He wrote to Lord Hillsborough that for some time he was bothered with "Bilious Disorders in [his] stomach and Bowels" and that the "Physical Gentlemen" had deemed it necessary for him to have a "Change of Climate"

99

and a "Sea Voyage."[22] Perhaps that was true; because of the water conditions in St. Augustine during this time, a great number of people suffered from dysentery and other similar diseases; and true perhaps was the situation of his private affairs in England. But it seems that among other reasons that induced him to leave Florida was the fact that he had had enough of the difficulties in an underdeveloped colony of America, that he felt nostalgic for his old country, that he did not like the restlessness and the rebellious climate of opinion prevailing over the colonies,[23] and that he saw possibilities of a successful political career back home on account of his military and administrative background. On May 9 he left Florida for England.[24] His leave of absence had been prolonged; and in April, 1773, when he had completed almost two years in England, Grant wrote to the Earl of Dartmouth, who had replaced Lord Hillsborough in the meantime: "The Election of the Northern District of Burroughs is to be the 26th of the Month—I shall have the concurring Votes of the five Towns, but as foreign Governors are precluded from sitting in Parliment, I must beg of your Lordship to lay me at the Kings Feet, and to ask His Majesty to permit me to resign the Government of East Florida, which I found a Wilderness, have had ten years and leave an useful Colony to the British Empire."[25]

The most important problem before Grant's departure from St. Augustine was the selection of the person who was to become the Acting Governor. Lord Hillsborough had noticed that of all members of East Florida's Royal Council, only three had been regularly appointed: "Mr. Woolridge, Dr. Turnbull and Mr. Jolly,"[26] and he suggested that the elder of them should replace the Governor during his absence. James Grant, however, had his own ideas. In a lengthy letter he discussed each of these gentlemen and he excluded all three of them. In connection with Turnbull he had found him "unexceptionable, but constant Residence at Smyrna is absolutely and indispensably necessary," and so "he is not to be thought of."[27]

Grant's own choice was John Moultrie, "the first and best Planter" of the province, as he called him.[28] In his letter the Governor offered many reasons for advocating Moultrie's appointment to the rank of Lieutenant Governor. The first was that Moultrie had been attracted to stay in Florida because for the last seven years he had been considered as the President of the Council. "It was that Feather," Grant explained, "that induced him to move into the Colony [because] he married a Woman of considerable property who would not have agreed to leave her favorite Carolina upon any other Terms."[29] Then Grant resorted to more persuasive arguments. In the New World the real value of a man was judged by what he could produce:

Mr. Moultry made the Salop which I sent Your Lordship last year— his indigo sold for six shillings and threepence which beat me by a shilling in the pound—he has made a small Cask of Wine this year has a Field of Sugar Cane ready to cut—and is to make Rum and a small quantity of Sugar by way of Experiment to see how the Cane produces—I intend to send Your Lordship some of each with Samples of this Year's Indigo and a bottle or two of Wine if I think it tolerable, such a man leaving the Province would be a great misfortune to the Country; I must therefore beg leave to recommend Mr. Moultry as a proper person to be appointed Lieutenant Governor.[30]

This was the *sui generis* but powerful and eloquent way Governor Grant recommended John Moultrie, the man who, with the fine quality of indigo he had produced, managed to beat him "by a shilling in the pound." Salop (or salep) is a thick, syrup-like drink, well known especially in the Middle East. It was usually served hot, with milk and sugar to which had been infused either certain powdered East India orchids, or in this case, Florida sassafras. Those who were very particular used to add powdered cinnamon for a more exquisite taste. Unless the Earl of Hillsborough was really fond of salop, the excessive sweetness of which had disposed him favorably toward Moultrie, it is almost certain that the qualities of the man, as were described by Governor Grant, impressed him.

The only other person who could have been appointed instead of Moultrie was Andrew Turnbull. But for reasons not very clear, Grant did not want to see him holding this responsibility. Grant had helped Turnbull in the past and liked his compatriot from Scotland a great deal. Moreover, a success in New Smyrna meant a success in Grant's province, and so by helping Turnbull, he was also helping himself. It seems, however, that the daring doctor with the grandiose plans and strong imagination did not inspire the Governor with confidence. The thoughtless transportation of so many Mediterraneans to Florida's wilderness without having made the necessary preparations, a heavy negligence for which Grant severely criticized him earlier; the peculiar handling of the colony's accounts, which had caused friction with his distinguished partners in London; and perhaps Turnbull's aggressiveness, all contributed to make Grant take a disparaging attitude. Later in London, Grant took an even more stern look at Turnbull, when he decided to be one of the witnesses supporting the claims of Turnbull's opponents.[31]

For the time being, however, Grant was concerned with the problem of keeping Turnbull out of the governorship. Without having asked him and, of course, without having Turnbull's views on this question, once again Governor Grant, on the eve of his departure from Florida, explained to Whitehall why Turnbull could not have been appointed Lieutenant Governor: "Doctor Turnbull obliged to constant Residence at Smyrnea could not with propriety think of entering into the Administration if he was to be continued in it, and of course as things are Circumstanced will not interfere with Mr. Moultrie, who may properly receive His Majesty's Mandamus in a few weeks, at any rate long enough before he can have any business of consequence to transact—for I shall leave him very little to do for some time."[32] The only trouble was that Turnbull could "think of entering into the Administration," and his thoughts were shared also by a few of his friends, who included William Drayton, the Chief Justice of East Florida.

When Grant's intentions for his replacement became known, and a little later on February 11, 1771, when it was learned that His Majesty had conferred upon John Moultrie the rank of Lieutenant Governor,[33] the Turnbull-Drayton circle developed a marked hostility toward the salopmaker. Perhaps up to that time they had felt only a kind of jealousy and dislike toward a rich, successful, and somewhat vain planter of their limited and provincial society of East Florida. But after Moultrie's elevation to Lieutenant Governor, they developed a contempt for him and became very antagonistic to his policies. However, it was not until after the Indian visit to New Smyrna that Moultrie became aware of the cleavage created between him and those who did not like him. In this way, the most catastrophic factional struggle in British East Florida had started. A few years later, William Drayton, speaking about his part in this feud, remarked that it had arisen "from some trivial cause between these two gentlemen [Drayton and Moultrie] (who were Countrymen & old Aquaintance), long before the first had been promoted to his Office, &, like most disputes between former Friends, had been carried rather to a degree of Excess and Rancour. It is immaterial, which of them was wrong at the Commencement of it; certain it is, that both are in some Degree censurable, if the Consequence affected the Public. But this ought to have been prevented."[34]

1. C. O. 5/548, pp. 113 ff.
2. *Ibid.*, pp. 449 ff.
3. C. O. 5/549, p. 25.
4. C. O. 5/544, p. 77.
5. Grant to Hillsborough, St. Augustine, Jan. 14, 1769, C. O. 5/544, p. 191.
6. *Ibid.*
7. *Ibid.*
8. C. O. 5/548, p. 265.
9. C. O. 5/549, p. 284.
10. C. O. 5/552, p. 94.
11. Don Joseph Antonio Gelabert, Representative of the Council of Indies, to the Crown, *Materias de la Real Hacienda*, Florida, 1752-64, A.I. 87-1-14/2, pp. 113-114, Stetson Collection, University of Florida.
12. Turnbull to Grant "or in his absence to the Lieut. Governor," New Smyrna, May 9, 1771, C. O. 5/552, p. 97.
13. Moultrie to Hillsborough, May 23, 1771, C. O. 5/552, p. 85.
14. C. O. 5/552, p. 95.
15. C. O. 5/552, p. 97.
16. St. Augustine, June 13, 1771, C. O. 5/552, p. 90.
17. C. O. 5/552, P. 92.
18. Moultrie to McKensie, St. Augustine, June 3, 1771, C. O. 5/552, p. 102.
19. McKensie to Moultrie, St. Augustine, June 6, 1771, C. O. 5/552, p. 105.
20. Hillsborough to Moultrie, Whitehall, Dec. 4, 1771, C. O. 5/552, p. 123.
21. Hillsborough to Grant, Whitehall, July 31, 1770, C. O. 5/551, p. 85.
22. St. Augustine, Mar. 20, 1771, C. O. 5/552, p. 69.
23. Grant to Hillsborough, St. Augustine, Feb. 9, 1769, C. O. 5/550, pp. 81-82.
24. Moultrie to Hillsborough, St. Augustine, May 12, 1771, C. O. 5/552, p. 77.
25. London, Apr. 22, 1773, C. O. 5/553, p. 37.
26. C. O. 5/551, p. 85.
27. *Ibid.*, p. 174.
28. *Ibid.*, pp. 172-73.
29. *Ibid.*
30. Grant to Hillsborough, St. Augustine, Oct. 19, 1770, C. O. 5/551, p. 171.
31. Treasury 77/7, The Memorial of Thomas Grenville, William Wyndham Grenville, and Lady Mary Duncan, Claim of Losses suffered in East Florida, No. 151, delivered Dec. 30, 1786.
32. Grant to Hillsborough, St. Augustine, Mar. 20, 1771, C. O. 5/552, p. 69.
33. Hillsborough to Grant, Whitehall, Feb. 11, 1771, C. O. 5/552, p. 5.
34. William Drayton in his unpublished *An Inquiry into the Present State and Administration of Affairs in the Province of East Florida; with some Observations on the case of the late Ch. Justice there (1778)*, in the Manuscript Division of the Library of Congress.

EIGHT

Worshiping God in the Wilderness

THE DEVELOPMENT OF A FACTIONAL STRIFE in the back-
stage of East Florida's political scene did not affect New
Smyrna at the beginning. People there lived and loved,
struggled and died, and in this part of the American wilderness a familiar pattern of frontier life was repeated.

Those who only a few years ago met for the first time when they
were packed in the hold of the same boat had now become friends.
The understanding of Spanish and English by more colonists made
them know each other better. Bound as they were by the same fate,
living under the same conditions, facing together the grave problem
of survival, they became steadily less aware of the contrasts of their
different backgrounds. A community of new attitudes and ideas developed among them. Romances started between men and women of
the colony. The Greek Orthodox Maniotes and the Uniate Corsicans
married dark-eyed Roman Catholic Minorcan girls and widows. And
soon Father Pedro Camps diligently began recording the baptisms of
the newly-born babies. This was a new generation, an American one,
the little roots of the colonists that started growing in this land.[1]

He was a good priest, this Father Pedro Camps. A native of Minorca, he had served for about 12 years as vicar and assistant parish priest
in the island's little town of Mercadal. He had studied at the University of Mallorca from which he had received the degree of Doctor of
Sacred Theology. He had preached during many Lents, and as he

was hardworking and devoted to his ministerial duties, he had commanded the profound respect of his parishioners. When in 1768 hundreds of Minorcans decided to join Dr. Turnbull, Father Pedro Camps also decided to go with them so that they would not be deprived of spiritual guidance in that faraway part of the world. He landed among the first colonists in New Smyrna, and he was the last to leave. The 9th of November, 1777, when he moved from New Smyrna to St. Augustine, marks the closing date of the history of this colony.[2]

The coming of Roman Catholics to the colony was unexpected. Originally, Turnbull planned to bring a Greek Orthodox priest, who would be required also to perform the duties of a teacher among the first 500 Greek settlers Turnbull intended to transport. In fact, he had asked the Board of Trade to approve a salary of £100 annually for such a purpose[3] from the unclaimed bounty of East Florida; and the Board of Trade, in turn, had authorized Lord Shelburne to decide on this matter.[4] But this plan never materialized. The last time the Maniotes had seen Greek Orthodox priests was when they were leaving the port of Coron. Wrapped in their long black robes, these priests stood solemnly among the excited crowd. They were the ones who finally gave the signal for the departure of the boats.[5] The Maniotes still remembered their black silhouettes on the docks, blessing them in benediction until, as the boats sailed away, they became small black dots which shortly disappeared over the horizon together with everything else that meant Greece to them.

One of the terms of the grants issued to Turnbull and his partners by the King in Council was that within ten years they should people their land with white Protestant inhabitants.[6] Turnbull's recruitment of Greek Orthodox did not raise any objection since their sect was always considered as a precursor and affiliate of the Anglican Church. Strangely enough, however, no objection was raised to the hundreds of Minorcan Roman Catholics who came to Florida. The reason was that Minorca was ceded to England by the Treaty of Utrecht in 1713; to this, a separate treaty of peace between England and Spain was adjusted, which in its eleventh article provided for the safe, peaceful, and honorable enjoyment of the Roman Catholic religion by the inhabitants of the island. Thus, the Minorcans were people living within the Empire, formally enjoying religious freedom, and being able to move from a British colony in the Mediterranean, like Minorca, to a British colony in America, like Florida, without changing their status. Underlying this reasoning there was, of course, the persuasion of expediency. Without settlers Florida was useless; and when it was so difficult to find immigrants for this part of the New World, it would seem unreasonable to argue about the religious affiliation of the few Christians who after so much trouble and expense had been brought to America.

Despite the terms of the treaty, the British had restricted the activities of the Roman Catholics in Minorca and had taken special care to isolate them from their spiritual leaders who were in Spain. Thus, the Bishop of Minorca, who resided in nearby Palma de Mallorca, was completely uninformed about the happenings in his diocese, and only from time to time did he receive news by word of mouth from his vicar-general, who lived in Mahón. So when Father Camps and a young Augustinian monk, Father Bartolome Casanovas, decided to join the Turnbull party, they could not communicate with their bishop and ask his permission to do so. The vicar-general in Minorca gave them leave to depart, but he could not answer the question of their powers and privileges in the New World. Since it was easier to contact Rome than Mallorca, the two clerics decided to submit a request for faculties directly to the Vatican. Evidently this request was also supported by an appeal made by the Minorcan families of the Turnbull expedition, begging that their own priest be allowed to make the journey.[7]

As the Vatican had no clear picture of what happened in Minorca, or of the situation in Florida after the departure of the Spaniards in 1763, their request came as a surprise; and it was not until June 18, 1768, that the faculties were granted to Father Camps and Father Casanovas. They were both empowered as Apostolic missionaries for the English province of East Florida. The faculties were for a period of three years within which the two clerics were instructed to contact the diocese nearest their American location.[8] The powers granted to them were wide, but arrived at Minorca too late—Turnbull's ships had already sailed for America. On them had sailed the two priests who, faithfully attached to their parishioners, possessed a feeling of uncertainty and guiltily believed there was a degree of irregularity in their departure. Moreover, they were afraid that in this unknown part of the New World where they were going, they would find themselves cut off from the Holy See—and they were.

Despite the difficulties of life in New Smyrna, a spacious church of brick was soon built, and its decent appearance later impressed a

Cuban fisherman who landed in the colony on his way to northern fisheries.⁹ The church was dedicated to Saint Peter, the Apostle who was a fisherman, like most of the colonists; perhaps some of them had thought it particularly proper to dedicate their church to the Saint who holds the keys of the kingdom of heaven, whose gates New Smyrna constantly kept so busy. Like another Aeneas, Father Camps had brought from his island two statues, one of Saint Peter and the other of Saint Anthony. Together with the figure of Christ over the high altar, they became the main decoration of the simple interior.¹⁰

The Roman Catholic parish of New Smyrna, which included the majority of the settlers, had been left free in all religious activities. But Father Camps soon realized that the isolation of the colony could become a hindrance to the normal function of his church. A year after their arrival, he was in grave need of holy oils to administer baptism and extreme unction. Luckily enough, in October of 1769, two Cuban fishermen, on their way north, put into the vicinity of the Mosquito Inlet. To them, Father Camps gave a brief note for the bishop of Santiago de Cuba who, according to every indication, was the superior closest to their parish. Father Camps explained the conditions in New Smyrna and his need for holy oils and two directories for the recitation of the divine office. He begged the bishop in his note to take them under his protection.¹¹

The bishop, Santiago Joseph Echevarria, had never heard of this colony at the Mosquitoes before. He did not know how much credit he should give to the story of the fishermen and to the note he had received. And so, an unbelievable search for the truth started, a search that lasted for years and reflected the highly bureaucratic mind of eighteenth century Spain. Echevarria contacted the Governor of Cuba. He also was ignorant of the Florida situation and after some preliminary investigation he decided to request the advice of the King's Council in Madrid. They too did not know anything about New Smyrna. A judicial authority was subsequently appointed to examine the whole case and issue a decree on the matter. Since he could not find any record substantiating Father Camps' account, he praised Echevarria and the Governor of Cuba for their prudence and asked for additional information from the bishop in Mallorca and from the representative of the King of Spain at the Vatican. But a special permission of the British Privy Council was needed for the bishop to communicate with the vicar-general in Minorca; and in the Vatican also an inquiry demanded time.

On October 12, 1771—two years after his first message—Father Camps managed to send two more letters; one to Echevarria expressing his anxiety about the difficult situation of the New Smyrna parish and one to the Holy See in Rome requesting the renewal of his faculties. Fortunately, the search in Spain, in which many more authorities had been involved, ended happily. All gathered information pointed to the integrity and excellence of the two clerics in New Smyrna and to the accuracy of Father Camps' story. Their faculties were renewed, and on December 3, 1771, a Cuban fisherman secretly brought Father Camps the good news and the holy oils. Two years later, in May of 1773, Father Camps was informed by Bishop Echevarria, in the same secret manner, that the Holy See had extended their faculties for 20 years and that his authority had been greatly increased.[12]

Both missionaries were very grateful for the attention given to their requests. The established contact with their superiors gave them a feeling of security. But they were not happy at all with the widespread misery and the continued maltreatment of the people in the colony. Toward this situation each one of them reacted in his own manner. Father Camps, older and more composed, believed that by concentrating his efforts in securing a regular function of his church he would offer a source of consolation and hope, so acutely needed in New Smyrna. The only person to whom he communicated his worries about conditions in the colony was Bishop Echevarria. To him at very rare intervals, Father Camps wrote about the sufferings and nostalgia of his parishioners.

Father Casanovas, however, was different. He was younger and more temperamental. His experience was not so extensive, although in Minorca he had been given the license and power to preach and to hear confessions, and he had preached for some time in the parish of Alazor. The bishop of Minorca had stated in March 22, 1773, after having examined his record, that "he had found nothing wrong in his conduct."[13] But about a year later Father Casanovas could not restrain himself any longer. He raised his voice in protest against the cruelty and tyranny that prevailed in the colony.

This outspoken censure irritated Turnbull. As long as the church could offer spiritual relief by diverting the parishioners' attention from their temporal, mundane troubles to their afterdeath life, the priests were tolerated. But when, instead, they denounced the cause of the misery around them and in so doing excited and demoralized the colonists, Turnbull thought that drastic measures should be taken.

He immediately notified the British authorities at St. Augustine regarding the secret visits made to the colony by the Cuban fishermen. He presented the whole affair as a "Spanish intrigue" involving the young Augustinian who, for this reason, should be sent back to his country.[14]

In this manner the anguish of six years ended for Father Casanovas.[15] When he was forced to leave for Europe in 1774, he left the tried and sick Father Camps alone and with doubled responsibilities. With the departing friar, Father Camps sent a letter to the vicar-general of Minorca requesting the dispatch of priests, so that he too could return to his island. He was afraid that his ill health would prevent him from performing his duties.[16] His superiors, however, responded very slowly. When two other priests, both Irish, finally arrived in Florida, it was much later, after the Spanish had returned. On May 22, 1790, the seventy-year-old Father Camps ended his days in St. Augustine without having seen his beloved Minorca again. But he had great satisfaction when he closed his eyes, surrounded by his heartbroken parishioners, whom he had not abandoned during the days of their "Babylonian captivity."[17] He was indeed a brave and good man, this Father Camps.

The Anglicans of the colony were not as fortunate as the Roman Catholics in enjoying the continuous services of devoted clergymen. For some time after their arrival, the Anglican minister of St. Augustine, Rev. John Forbes, visited New Smyrna at intervals and conducted religious services. A young Scotsman, about twenty-eight years old in 1768, Mr. Forbes had received his Master of Arts degree ten years earlier from the University of Aberdeen. He was the first Anglican minister to come to Florida after the Treaty of Paris of 1763, and since he was one of the few educated men in the province, with a distinguished personality, he was appointed to a seat on the Colonial Council of East Florida on November 22, 1764.[18] Ambitious, and being much involved in local affairs, he became known more for the performance of his administrative and judicial affairs than for his religious activities.

These additional responsibilities and the fact that he resided in St. Augustine did not allow Mr. Forbes the time to meet the spiritual needs of the remote parishioners at New Smyrna. Moreover, other reasons, sometimes happy and sometimes unhappy, also contributed to make his visitations to the colony rare. His health had been impaired, and after his being "dangerously ill" in 1767, Governor Grant had given him a leave of absence to go north for his complete recovery. In the autumn of 1768 he left again "to go to Boston to be married to a young Lady with some Fortune," as Governor Grant reported to Whitehall.[19] Thus, on February 2, 1769, the Rev. John Forbes married Miss Dorothy Murray, with whom he returned to Florida after some time.[20]

During his absence the chaplain of the 21st Regiment acted as the clergyman of the town of St. Augustine. New Smyrna, however, was left without an Anglican priest for months. Governor Grant was seriously concerned about this problem. He wrote to his government and, as a solution, asked the transfer of the appointed clergyman to St. Marks because "he may be of great use at New Smyrna, which in the future I should imagine will be the proper place of residence for the clergyman and schoolmaster intended for St. Marks."[21]

After some time there arrived the Rev. John Frazer, who, on March 23, 1769, had been licensed to East Florida. He immediately established himself in New Smyrna.[22] The Protestant parish was reorganized and by 1771 the Anglican church was built which, with the Roman Catholic St. Peter's, was mentioned in the description of the colony by William Gerald de Brahm.[23] This Protestant revival did not last very long. The life of the wilderness, its hardships, and its misery were too arduous for the good missionary, Mr. Frazer. In 1772 he migrated, like so many of his parishioners, from the sandy shores of the Mosquitoes to his heavenly home.

The death of Mr. Frazer meant again that there was no resident Protestant clergyman in the colony. And so again Lieutenant Governor Moultrie asked the Rev. John Forbes to visit New Smyrna regularly and officiate there as he had a few years earlier. Moultrie explained to Lord Dartmouth that in this manner he would be "glad to give the people not only the benefit of a clergyman, but to keep up a decent and proper appearance of religion in the quarter." Because Mr. Forbes had to "incur some expense and a good deal of trouble," Moultrie asked for the approval of the payment to him of the salary appropriated for the colony's clergyman until, of course, another one would be appointed.[24] This request was promptly approved.[25]

Finally, in November of 1773, the replacement of the late Mr. Frazer arrived. He was Rev. John Leadbeater who, on May 18, 1773, had been appointed for St. Marks. As soon as he set foot in Florida, he was directed to New Smyrna.[26] He stayed there only a few months, which were enough, however, to shock him and to undermine his health. In the summer of 1774, after suffering an infection of boils, he decided to return to England. In vain Governor Tonyn tried to induce him to stay by making him attractive offers, but Mr. Leadbeater was determined to avoid the fate of his predecessor. And so, after some time in St. Augustine, he left for England in 1775.[27]

For three more years the colony was left without an Anglican minister. The young Rev. John Kennedy, who was originally nominated as Mr. Leadbeater's curate in St. Marks parish, arrived in Florida in 1778.[28] But by that time there was no New Smyrna Colony.

Seal of St. Peter's Church at Mosquitoes and signature of Father Pedro Camps

NOTES — Chapter Eight

1. This important record of baptisms is known as *Father Pedro Camps' Register* or, as the descendants of this tormented generation call it, "The Golden Rule Book of the Minorcans." The original is found in the library of the Roman Catholic bishop of St. Augustine, while a copy of it has been deposited in the Archives of the St. Augustine Historical Society.

2. All biographical data and the account of the activities of the Roman Catholic Church in New Smyrna are based on the documents deposited in the *Archivo General de Indias*, Seville, and especially in the following two *legajos:* Audiencia de Santo Domingo 2594 and 2673. Several of them have been published in *The Unwritten History of Old St. Augustine*, already cited, pp. 191-228; they have been also quoted, together with several others, in Curley, *op. cit.*, pp. 23-49.

3. "Narrative of Dr. Turnbull," *op. cit.*, and C. O. 5/541, p. 211.

4. C. O. 5/548, pp. 305, 313.

5. Pouqueville, *op. cit.*, p. 332.

6. C. O. 5/548, p. 23.

7. "Proceedings of the Council of the King of Spain," 1773, in *The Unwritten History of Old St. Augustine, op. cit.*, p. 217.

8. In connection with the faculties see *ibid.*, pp. 217-21; also, for a copy of them in Latin in Curley, *op. cit.*, pp. 26-27, fn. 29.

9. "Proceedings of the Council of the King of Spain," *op. cit.*, p. 223.

10. Curley, *op. cit.*, p. 35.

11. *Ibid.*, pp., 41-49.

12. *Ibid.*, p. 44.

13. "Proceedings of the Council of the King of Spain," *op. cit.*, p. 222.

14. The myth of the "Spanish intrigue" had been later repeated by Corse, *op. cit.*, p. 95 ff. The correspondence between Father Camps and Echevarria, as well as of all Spanish authorities involved, is now known and deposited in the Spanish Archives in Seville. It shows clearly that any statement about a Spanish intrigue is completely unfounded. On the contrary this collection of documents makes evident that all responsible Spanish authorities were completely uninformed on the establishment of New Smyrna; that they reacted in a very leisurely manner; that the established contact intended only to secure the regular function of the church; and that the secrecy kept in those contacts had been adopted in order to avoid diplomatic complications since, despite the established treaties, the British did not favor the growth of Catholicism.

15. Siebert says that "the immediate result" of the seizure of a vessel in Mosquito Inlet and the revelation of the unlawful correspondence "was the conviction and execution at St. Augustine of the priest and several Minorcans on the charge of high treason." Siebert, *op. cit.*, p. 6. This is completely inaccurate. It is evident that Siebert took this information from Corse, *op. cit.*, p. 99.

16. Curley, *op. cit.*, p. 35.

17. *Ibid.*, p. 218. On Father Camps' life and work see also Michael V. Gannon, *The Cross in the Sand, The Early Catholic Church in Florida, 1513-1870* (Gainesville, University of Florida Press, 1965), p. 86 ff. An excellent account of Father Camps' death and burial is found in Eugenia B. Arana and Doris Wiles, "Burials in the Cathedral," *El Escribano* (A Quarterly of the Saint Augustine Historical Society), III (Jan., 1966), 15-19.

18. Edgar Legare Pennington, "The Church in Florida, 1763-1892," *Historical Magazine of the Protestant Episcopal Church*, III (Mar., 1938), 4 ff.

19. St. Augustine, Dec. 1, 1768, C. O. 5/550, p. 8.

20. Pennington, *op. cit.*, p. 11.

21. C. O. 5/550, p. 8.

22. Pennington, *op. cit.*, p. 10; also, Siebert, *op. cit.*, I, 6.

23. De Brahm, *op. cit.*

24. Moultrie to Dartmouth, St. Augustine, Aug. 25, 1772, C. O. 5/552, pp. 379-80.

25. Dartmouth to Moultrie, Whitehall, Dec. 9, 1772, C. O. 5/552, p. 383. See also, Moultrie to Dartmouth, St. Augustine, Feb. 19, 1773, C. O. 5/553, p. 33.

26. Pennington, *op. cit.*, p. 12; Siebert, *op. cit.*, p. 6.

27. Siebert, *op. cit.*, pp. 6-7.

28. Pennington, *op. cit.*, p. 8.

NINE

The American Revolution at Florida's Door

JOHN MOULTRIE DILIGENTLY CONTINUED to perform the duties of the Lieutenant Governor of the province. But Andrew Turnbull, William Drayton, and their friends persistently opposed his measures.

Actually Turnbull ought to have been satisfied with some of Moultrie's achievements. For instance, the 20-mile roadway south of St. Augustine toward New Smyrna, completed by September 25, 1771, was a great convenience for all planters of the area, but most especially for Turnbull himself. The lack of a road through the wild, hazardous terrain made transportation a risky undertaking, as Governor Grant had asserted when he first advocated this improvement.[1] But now bridges and causeways were built; carts and wagons could roll to the south through areas previously covered by marshes which had fatally trapped horses and forced travellers to walk long distances on foot.[2] The Lieutenant Governor proudly reported to his government that this new road was constructed in such a manner "as not to need repairs for many years."[3]

The seriousness with which Moultrie tended to his duties, the care he displayed in coping with problems such as defense against the Indians and protection of the province, did not appease the sentiments of his opponents. What at the beginning was confined to a personal antipathy toward the new Lieutenant Governor was soon channelled into a wider feeling of general discontent. A profound change in the attitude of the inhabitants took place when the Grand Jury of the province, inspired perhaps by Chief Justice William Drayton, demanded the call of the representatives of the people to form a provincial legislature, which His Majesty, by the Proclamation of October 7, 1763, had promised to his subjects of East Florida.[4] Moultrie, conscious of the temporal character of his interregnum, remained adamant against such a demand which reminded him of the rebellious *vox populi* of the colonies to the north.

Other grievances were soon added, resulting in a near crisis when on October 19, 1771, Drayton first,[5] and Turnbull immediately thereafter, submitted their resignations from the Board of His Majesty's Council.[6] Poor Moultrie! With his Council crippled, he could hardly act as the head of his government. "By these transactions," he confessed to Lord Hillsborough, "I was left without a sufficient number of Councilors to transact business."[7] Yet these were hard times, when efficiency in government was badly needed.

For the past ten years an American consciousness had been awakening, and people in the colonies—sometimes in the name of their rights as British subjects, sometimes simply in the spirit of defiant colonials—resented the measures for imperial reorganization. The colonies decidedly had come of age.

All colonies were by that time moving in the direction of the Revolution—all but Florida. To say that this thinly populated and quite isolated province stayed aloof from the inflammatory agitation of the other colonies would not be accurate. There was excitement and nervousness among the inhabitants; some of them were accused of being rebels or sympathizers with the rebels' cause; officials feared that great parts of the population, such as the colonists of New Smyrna, would join the Georgia patriots; and even the quest for a legislature, around which the most significant political fermentation of the colony took place, was not unrelated to the spirit that reigned over the other colonies.

That finally Florida did not follow the path of the northern provinces, that in 1775 John Adams and John Hancock were burned in effigy in St. Augustine,[8] and that later Florida became the stronghold of the Loyalists—all was due to local developments which were different from those of other colonies. Most of Florida's settlers were newcomers who, migrating after 1763, did not have time to develop roots in the new land and feel that they were "Americans"; they were few and dispersed, with no political or other organization to bind them together; their only church in the province, besides the Roman Catholic, was the Anglican, a pillar of the Crown in itself; their only town in the whole colony, St. Augustine, where people could gather together, talk, and exchange goods and ideas, was inhabited mainly by Crown officials and army. Furthermore, they had a government which, with an iron hand, had managed to curtail freedom and keep people in line.

During those days, when the fire of the rebellion was approaching Florida, Whitehall thought that the colony's government should be entrusted to stronger hands. Thus, on August 4, 1773, Lord Dartmouth informed Moultrie that His Majesty had been pleased to appoint Colonel Patrick Tonyn to be Governor and that he expected to embark early in the month of October.

Tonyn was a person well fitted for this post. He had good connections in London (being a protégé of Lord Marchmont),[9] professional military experience so necessary during those days of turmoil, and a vested interest in Florida's welfare, since he was an absentee landlord—one of the first after 1763 to receive land grants in the province.

On December 22, just before Christmas of 1773, Tonyn sailed for America; and on March 7, after a rough winter journey, he wrote to London with relief that "it had pleased God to set me on shore at St. Augustine the 1st instant [March, 1774]."[10]

His first impression revealed mixed feelings. He was happy to note that Indian restlessness, quite alarming before his arrival, had ceased in Florida and in Georgia. But the situation in his capital of St. Augustine was far from being satisfactory. The Castillo de San Marcos needed repairs, as well as the beautiful Governor's Mansion, whose roof leaked. Ordnance was lacking, and ammunition was scarce.[11] Worst of all, after the rebellious activities of the northern colonies, the morale of the people was very low. Seeking to strengthen the colonists' confidence in British sovereignty and to reaffirm publicly the Empire's prestige, Tonyn determined to make his installation an august occasion. He decided that it should take place "with the most respectful and dutiful Solemnities that can be devised, that the strongest impression may be given of its great Dignity and Importance."[12]

It was the first time since the British had come to Florida that St. Augustine had lived in such a festive and ceremonious atmosphere. On the morning of March 9, in the presence of the Lieutenant Governor, the other officers of the Crown, a great number of local notables, and the men of the garrison, the Deputy Clerk of the Council with all due solemnity read publicly "the Commission appointing his Excellency Patrick Tonyn Esquire Captain General, Governor, Commander in Chief, and Vice Admiral in and over His Majesty's Province of East Florida."[13] The great guns from the fort were fired, and the salute was continued by three volleys from the troops. The commission was then escorted by the grenadiers of the 14th Regiment to the church, followed in proper order by all officials who attended the services performed by two Anglican ministers, the Rev. Mr. Forbes and the Rev. Mr. Leadbeater. These dignitaries, passing between two rows of grenadiers presenting arms, escorted the commission to the Council Chamber. A reception for the members of the Council followed. Welcoming addresses were delivered, to which the new Governor answered; and the Cowkeeper, the head and representative of about a hundred Indians, talked on behalf of his nation.

There were two problems, however, that made the new Governor uneasy: the military preparedness of East Florida—an important task during those troubled times—and the establishment of political tranquillity which would terminate the inherited factional fight within his colonial government. The problems were related, and eventually the British government thought that Tonyn had successfully solved them. His opponents, however, felt that he had done so only by adopting ruthless tactics and unethical measures.

Tonyn was quite well briefed about the situation in Florida before his departure for America,[14] but after his arrival it seems that it was Moultrie who informed him about specific persons and situations. It did not take the Irish Patrick Tonyn long to decide whom he would favor; to him the attitude of the Scottish Andrew Turnbull and William Drayton was unacceptable. But both continued as members of his Council, since their resignations had never been accepted by the Crown. With his Lieutenant Governor, always a devoted collaborator, Tonyn waited for the right moment at which he planned to deal the fatal blow that would rid his government of them both, and this moment came a few months later.

In Georgia lived Jonathan Bryan, a former member of Georgia's Council and a great man, both in size and wealth. In 1771, he realized he could obtain a 99-year lease from the Creek nation for a great body of land lying south of Georgia and including, perhaps, the best soil of Florida. The payment would be 100 bushels of corn yearly, besides initial gifts to the headmen.

The scheme was grandiose, but not without difficulties. The tract lay exactly south of the line drawn after the Treaty of Lochaber of 1770, its western boundaries being the Gulf of Mexico and the Apalachicola River; the northern, a line from this river to the confluence of the Chattahoochee and Flint rivers and from there to St. Marys; and the eastern and southern limits a line from St. Marys to the Gulf of Mexico.[15] This was Indian territory, clearly prescribed as such by the Proclamation of 1763. Therefore, Bryan could not advance his plans without the help of Florida's government.

It happened that during this time William Drayton was visiting his relatives in Charleston. Bryan, an old acquaintance of Drayton's father, grandfather, and uncle,[16] asked Florida's Chief Justice to give him his opinion about this possible acquisition of Indian land. Drayton found the plan extremely interesting and advised him to see Governor Grant about it, but Bryan negated this suggestion, answering that "Grant was too hard a man in bargains."[17] Drayton then told him to proceed with his plans and even agreed to give him the necessary £400, thinking that when the agreement would be accomplished, the government would consent to such an addition of territory; but "he never intended to carry the scheme into execution, without the consent of government."[18]

Drayton further promised Bryan to ask the help of his confidant, Dr. Turnbull, who could exercise an influence on the government's decision on the matter through his powerful London connections. After all, Lord Shelburne, author of the Proclamation of 1763, was Turnbull's personal friend. Drayton also suggested that as the man who would help to secure the government's support he deserved a reward of 20,000 acres for himself.[19] Bryan agreed.

Soon the agreement with the Indians was completed and Bryan left the lease in the hands of their headmen to be publicly displayed in all their villages for the approbation of the whole nation.[20] But by the time all this was accomplished, other Indian troubles broke out, unrelated to this deal, and during their suppression Governor Wright of Georgia somehow managed to take possession of the lease. Wright, angered by Bryan's act, tore the Indian seals and notified Governor Tonyn immediately of the affair. Here was the moment for which Tonyn had waited to declare open war against Turnbull and Drayton.

In the eyes of every colonist, Bryan's speculative activities were very natural. It is true that they were not in accord with the Proclamation of 1763, but most of the colonists never understood the utility of this Proclamation; no one agreed with it, and very few took it seriously as a permanent arrangement. Its critics could be found among great men in both England and America; and George Washington simply expressed a *consensus universalis* when he declared that he could never look upon that Proclamation in any other light than as a temporary expedient to quiet the minds of the Indians; and he had concluded that "any person, therefore, who neglects the present opportunity of hunting out good lands, and in some measure marking and distinguishing them for his own (in order to keep others from settling them) will never regain it." This is what he personally did; this is what Benjamin Franklin and other wise and distinguished men, as well as several land companies, did. Bryan was not unique.

As soon as Governor Wright took possession of the document of the lease, the Creeks assured Bryan that his "Right to the Land did not lye in that Bit of Paper but in their Hearts and that they would renew the Lease,"[21] which they did. And so, in November of 1774, heading a small party of gentlemen accompanied by two Indians, Bryan was on his way to inspect these lands and to endeavor to find a navigable river for the entrance of vessels.

Being in sympathy with Bryan's transactions of the lease, William Drayton found himself in a very difficult position when Tonyn asked his legal opinion on grounds for prosecuting Bryan. The Chief Justice of Florida asked for time to consider the case. Then he visited Tonyn and, in good faith, told him everything he knew about the affair and surrendered all the correspondence he had had with Bryan. He added that he saw no culpability at all in this transaction. When Tonyn heard Drayton's statement, he "made no reply but silent amazement," as he wrote to Lord Dartmouth. He finally told Drayton, however, that "Bryan must be proceeded against directly."[22]

Tonyn could found his accusations on solid grounds. The Proclamation of 1763 was explicit in forbidding individual land purchases from the Indians. He told Drayton, therefore, that he would never "give countenance to a fellow that had the impudence to fly in the face of the King's proclamation, had daringly violated his prerogative, was doing all in his power to rob His Majesty of his land and to get into possession of it."[23] He considered particularly incriminating two newspaper articles, one signed with Bryan's name and the other by *Veritas*, which Tonyn thought was Bryan's pen name. In them there was an attack against the provisions of the Proclamation and Governor Wright's attitude toward this land deal. "Nothing can show more visibly Bryan's designs and his opposition to all government than these inflammatory articles,"[24] explained Tonyn, sensing in them the revolutionary spirit of the North.

Toward the closing days of December of 1774, the Governor asked Drayton to sign the writs against Bryan for all the above reasons and additionally for £10,000 damages. Drayton refused and pointed out that he was ready to leave for the Mosquitoes and that his associate, Mr. Forbes, would sign them. Indeed, he departed immediately for a prolonged stay at New Smyrna. Tonyn was infuriated. He sent his Provost Marshal after Bryan, but the latter's good luck and the immense weight that caused his slow locomotion virtually saved him.

While Tonyn's men were chasing Bryan he, unaware of the danger, was coming to St. Augustine to talk about the matter with the Governor. A few gentlemen of his party came to town first and waited for the Governor, explaining "the Reason of Mr. Bryan's not coming with them, his Bulk, and not being able to procure a strong horse to bring him from St. John's River."[25]

But Bryan was destined never to arrive. A note of his, written in a great haste, reached his waiting friends and informed them that he had escaped north. This is what he wrote to them: Mr. James Penman, a friend of Mr. Drayton, at Gimell's place on St. Johns River, on his way to Georgia, had mentioned the Governor's plan to arrest Bryan and confine him in a dungeon. It was then that the Provost Marshal, Mr. Skinner, arrived with the writs against Bryan. And while Mr. Skinner had stopped to rest a little and play a game of backgammon, a young man saw Bryan's imposing silhouette landing and slowly moving up the hill to Gimell's place. He sent his Negro immediately and notified Bryan of what had happened. Bryan reversed his course and northward he sped.[26]

Tonyn read the note. With Bryan now beyond his reach, he directed his wrath against Drayton and Turnbull. He accused Drayton of attempting to persuade the Governor to adopt Bryan's plan and of violating his oath by not signing the writs against Bryan, thus giving Bryan time to escape. And turning against Turnbull, he added in his official report to his government that "private persons entering into treatys with the Indians for portions of land, and that the leases would be valid, are notions, my Lord, imported into the Province by Doctor Turnbull, about three years ago as I am informed; that the Doctor took Councel's opinion upon that question in England, when last there, and he came out here full of it."[27]

119

What really was a serious accusation against Drayton and Turnbull was Tonyn's assertion that behind the whole affair lay revolutionary ideas similar to those expressed in the other colonies. He maintained that in the past Drayton had declared the Proclamation of 1763 illegal and that he had criticized the government. "I have had opportunities to observe, my Lord," Tonyn continued in his report, "that Mr. Drayton is at the head of a faction that have been in opposition to the Government. It is also pretty well known, my Lord, that Mr. Drayton has discovered principles, strongly on the side of the question, which the people of Carolina have adopted with the other colonies in opposition to the authority of Great Britain over them and that all his relations and friends in Carolina are attached to those measures, and are all of that way of thinking. It has, my Lord, been very evident in several little matters too trifling to take notice of them, that he inclines too much to the pernicious ideas of those who mistake true liberty for unrestrained licentiousness."[28]

In this manner Tonyn had placed Drayton's loyalty in question a very dangerous insinuation during those days. And as it has happened in centuries before and after, since Drayton's subversiveness was evident only "in several little matters too trifling to take notice of them," or perhaps it was not evident at all, Tonyn accused Drayton of being a rebel by "association."

It was true that the Chief Justice's relatives in South Carolina were among the leaders of the American patriots in that colony, but nothing was more untrue than a notion that Drayton was a rebel. During that time his tormented soul lived an unspeakable drama. While his dearest relatives and friends in his native Carolina were fighting for ideals— such as justice and freedom and independence—that could move every honest man, while in his own *American* eyes it seemed that reason and common sense undoubtedly supported the colonial views, there was a formidable force that paralyzed his will to side with his beloved and kept him numb: this force was a solid quality of loyalty toward his mother country.

Four years of study at the Middle Temple, in London, had deeply imbedded in his consciousness the notions of law and order. All these years after his London training in law, presiding over the highest court of his colony, he had dispensed a justice identified with the English law; his standard of reference, on the basis of which he rewarded or condemned people, was nothing else but the English principles of right and wrong. Thus, in the current dispute the mother country, for

120

him, could not be wrong; nor could his fellow Americans. Something else was the cause of this trouble, but he could not identify it. His ignorance of this matter kept him in confusion and engrossed his inner struggle. A few years later, he thought that he had found it. In his *Inquiry etc.*, a little pamphlet which he wrote in 1782, he asserted that it was the mean and tyrannical administration of the colonial governors which ruined the cause of his mother country and, at the same time, made the Americans suffer. But this avowal came later. Earlier he lived the agony of those who could say neither the great "yes," nor the great "no."

Tonyn could not suspect this condition, which was too subtle for him. He was blinded by his determination to establish a monolithic government in that period of imperial crisis. Thus his verdict was vengefully pronounced: "From these circumstances, it is not unnatural, my Lord, to form these observations. That Mr. Drayton and Dr. Turnbull have associated with Bryan in his scandalous undertaking. That, my Lord, the blame must fall with an oppressive weight."[29]

Tonyn hoped that the dismissal of Turnbull and Drayton from the Provincial Council would come from London after his artful exposure and convincing enclosures. But events did not follow so. Lord Dartmouth agreed with Tonyn that "the fraudulent Purchase of Lands from the Indians by Jonathan Bryan is big with the greatest Mischiefs, and being subversion of every Principle, upon which the crown claims a Right to the Disposal of all unappropriated Lands, it cannot be too strenuously opposed; and I have the Satisfaction to acquaint you, that the King approves every step you have taken in that Business."[30] But in connection with Drayton's part in this affair, he was more lenient. He found that the Chief Justice's attitude was diametrically opposed to the duty he owed to the King and he hoped that by that time "he will have seen his Error & repented of his rash Proceeding."[31]

This action ended Tonyn's first assault but not his fight. This persistent Irishman intended to stop only when his opponents were completely destroyed or somehow erased from the face of Florida.

The more the revolutionary tide swept the southern colonies, the more an unusual restlessness was noticed in St. Augustine. People there thought that they were treated harshly and that they were deprived of an instrument of their own in the local government to frame "a number of Provincial Regulations necessary to their local circumstances, to which the laws of England did not extend."[32] Being at the mercy of a military government, they felt that both their freedoms and their property were in danger. Hence they repeated their demand for a local legislature, because "in the first place, the want of an established Legislature in the Province, by the Formation of a Body to represent the Inhabitants, left a Doubt in the minds of many, under what Government (whether civil, or military), the public Affairs of the Province were to be regulated."[33] And fear was rampant that a great number of the inhabitants would sell their property and migrate to other colonies; they "will spread their Disgusts, wherever they go: they will neither return; nor encourage others to seek the Place, which they themselves have abandoned: and the Governor in all the gloomy Pomp of an Asiatic Tyrant will have no subjects in his sight, but the few officers of Government who shall prefer a sinecure Post in a Desert with a Salary to the Blessings of Society and Plenty without one."[34]

In the June session of the province's Grand Jury, the demand for a legislature was strongly renewed. A significant document, reflecting the inhabitants' mind on the matter, was presented to the Governor and his Council:

Presentments of the Grand Jury for the Province
of East-Florida
June 21, 1775

We do now for the fourth Time repeat that we consider it, as a very great Grievance, & one that has much retarded the Settlement of this Country, that East-Florida is the only Province, (Canada excepted), where a general Assembly of the People by their Representatives has not been called for the Purpose of enacting Laws & making such Regulations, as their particular local circumstances render absolutely necessary; which constitutional Rights was most graciously engaged to us by His Majesty's Proclamation of 7th Oct. 1763; when relying upon his royal Promise and Protection we left our friends, & the Country, where we enjoyed the valuable Privilege of Representation, to settle in a Wilderness.

Considering the present Situation of Public Affairs upon the Continent, we think it more than probable, that this Measure may induce many to seek that Asylum among us, they cannot now enjoy in older Provinces, & thereby forward the Settlement of this Country many years. And as the Property of the Subject is by no means secure under the present Insufficiency of Laws, & that numberless Grievances would then be redressed, which without it the Inhabitants must continue to endure; we therefore recommend it to the serious Attention of Government.

We request, that this our Presentment may be published in the Georgia & Carolina Gazettes. At the same Time we lament, that so little Regard has been paid to the Presentments of former Grand Juries; & in particular, that no Notice has been taken of the only Presentment made at the last Sessions.[35]

These grievances disturbed Tonyn. Without inviting the Chief Justice, he summoned his Council which issued a resolution stating that "the Grievances complained of was imaginery." Moreover, the blame should fall on the Chief Justice, who did not prevent such an act of the Grand Jury: "As it might be considered as a Complaint against the Administration in the Colony, the judge should have softened matters, & given support to the Authority of Government; & at least, if he had not quashed the Presentment, that he should have discouraged the Language of it."[36] Finally the Council condemned Drayton, because he acted upon measures and motives that were not consonant with the peace and good order of the province, and his duty to the King and the Constitution.

To the Bryan affair, the movement for a provincial legislature was now added. Tonyn thought that he should not wait for his government's opinion and he instructed his Council to proceed with the suspension of Chief Justice Drayton from his office. In the few days following he had one more reason to insist on Drayton's suspension.

With the opening of July, 1775, the Revolution had come quite close to East Florida. "Common fame has blown it out that the Carolina people intend to visit this Province,"[37] Tonyn informed Whitehall with great anxiety. He frantically started "preparing to put everything on the best state of defense."[38] He repaired St. Augustine's fort, ordered his engineers to mark on maps roads and paths and all passes through the swamps which could be used by the Carolina rebels. He used all the tactical steps that would "make their advancing into the country as difficult as possible."[39] Anticipating this hurricane from the north, Sir James Wright, the governor of Georgia, found himself short of gunpowder and asked Tonyn for supplies. Tonyn informed him that "he could not in prudence spare any powder from [his] Province in [its] present situation." However, he told Wright that the merchants of the town were soon expecting a cargo of gunpowder and that he could purchase any quantity of it, as soon as the shipment arrived.[40]

But this cargo never came. A few days later in July, Tonyn gravely reported to his government in London that the ship *Phillips,* Captain Maitland, bound for St. Augustine and carrying six tons of gunpowder

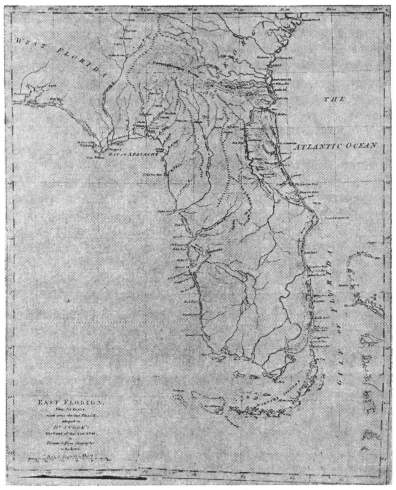

THOMAS JEFFERY'S MAP OF EAST FLORIDA (*c.* 1770)

had been taken off the bar of Georgia by one of the rebel cruisers and carried to Savannah, where the powder was secured for the rebels.[41]

This was a serious blow for the defense of East Florida. However, what really infuriated Tonyn was the fact that no mail could safely go to and from England through Charleston. The rebels had begun to intercept all letters, official and private. "Was there ever an event more

savage," wrote Tonyn to William Knox on July 18, 1775, "many of
my private letters were crammed into public packets, without their
[the revolutionists] being at the trouble to close the seals they had
broke open. Oh, shocking. I hope a day of retribution is not far off."[42]
He had reasons to hope so. Lord Dartmouth only recently had assured
him in a letter that "it is the King's firm resolution that the most vigorous efforts should be made by sea & Land to reduce his Rebellious
Subjects to obedience."[43]

Tonyn was very much upset. A few days earlier an incident had
happened that made him aware of how near the danger had crept. It
was ten o'clock at night on Thursday, July 13th, when a messenger
brought him a letter from Chief Justice Drayton,[44] who informed
him that he had received the enclosed from a near relative of his in
Carolina. This was an intercepted letter sent by Lord Dartmouth to
Governor Tonyn, in which Drayton's name was conspicuously mentioned. "I hold it my Duty both to Government and your Excellency,
to send you immediately the intercepted Letter, and as it is now late
in the Evening, I shall wait upon your Excellency in the Morning
to inform you further on the Subject,"[45] explained Drayton in his
note that accompanied the intercepted letter.

Indeed, the next morning he visited the Governor and told him
that his relative's letter to him included excerpts from other official
correspondence. He proceeded to read Tonyn all these quotations,
adding that the rest was of a private character.

Drayton's actions stemmed from loyalty. He believed the government of London and of East Florida should know these things. And
though he could have kept everything to himself, he spontaneously,
with a sincere concern for his country's fate, gave the information to
Governor Tonyn.

In the eyes of the Governor, however, there stood before him an
official of his own Council, in contact with the rebels, who all circumstances agreed could be a sympathizer to their cause. While he was
listening to the various quotations read by Drayton from his relative's
letter, his mind was busy on how to secure this letter for himself. He
could, perhaps, find in it more incriminating information. "I reasoned
in my own mind whether I should immediately secure the letter, or
whether I should proceed to get possession of it, in the manner I have
done; which has succeeded, as your Lordship will find, in the most
complete manner," wrote he to Lord Dartmouth as he narrated the
incident; "Securing the letter would alarm, occasion much noise, if

125

there proved to be nothing in it material, would likewise put Mr. Drayton in apprehensions, make him circumspect and cautious, and upon his guard. I thought the wisest way, to let Mr. Drayton remain in full confidence, and security, to say myself little, to let Mr. Drayton say much. He left me in his own ideas satisfied."[46] And Tonyn trapped Drayton in a Council's meeting making him voluntarily relinquish his relative's letter.

As Tonyn read, he thought he had found all he was looking for. The name of the relative was "William Henry Drayton, who stiles himself a member of the (Rebel) Congress, the general Committee, the Council of Safety, the Secret Committee, and the Committee of Intelligence, which last acts as Secretary of State."[47] He was the cousin of East Florida's Chief Justice with whom he shared the same name. In his letter, after informing the Chief Justice that he had received his last two letters of May 18 and 30, he stated that in connection with a certain Doran, a loyalist for whom Florida's Chief Justice had asked his cousin's special protection, "it was impossible to save him from being declared a Public Enemy." He had helped him, nevertheless, to escape. Then the cousin went on explaining the situation from the Revolutionists' point of view:

Peace, Peace, is now not even an Idea. A Civil War, in my opinion, is absolutely unavoidable—We already have an Army and a Treasury with a Million of Money. In short a new Government is in effect errected. The Congress is the Legislative—the Council of Safety the executive power—the General Committee as Westminster Hall—and the District and Parochial Committees as County Courts—See the effects of oppresion!

The proceedings of the General Congress do not transpire. But, depend upon two pieces of information. They are proceeding upon the Stupendous Subject—and there will be a Continental Army—Affairs are now hurrying to extremety—where they will stop I know not—We are under some apprehension of Troops coming here. If they arrive—bloodshed will be the consequence—This afternoon I go up to Dorchester to reconnoitre the Situation—It is almost surrounded by the River . . . for the news of the day, I beg leave to refer you to the prints I enclose, and particularly to our Circular Letter—Our former Circular, which I think I sent you has been reprinted generally in the Northern Colonies.[48]

The letter contained, of course, all the quotations from the official correspondence of the months of April and May, 1775, intercepted by the revolutionists, which already the Chief Justice had read to Tonyn.

The Governor felt provoked. His own Chief Justice was in frequent contact with leaders of the Revolution and he was a regular recipient of the inflammatory circular letters of South Carolina's Committee of Correspondence. In this light, Drayton's past obtrusive tactics toward Moultrie; his role in the Bryan affair; his peculiar leadership of Florida's Grand Jury which spearheaded the movement for a provincial assembly; his part in the faction of Andrew Turnbull, James Penman, and the others were all illuminated, and now Tonyn thought he saw the truth: Drayton was not a mere opponent in the game of politics; he was an enemy of his own country! And Tonyn made up his mind: Drayton and his faction should be exterminated!

This was perhaps a harsh sentence and Tonyn considered the possibility of some error in his judgment. But a revolution was going on. How could he take a risk, when his government in London expected him to do everything he could in order to keep his province loyal? Was not this the meaning of Lord Dartmouth's statement that "there is still some room to hope that the Coloniae to the southwest may not proceed to the same lengths with those of New England"?[49] To him Tonyn explained his attitude toward Drayton: "My warm zeal for the good of my Country, my Lord, may push me too far. In my situation, I feel this measure to be perfectly right. I am weak in Knowledge and Judgment, far from infallible, I may be doing wrong, but whatever sentence be passed or pronounced on this conduct, I shall have in my own breast a consolation, that it was done in sincerity and purity of heart, to the very best of my understanding, purely in uprightness to serve my King and Country."[50]

To General Gage and the neighboring governors Tonyn sent immediately all information he had from Drayton's letter. He gave instruction for a speedy dispatch of troops to the assistance of the Earl of Dunmore, and he took various steps deemed necessary under the circumstances. On that night of June 21, 1775, after having informed his government in London on the measures he had taken, his exhaustion was evident in the concluding lines of his report: "It is now very late at night, or rather early in the morning. I am so much fatigued I can scarcely prevent myself from falling asleep."[51] '

1. Grant to Hillsborough, St. Augustine, Dec. 14, 1770, C. O. 5/545, p. 74. 2. *Ibid.*
3. Moultrie to Hillsborough, St. Augustine, Sept. 25, 1771, C. O. 5/544, p. 100.
4. Drayton, *op. cit.,* Appendices I and II.
5. Moultrie to Hillsborough, St. Augustine, Oct. 20, 1771, C. O. 5/552, p. 135.
6. Moultrie to Hillsborough, St. Augustine, Dec. 28, 1771, C. O. 5/552, p. 227.
7. *Ibid.* 8. Siebert, *op. cit.,* I, 34. 9. Corse, *op. cit.,* p. 106.
10. Tonyn to Dartmouth, St. Augustine, Mar. 7, 1774, C. O. 5/554.
11. *Ibid.* 12. *Ibid.*
13. Tonyn to Dartmouth (not dated, received in London on June 10, 1774), C. O. 5/554.
14. Tonyn to Pownall, Radnage near High Wycomb, Dec. 5, 1773, C. O. 5/553.
15. Tonyn to Dartmouth, St. Augustine, Dec. 14, 1774, C. O. 5/555.
16. *Ibid.*
17. Tonyn to Dartmouth, St. Augustine, Dec. 30, 1774, C. O. 5/555, p. 53. 18. *Ibid.* 19. *Ibid.*
20. Bryan to Drayton, Mr. Williamson's Cowpen, Nov. 23, 1774, enclosed in Drayton's memorial, C. O. 5/555, pp. 227-81. 21. *Ibid.*
22. St. Augustine, Dec. 30, 1774, C. O. 5/555, p. 54. 23. *Ibid.,* p. 55.
24. *Ibid.,* p. 54. 25. C. O. 5/556, pp. 320-21. 26. *Ibid.*
27. *Ibid.,* p. 57. 28. *Ibid.,* p. 58. 29. *Ibid.*
30. Dartmouth to Tonyn, Whitehall, May 3, 1775, C. O. 5/555, p. 123.
31. *Ibid.*
32. Drayton, *op. cit.,* p. 13.
33. *Ibid.,* p. 11.
34. *Ibid.,* p. 14.
35. *Ibid.,* Appendices I-III.
36. The Council's Resolution, in *ibid.,* p. 23-25.
37. Tonyn to Dartmouth, St. Augustine, July 1, 1775, C. O. 5/555, p. 191. 38. *Ibid.* 39. *Ibid.* 40. *Ibid.,* p. 188.
41. Tonyn to Dartmouth, St. Augustine, July 21, 1775, C. O. 5/555, p. 227.
42. St. Augustine, July 18, 1775, C. O. 5/555, p. 239.
43. Whitehall, July 5, 1775, C. O. 5/555.
44. Tonyn to Dartmouth, St. Augustine, July 21, 1775, C. O. 5/555, p. 251.
45. Drayton to Tonyn, St. Augustine, July 13, 1775, C. O. 5/555, p. 251.
46. St. Augustine, July 21, 1775, C. O. 5/555, pp. 244-45.
47. *Ibid.,* p. 245.
48. Drayton to Chief Justice William Drayton, Charleston, S. C., July 4, 1775, C. O. 5/555, pp. 255-57. Underlining and separation of phrases with dashes of the original.
49. Whitehall, July 5, 1775, C. O. 5/555, No. 9.
50. St. Augustine, July 21, 1775, C. O. 5/555, p. 246-47.
51. C. O. 5/555, p. 248.

TEN

The Death of New Smyrna

DURING THE LAST SIX MONTHS OF 1775, nervousness and tension prevailed in St. Augustine. The news from the North caused excitement, confusion, and anxiety, and the draining of the castle's garrison of its men produced grave concern.

The detachments that left St. Augustine to reinforce the British forces in Georgia and South Carolina had "put the King's Fort and Ordnance stores into a totally useless defenceless Situation," reported Tonyn to London.[1] "The detachments drawn away nearly reduce things to that very state. At large the Province is absolutely defenceless. The Garrison so inconsiderable. The Fort alone can be guarded, not defended in any formidable manner."

From the point of view of East Florida's government, the main problem during those days appeared to be the enlistment of new men in the little garrison of the province. Tonyn undertook this difficult task with vigor, despite the fact that manpower was a most rare commodity. The way he performed it contributed a great deal to the final destruction of New Smyrna.

At the beginning, Tonyn decided to solve the problem by enlisting Creek Indians. In September of 1775, he invited their headmen to St. Augustine, and after offering them gifts, he asked them to fight against the rebels. The Indian chiefs were not overanxious to agree, but what actually persuaded them was an incident that happened as soon as they departed from the meeting with the Governor. A

129

band of Georgians waylaid them and took all the gunpowder and ball which had been given to them by Tonyn.[2] In their eyes, there was no doubt now that the Georgian patriots were as bad as the Governor had told them they were. And from that moment on, the Indians participated in all raids against them. The scalpings, burnings, killings, and the atrocities they committed soon caused disapprobation and protest even among the Floridians.

Tonyn's use of Indians against British colonists was quite unorthodox. But during this period, he was not in a position to pay attention to such scruples. Only a few weeks before his conference with the Indians he had experienced a painful humiliation that was enough to make him resort to any method against the rebels.

On the evening of August 3, 1775, the brig with the much-needed ordnance finally arrived off the St. Augustine port. The sand bar was high and dangerous, and since the brig was overloaded it had to stay out of the port. The following day the brig's captain, Lofthouse, came on shore to ask the Governor to lighten the ship so that she would be able to sail over the bar. The *Provincial Vessel* was immediately sent for this purpose and by August 6, it had carried ashore 293 barrels of gunpowder. The brig was now light enough to float over the barrier, but she did not do so. That day was calm, and she could not move. Early in the morning of August 7, when the tide was still low, a sloop, taken first for a Negro vessel, ran on board the brig, and her 26 armed men took away not only the gunpowder carried for the merchants of St. Augustine but also 111 barrels of it that belonged to the government.

On the brig were ten unarmed soldiers used as laborers for the unloading of the ship. By the time these men realized that the men of the sloop were rebels from Carolina, the raiders were ready to leave. The Commander of the sloop, Clement Lempriere, identified himself and gave them a copy of his orders, issued by the Carolina President of the Council of Safety, Henry Laurens, authorizing him to "buy" from the brig any quantity of gunpowder, muskets, and ball. Whereupon he paid them for the gunpowder taken with a draft of £1000 sterling on Mr. Miles Brouton, merchant of Charleston, South Carolina, which he signed.[3]

All of these events took place just under the cannons of the Castillo de San Marcos! When the Governor realized what had happened, he equipped the *Provincial Vessel* with eight pieces of small ordnance, manned it with one officer and 30 men of the 14th Regiment, and sent it after the sloop. The soldiers chased the sloop to Georgia, then through the inland passage to Beaufort, South Carolina, but there they lost trace of it.[4]

The raid was bold and the blow it dealt heavy. When a few days later on September 14, 1775, the Earl of Dunmore sent a sloop and a snow to carry to Virginia[5] the 14th Regiment that was stationed in St. Augustine, Florida's defense was suffering from an acute shortage of both men and ordnance. The use of Indians thus appeared to be a necessity.

In this manner the military preparedness of Florida had suffered many setbacks, and it was then that Tonyn thought it imperative to clear at least the political situation of his capital and safeguard his back. The two members of his Council who opposed his administration were Turnbull and Drayton. Since Tonyn did not have obvious grounds to justify a dismissal of Turnbull, he turned his wrath toward Drayton, whom he considered as the leader of the pro-American faction. With the opening of 1776, he dismissed him from his post as the Chief Justice of Florida.

Nothing was more inaccurate than Tonyn's notion of Drayton's disloyalty. On December 27, 1775, a few days before his dismissal, Drayton had sent a long letter to the Earl of Dartmouth, explaining his attitude toward the "Unhappy Contest" between the mother country and the American colonies. "I am a Native of America descended from one of the first Settlers in my Province and am consequently allied to numerous Families in it. The Love to one's native soil & the indissoluble Ties of Affection, which mark the Feelings of Humanity have often prevented me from joining in the sanguinary wishes form'd by others in conversing on the Subject so interesting both to Britain and America. I devoutly wish for a Reunion & that it might be effected without Ruin to the Persons of some of my nearest Conexions & the Desolation of my Country. But that I have any Way, by Word or Deed, promoted or participated in the present unhappy Opposition to Government, or that any Instance in my Conduct can plainly show such Disaffection in my Person, I defy both the Malice of Enemies & the Treachery of Friends to prove."[6]

In the same letter Drayton enclosed the text of the censure passed upon him by the Governor and a lengthy answer to all charges; a copy of the presentments by the Grand Jury at the June session of 1775, in which the demand for elections of a provincial legislature was renewed; and two more resolutions of the same Grand Jury: one concerning the imposed censure, and the other a citizens' address to him made after his censure became known. All these documents showed one thing: that Drayton was far from being pro-rebel, that he was a man of great personal integrity, a Chief Justice who was highly respected by the Floridians.

Tonyn perhaps knew all these facts. But it was only natural for a man of his mentality to consider as a security risk every member of his government who, in such moments of an armed clash, was not actively engaged in the suppression of the rebellion. For this reason, he unceremoniously had replaced Drayton with a more trustworthy person—the Rev. John Forbes. The official grounds of the Chief Justice's suspension was, "Deficiency in point of duty to His Majesty, and His Government."[7]

In the little society of St. Augustine this development was an important event. The many friends of the Chief Justice reacted fast and in a determined way. A meeting took place, on February 27, 1776, at Wood's Tavern, where the whole affair was discussed. Such a gathering, during those days of suspicion and hard feelings, could be easily labelled as subversive. Therefore, the first part of the meeting was spent in framing a loyalty address to the King in which the participants declared that "'we will not only studiously avoid every Connexion, and Correspondence with, or Support of, the Persons engaged therein, (not withstanding the very great Distress which many of us do now feel from the Want of those necessary supplies which we used to derive from the Colonies); but that we shall be always ready and willing to the utmost of our weak abilities to manifest our Loyalty to Your Majesty's Government, and the Legislature of Great Britain."[8]

They concluded with a wish "for a speedy and happy Reunion" of the colonies with the mother country and then some 75 persons signed it. Among them were wealthy planters, merchants, and many men of distinction who enjoyed great prestige in the province. Dr. Turnbull, who was the chairman of the meeting, signed also "for upwards of two hundred families of Greeks and other Foreigners on the Smyrna Settlement."[9]

When this was done, the meeting came to the important topic of Drayton's dismissal. A document was read which was an answer by the former Chief Justice to the various charges pronounced against him by Tonyn, and after a discussion, they all agreed that his suspension from office was completely unjustifiable. Whereupon they drew up an address to William Drayton assuring him of their warm feelings and of the confidence they had toward his judicious character. They finally decided that Dr. Turnbull should carry the original address to London and submit it to the King, while a copy of it should be given to Governor Tonyn.

Next day, February 28, 1776, at ten in the morning, the Governor received Turnbull and six other gentlemen, who delivered to him the copy of the loyalty address to the King. Tonyn saw it and became infuriated. He told them that this act to bypass him and send the original signed address directly to His Majesty was an insult to him and to his government. He made a few more angry remarks and then abruptly retired into another room.[10]

When a few days later, on March 22, 1776, Tonyn reported the incident to Whitehall, he included another loyalty address signed by 85 persons, among whom were all the members of the Council (with the exception of Turnbull, of course), other inhabitants of Florida, and a number of people engaged in the construction of public works. He also included another address, signed by the same people, toward him as the Royal Governor of Florida.[11] Tonyn explained that he could vouch for all of them, that they were truly reliable persons "and in case of an attack can depend upon their persons, assistance in cooperating with His Majesty's troops for the defense of the Province and upon a considerable number of their Negroes who may be trusted with arms, and rendered on such emergency very useful to His Majesty's service."[12] Turnbull, however, thought differently about them; while they were all insignificant people, the ones who had signed the Wood's Tavern loyalty address included many of "the oldest and principal inhabitants" of the province, and most of them owned more property singly than the Governor and Council collectively, with the single exception of Lieutenant Governor Moultrie.[13]

The use of Negro slaves in case of emergency had occupied Tonyn's thought very seriously. A month earlier, among other defense measures he had proposed at several of the Council's meetings, was also the establishment of a volunteer company, headed by a captain, with officers and 25 privates, a troop of light horse, and a militia.[14] The scarcity of men, however, had made difficult the formation of these units and had made him think not only of using Indians, but also slaves. For this purpose he had asked all planters to report how many of their slaves could be trusted with arms. In connection with this plan, on February 27, 1776, he had asked Turnbull to report on the military fitness of the New Smyrna colonists. Turnbull, disturbed, and fearing that such a recruiting of his men would have disastrous effects on the colony, answered that there were 200 males from the age of sixteen to fifty. "I do not pretend to be a Judge of their Military Abilities; but can safely vouch for their Loyalty to his Majesty, for their diligent and honest endeavours to fulfil their contracts with me; and for their affectionate care in supplying their Families with the dayly necessaries of Life. And I think it is a duty incumbent on me to beg that Your Excellency would please grant such a Protection for these industrious Foreigners, as may prevent their being disturbed from Agriculture, without which they, with their Families must starve."[15]

The March meetings of the Council were approaching and the main topic to be discussed there was the recent storm in St. Augustine's political scene. Tonyn, expecting perhaps that Turnbull would admit something incriminating, asked him on March 4, 1776, to report if anything had been discussed at the meeting at Wood's Tavern in connection with the Drayton affair. This was a legitimate inquiry, since the doctor was a member of his Council and the Clerk of his provincial government. The answer was a dramatic refusal: "I am desired to give information against myself, on a subject which your Excellency seems to think culpable." He knew very well that he was innocent, but he told Tonyn that on account of the Governor's threats during their last meeting, when he submitted to him the copy of the loyalty address, he had become very cautious. Turnbull indicated that he knew about Tonyn's plans to destroy him, and he solemnly warned him that "by destroying me you involve in my ruin hundreds of His Majesty's most loyal and industrious Subjects, who look up to me, and depend on me for every necessary of Life. I beg leave also to remind your Excellency that I settled here under the Auspices of His present Majesty. I was even made happy by His most gracious wishes for my success in an undertaking never before attempted on so large a Scale by any private person, and that His Majesty was pleased to order His Governor of this Province to assist me as much as was in his power."[16]

It seems that his letter gravely concerned Tonyn. He answered him immediately and explained to Turnbull that it was the "improper and unconstitutional" mode of submitting the loyalty address to the King with which he disagreed, but that he had not threatened anyone. "Pray, Sir, what threats do you pretend I made use of? I mentioned no threats, I meant none: Nor do I harbour or entertain the least personal Resentment against any of those Gentlemen who brought me the Address to His Majesty."[17] Then, remembering perhaps that Turnbull had very powerful friends in London and that *scripta manent,* he reminded him of his friendly attitude of the past and the interest he had shown in the growth of New Smyrna. "If to this moment I have not shown you marks of Civility and Attention it is owing to yourself, as you have not done me the favour of calling upon me, on the several Times you have been lately in Town. I do not Know that I am acquainted with any of your Enemies, if I am I study to guard against prejudices, and always collect and deduce my opinion from the Actions the Conduct and the Facts. I sincerely wish for your success as a Planter and that of your Settlement. I shall always be ready by every means in my power to give it and you every protection and assistance. I cannot help expressing my surprise that you seem to have totally forgot my early attention to it immediately upon my arrival in the Province, when I visited your Settlement before I did my own Plantation, recommended Regulations and was at pains to satisfy the murmuring discontent of your people, and to suppress loud Complaints of Tyranny and Oppression, which were not entirely concealed to, or confined within the Knowledge of the people of this Province."[18]

All this happened in St. Augustine while the revolutionary tide was constantly growing in the other colonies. In this factional strife, where the events of the North had provoked strong reactions and where personal issues had been confused with political, Turnbull was becoming daily more and more involved. A frightful element of tragic irony, however, was evident in the developments that followed Drayton's suspension. The more Turnbull tried to win in this struggle, the more he failed. Every step he made brought him closer to his own catastrophe. It was as if he had been trapped in one of the many quicksand holes around New Smyrna: every attempt to escape buried him deeper and with him the fate of his colony.

The month of March of 1776 found William Drayton in New Smyrna, where he had gone to recover from the strain of the late events. There he could also plan the strategy for the future with his friend and fellow Scotsman, Andrew Turnbull. By that time both men had reached the conclusion that as long as Tonyn remained Governor of East Florida, not only their property but also their own personal safety was in danger. And as Turnbull asserted later, "I had received information from undoubted authority, that Governor Tonyn intended to throw me with some others into the Dungeon in the fort, where we must have perished in the hot season from the damp and a total exclusion of all circulating air."[19] There was only one solution: to make the London government replace Tonyn with another, more sensible, man. For this, both men had to go to England. There Drayton hoped to prove his loyalty and to be reinstated as Chief Justice, dealing in this way a decisive blow against Tonyn. Turnbull also hoped that by mobilizing his patron Lord Shelburne and his powerful connections he could persuade the British government to recall Tonyn.

For Turnbull such a trip meant enormous expenses, a tedious crossing, and a long absence from New Smyrna. Besides these difficulties there was always the problem of how to escape the watchful eye of the Governor who was determined to keep both men in Florida. Tonyn knew that the outcome of their activities in London could not be pleasant for him. So he kept an eye on them, spying on their movements and trying to detect possible preparations.

Turnbull and Drayton kept their plans secret until the end of March, when a ship was ready to leave for England. Tonyn suspected that this was the one on which the two men planned to leave and asked the captain about it. From him he learned that Turnbull had indeed paid for his passage, but later changed his mind and withdrew his reservation. When the ship was ready to sail, however, Turnbull appeared in town. David Yeats, the Deputy Clerk of the Council, told him that the Governor wanted to see him. Turnbull knew that Yeats was one of Tonyn's men and through him informed the Governor "that he was going to see his son on board." And indeed on board he went, and there he stayed with his friend Drayton while the ship was leaving the port of St. Augustine.

The two men arrived in London sometime during the first days of May, 1776, determined to make their trip a success. Drayton's case progressed rapidly and successfully. Within two weeks after their arrival, Lord Germain, the Principal Secretary of State, appeared before the Lords Commissioners of Trade and Plantations, and on May 24, 1776, laid the charges exhibited by Tonyn against Drayton.[20] The Lords of the Board postponed the discussion to June 3 and suggested that Drayton should attend the next meeting.[21]

To the same Board on June 1, 1776, Drayton submitted a lengthy petition in which he answered Tonyn's charges.[22] He dealt chiefly with three topics: the Bryan affair, the complaint of Florida's Grand

Jury for not having "a General Assembly of the People by their Representatives," and his relation with his patriot cousin from South Carolina, William Henry Drayton. In all points he showed his innocence and he expressed his hope that their Lordships would recommend his restoration to his old position as Chief Justice of Florida. Moreover, because "of his long and hazardous Voyage & of the Expences attending the same, that he may receive the whole of the Salary annex'd to the said Office from the Day of his Suspension."[23]

On June 3, the Board of Trade discussed the case, heard Drayton himself, and a week later, on June 10, 1776, they signed their Representation to the King,[24] on the basis of which Lord Germain informed Tonyn that the "Lords of Trade have considered Mr. Drayton's conduct towards you & their Lordships have, upon a full Examination of the Charges brought against him, reported to His Majesty their Opinion that his Suspension from his Office of Chief Justice ought to be removed, and that his whole Salary during the time of his Suspension should be restored to him, and I am commanded by the King to signify to you His Majesty's Pleasure that you do accordingly remove his Suspension, and reinstate him in his Office of Chief Justice, and that no part of his Salary be withheld on account of his Suspension, and the Agent has received Orders not to pay any Bills which may be drawn by any other person for part of that Salary."[25]

Lord Germain further assured Tonyn that he had very strong reasons to believe that Drayton's conduct in the future would be satisfactory to the Governor and that he had made known to Drayton in a letter how he was expected to behave in Florida, a copy of which letter he enclosed. Lord Germain was perhaps afraid that Drayton's reinstatement would make the Governor turn his wrath against New Smyrna, and he added: "The very great Advantage, which the Public must derive from the valuable Settlement at Smyrnea, gives it a Claim to particular Attention; and as, in the absence of Doctor Turnbull, Occurences may arise, which will require the Aid and Protection of Government, I must recommend it to you to be very watchful to prevent any Injury or Detriment happening to the Settlement, & to give every Encouragement in your power to promote its growth, & the Advantage of the Proprietors."[26]

This was a terrible blow against Tonyn and the first real success of Turnbull and Drayton. After this triumph, the latter was ready to return home. By September 3, 1776, he was in St. Augustine, back in his old position of the Chief Justice of the province.

Turnbull had stayed in London. His original aim was not the satisfaction of a personal claim but the forthright replacement of Florida's Governor. His task was extremely difficult, especially on account of the imperial crisis, which had made every responsible loyalist of the colonies, like Tonyn, indispensable.

Immediately after his arrival, on May 10, 1776, he forwarded the original loyalty address, signed at Wood's Tavern, to Lord Germain.[27] Then he probably thought that he should wait for the outcome of the Drayton case, which definitely would carry a great weight on his own claim. But somehow, on May 24, 1776, Lord Germain laid before the Lords of the Board of Trade Tonyn's charges against Turnbull related to his conduct in New Smyrna; therefore the Board, on June 3, 1776, prepared a "Draught of a Representation to his Majesty upon the Memorials and papers relative to the misconduct and oppression of the Superintendent of the Mosquito Shore."[28] When he found himself in the same position as his friend Drayton, Turnbull changed his offensive tactics to defensive ones.

When Tonyn heard about Turnbull's escape from Florida, he summoned his Council and pointed out the illegal departure of Turnbull from the province without a written leave of absence. Moreover, it was clear that Turnbull was a leading figure of a pro-American faction. Tonyn had notified the Crown about it, and only recently he had written to Lord Germain: "I am properly informed that Doctor Turnbull, Mr. Penman, with a few more of the Chief Justice's creatures are intriguing and endeavoring to raise a faction from which I expect hostile proceedings in our next general sessions in December";[29] and that "should this faction lift up its head," he would take very drastic measures. The time had now come to do so. Hence he and his Council, on March 30, 1776, decided to suspend Turnbull from office as the Secretary and Clerk of the Council.[30]

Tonyn explained to Lord Germain that there was no doubt about Turnbull's anti-British attitude. He asserted that in a debate with Lieutenant Governor Moultrie, Turnbull had declared openly "that America was in the right," and moreover he had stated in public that there would be a famine caused by the stopping of the economic intercourse with the rebels in Georgia. His faction had sabotaged the defense effort of Florida: when Tonyn faced a shortage of food and tried to provide his garrison with rice from Savannah, he detected members of this faction shipping rice to the West Indies from St. Marys.[31]

The truth is that not all members of the Council shared this opinion. Two of them, Stuart and Malcuster, were absent from the meetings of March 30. Turnbull thought that they were both "of the ablest most upright men of that Board," and that since they had previously voted against Drayton's suspension they would have probably done the same for his case.[32] Martin Jollie, member of the Council and Assistant Judge, refused to believe all these charges, voted against Turnbull's suspension, and in the next Council meetings of April 8, 1776, obviously hurt by the proceedings, submitted his resignation.[33] The other three members of the Council—Holmes, Catherwood, and Forbes—were Tonyn's obedient men for whom Turnbull, reporting to the Board of Trade, could not use any kind words. "The first of the list has rose from being a bad apothecary to be a worse surgeon and is a man who has shown bad regard to truth, that his Want of it has become proverbial. The second is a searcher of the custom house, which is the meanest office in that department. He does not think it dishonorable to board kept women. The third is deputy chaplain of the garrison and a man of a most infamous character in many respects. It is by these men that I am condemned without examining a witness or giving me the least opportunity of defending myself."[34]

Turnbull justified his illegal departure from Florida by the fact that as early as in November, 1775, he had written to the Governor from New Smyrna that he planned to go to England at the first opportunity. The Governor did not answer the letter, but he apologized to him when Turnbull returned to St. Augustine. It was then that he told Turnbull that he did not have any objection to his going and that he might prepare himself to go by the first ship. Moreover, written permission had not been thought necessary since Governor Grant's administration, and Turnbull himself in the past had more than once come to England without such a leave. Explaining his departure from Florida in March, 1776, he stated that it was "absolutely necessary for me to withdraw myself from the wrath of a man who sets no bounds to his resentment and cruelties. I was informed of his intention by a gentleman of trust and honor, to whom the governor had trusted this secret. I have leave to mention his name if necessary; for he acquainted us all with Governor Tonyn's designs against us. I was also advised of it in a letter sent by express to me. That letter is now in my custody. This imprisonment was intended, because we had said that in our opinion Governor Tonyn had suspended Mr. Drayton to gratify a private resentment and not for anything for which he had done to deserve such punishment."[35]

While in London, however, Turnbull reasserted his point of view that he was there regularly on a leave of absence, and on July 1, 1776, before he was informed of his suspension, he applied to the Crown for a year's extension of his leave which, he stated, had expired. Lord Germain, by His Majesty's command, gave obligingly, on July 11, 1776, to "Our Trusty and well beloved Andrew Turnbull, Esq., Secretary and Clerk of the Council of Our Province of East Florida . . . full and free Leave, License and Permission to be absent from our Province of East Florida for the space of Twelve Months."[36] When a little later, Turnbull's suspension became known in London, this extension considerably weakened the argument that he had left Florida illegally.

But this time the American affairs had taken an abrupt turn for the worse. The Declaration of Independence which brought the American Revolution formally before the eyes of the world, the rapid developments in the colonies, and the determination of the patriots made hopes for a speedy settlement of the "unnatural contest" fade away. The London government was constantly becoming more involved, mobilizing the Empire's war machine; and under the circumstances, Turnbull could not hope for a fast conclusion of his own affair. It was mainly for this reason that not until September 19, 1776, did he manage to submit his lengthy memorial to the Lords of the Board of Trade through Lord Germain.[37]

This memorial had only one purpose: to persuade the Board of Trade to remove Governor Patrick Tonyn from East Florida. His own dismissal from his office appeared in it in an incidental manner, and Turnbull did not make a point of asking for his own restoration. He figured, perhaps, that with Tonyn out of the way he would automatically be reinstated.

In the memorial, Turnbull charged that the Governor had disregarded the rights of the King's subjects in his province and that he followed an unjust and arbitrary policy in connection with land grants; that he interfered with the administration of justice, dictating his commands to the courts and the Grand Jury; that he meddled in judicial matters by examining the validity of contracts, and by doing so in New Smyrna disturbed the order, peace, and industry of the settlement bringing it to a near ruin; that he received money from various persons in Florida issuing them bills of credit payable in

London, where, however, they were protested because Tonyn did not have deposits there: "This mode of raising Money on false Pretexts, called swindling, is a species of Fraud introduced into the Province by Governor Tonyn, for it never was attempted before in that Colony"; that he committed a fraud by not paying the artificers engaged in the construction of public works despite the fact that he had received their receipts in advance, and for this reason the chief master builder in St. Augustine refused to repair the platform for the guns in the fort; that he established a monopoly through which he distributed provisions for the poor at double price; that he was cruel, with no regard for decency, in punishing his servants, whose cries and inhuman treatment had caused great distress in St. Augustine; that on frivolous pretexts he had suspended both the Chief Justice and himself, "resolved to destroy all, whose characters are a contrast to his"; that the people in the province had lost confidence in him, being afraid of their lives and property "by his acting in everything like a Man lost to all sense of Honour, Humanity, Decency, Credit & Reputation." For all these reasons and for the "Advantage of His Majesty's Service and for Restoring the Peace and Tranquility of the Province of East Florida" Governor Tonyn ought to be removed from the government.[38]

Turnbull had thoroughly exposed the Governor, and his memorial was deposited before the Board of Trade by Lord Germain on September 20, 1776. Their lordships read it, discussed it, invited Turnbull in, and heard an oral elaboration of the various charges, but they failed to see things in his way. For them a rebellion was going on. All colonies had severed their ties with their mother country except Florida, where the Governor was defending the interests of the Empire in a loyal and determined manner. Perhaps Tonyn was more arbitrary in his measures than he ought to have been and perhaps he was involved in monetary anomalies. But one thing was certain: he was devoted to the Crown and its government, wholeheartedly striving for the success of the British interests in America. In their decision their Lordships made it clear that unless something more specific was brought forth and the general charges contained in the memorial were reduced, Turnbull's complaints would not be attended to.[39]

This must have been a painful experience for Turnbull. After waiting for such a long time in London and after finally having the opportunity to be heard by the Lord Commissioners, he had not been able to persuade them. But Turnbull was a fighter. He came back with another memorial, on December 6, 1776.[40] In it he repeated the same charges, only in a more condensed form. He was also somewhat more specific. For instance, speaking of Tonyn's arbitrary land policies, he mentioned a few names of people who had been unjustly deprived of land grants and of others who had received such grants as a matter of Tonyn's favoritism. The real difference, however, between the two memorials was that in the second Turnbull appeared as representing a large number of oppressed Englishmen. He concluded by stating "that your Memorialist in behalf of himself and the said settlers takes the Liberty to represent that he and others, who settled in that Province under a Persuasion that their Rights and Properties would be effectically secured and protected, have by the flagrant and unwarrantable Misconduct of the said Governour, been greatly injured in their private Property. And that the Peace and Quiet of His Majesty's Subjects in that Province cannot, in your Memorialists opinion be restored unless the present Governour is removed."[41]

This sounded very "American," indeed, and the Lord Commissioners must have heard several times during the last years, from people of many colonies, the argument that the oppression of the rights of the King's subjects by a selfish and tyrannical governor was the cause of the colonial troubles. This second memorial was nervously written, a fact evident even in Turnbull's handwriting. Turnbull had put all grievances in four categories but, hurriedly, he numbered the last as fifth instead of fourth. And, again, he did not ask for his own reinstatement.

On December 10, 1776, the Lords of the Board of Trade "ordered that a Draught of a Letter to Governor Tonyn be prepared, transmitting a copy of the memorial above mentioned [the one of December 6, 1776] and directing him to lose no time in preparing such proofs and depositions as he may think necessary for his own defense, and to give full license for the same purpose to all persons on behalf of the memorialist."[42]

Once again the Board of Trade had refused to remove Tonyn on the basis of Turnbull's complaints. Instead it ordered a regular examination of the case. With the slow communications of the time— even slower on account of the war—at least six more months were needed for an answer from Tonyn. And after this, nothing was certain about what their Lordships would decide. Turnbull had been close to a year in London and was far from succeeding in his objectives. Each day was lost and costly. In February of 1777, Turnbull had every reason to be in low spirits. He seems at this time to have been advised to abandon his efforts for the removal of Tonyn and to concentrate on his own reinstatement, which was more feasible. A copy of the minutes of East Florida's Council had informed him of the grounds of his suspension. Therefore on February 17, 1777, Turnbull submitted to the Lords Commissioners of Trade and Plantations not a "memorial," but a "Defense" against Tonyn's charges. This was a dramatic and lengthy vindication not aiming this time at Tonyn's removal. In it Turnbull "humbly prays that your Lordships would please to advise his Majesty, to direct his Governour in East Florida to reinstate Your Memorialist in his offices."[43]

Two months later, their Lordships were still undecided, whereupon Lord Germain took the initiative to terminate this dragging affair. On April 14, 1777, he wrote a long letter to Governor Tonyn in which he warned him about the serious consequences which Turnbull's complaints before the Board of Trade would have for him. "A Discussion of this nature, especially where the Parties have many & powerful Friends who on account of their Property in Florida, will naturally interest themselves in the Decision, soon becomes a more serious Business than the original Matter seemed to promise; and in this case, whatever the final Determination might have been the Consequences of the proceeding must unavoidably have proved disagreeably to you." Then he mentioned his possible replacement and added: "To avoid the necessity of so disagreeable a Step, I thought it best to endeavour to get rid of the whole Matter, and which I was more desirous of doing, as from what I had seen of it, there did not appear to be any sufficient Ground for a serious inquiry." For this reason he asked him—and he expressed his confidence that he would do so—"to bury in Oblivion every past Offence & to show him [Turnbull] that Civility & Attention which his great Share in the public Stake so well entitled him to, and that if he conducted himself with the same Propriety towards you, mutual Confidence & Friendship must be the happy effect, an Event which must greatly serve to promote the public prosperity, by restoring Harmony among the principal people of the Province." Then Lord Germain informed Tonyn: "I proposed to him, that he should take the first step towards a Reconciliation, and withdraw his Complaint against you; That I would then withhold from the Lords of Trade all Cognizance of your

Charges against him, and recommend to you to remove his suspension, upon Condition of his making a suitable Aknowledgement of the Impropriety of his Conduct, in quitting the Province without your Leave in Writing, & giving Assurances of a candid & respectful Behavior towards you in future. This proposal he very readily embraced, and as I cannot doubt his Sincerety, it now only remains with you to accept of the conditions, and to put an End to an Altercation which must, in the present circumstances of Affairs be very injurious to the King's Service, and highly detrimental to the Province. To Afford a proper Opportunity for so desirable an Issue, I make Dr. Turnbull the Bearer of this letter: and I shall extend it no further than to add My sincere wishes that it may be the Occasion of restoring that good Humour & mutual Confidence among the King's Officers, which is at all times necessary, but at present is so essential to the public Safety and advantage."[44]

And so Turnbull withdrew his charges against Tonyn who remained Governor of East Florida. He must have felt very unhappy seeing that all this time- and money-consuming effort ended in nothing. Nevertheless, he was restored to the offices he had held before his departure for England. When later Tonyn received his instructions to reinstate him, he must have felt humiliated and depressed. And yet, this was not a return to an *ante bellum* situation. Despite the temporary reinstatement of Turnbull, great changes had taken place during his absence in London which made him the loser in the long run.

After Lord Germain gave him the letter for Tonyn, there was no reason for him to stay in London. However, with most of the ships engaged in the war effort, Turnbull had to wait for more than two months until he was taken on one of them sailing for America. It was on September 25, 1777, that "after a most tedious Convoy passage"[45] he arrived in New York. There again was an embargo; all ships were tied up in the port and he had to wait once more before he was able to leave for Florida. In New York, however, he was informed about what had happened to New Smyrna since March, 1776, a year and a half earlier, when he had left Florida for England to pursue the removal of Governor Tonyn.

For some time after Turnbull's departure from Florida in March, 1776, everything was normal in New Smyrna. The management of the colony was in the hands of his nephew, also named Andrew Turnbull, and the agricultural output of that year was very impressive: 6,390 pounds of indigo, more than ever before, were shipped to England;[46] and out of that year's corn production, 5,000 bushels were sold in the area of St. Augustine, when a sharp shortage of food was noted during the winter of 1776-77.[47] The produce of naval stores and sugar was good, and everything pointed to the fact that New Smyrna had definitely entered the road to recovery.

Then a series of events happened that caused great distress to the colony. In July, 1776, 22 Indian warriors of a large war party came down to Indian River and from there to New Smyrna. There, they broke open several houses of the colonists, stole their property and especially "women apparel," robbed beehives, and took with them corn from the fields.[48] The settlers were terrorized and notified St. Augustine about the incident. Tonyn immediately summoned the headmen of those Indians in the vicinity and warned them concerning the future. He told them that such crimes among the whites were punished with death, and he asked them to give him the names of the braves who went to New Smyrna so that he might know them. The chief of the Creek nation was informed and asked to punish these men. The Indians promised that they would not repeat the incident.[49] Tonyn, of course, was careful in handling this affair, since he had employed the Creeks in his operations against the Georgian patriots. The results of his quick intervention, however, were not effective, because the Indians did attack New Smyrna again.

Then the next month, in August of 1776, an American privateer which was daringly active in Florida's waters sailed toward the Mosquitoes coast. Tonyn by speed express informed the doctor's nephew, Andrew Turnbull, as well as the other neighboring plantation owners, to take the necessary measures for the protection of their property and especially for the safeguarding of their Negro slaves.

Young Turnbull became "a good deal alarmed," especially because the American privateer had on board a pilot named Warner who knew the coast. Turnbull had a plan to save the Negroes by taking them either down the Indian River or back into the woods, but he was very anxious about the white settlers of the colony. In a letter to Arthur Gordon, in St. Augustine, he confessed that in case the privateer appeared, "I cannot say what might be the consequence regarding the white people as there is a good number of them at present a little discontented, and I am fully persuaded would join the Rebels immediately on their landing at Smyrnea. I therefore beg you and Mr. Penman would make application to the Govr. and Commanding Officer at St. Augustine to reinforce the party here with a few more men if it is eight or ten only, for it is absolutely necessary, if it was for no other end but keep our own people a little more at awe. If this cannot be done I see plainly they will grow very insolent and unruly for the Georgians being so successful in their excursions in this Province."⁵⁰ As soon as Colonel Bisset, whose plantation was quite close to New Smyrna, received the Governor's warning about the coming of the privateer, he found it "very alarming especially with regard to Dr. Turnbull's people, a great many of whom would certainly join them," as he informed the Governor immediately.⁵¹ He thought that they could get the Negroes out of the way, but he was afraid that if a landing "should happen, most probably those that joined them of the Smyrna settlements, would endeavour to plunder our Plantations. However I have great confidence in the badness of our bar, which I hope will detain them from attempting anything here. I shall set out immediately for Smyrnea & will make the best disposition I can for the defence of the place by arming those we can trust & disarming the suspected."⁵²

The Governor found himself in a difficult position. A few weeks earlier, on August 21, 1776, he had reported to Lord Germain that out of Turnbull's men he could raise one company of militia and not more.⁵³ Now, with the crisis which the privateer caused, it became evident that he had to abandon temporarily the idea of receiving aid from New Smyrna. Instead he had to send aid to it. There were many "discontented" settlers and the possibility of a large number of them joining the rebels was indeed great.

"Such my Lord has been the state of the settlement from its commencement," he wrote to Lord Germain on September 8, 1776, "that it has been always necessary to post a military guard there, to prevent tumult and insurrection, and I am sorry to acquaint your Lordship, that at this critical Juncture, it is a thorn in our side, as I am just now obliged to reinforce that Guard to preserve internal good order, when the Troops are much wanted to oppose the depredations of the Rebels in our north frontiers."⁵⁴

By that time, however, Tonyn was bitter. Drayton's reinstatement had hurt him, but the contempt that the Chief Justice showed toward his person was even more painful. When Drayton had returned from London on September 3, 1776, he did not pay him a visit, as he ought to have done, and did not display the courtesy and change of attitude toward the Governor that he had promised to Lord Germain. Several times in open court he also declared that he had been "by His Majesty's Justice honorably cleared of the false and groundless charges" brought against him by the Governor, and in this way Tonyn thought that Drayton endeavored to keep alive animosities instead of burying them in oblivion.[55] Besides Drayton's attitude, in the fall of 1776 the news from London in relation to Turnbull's efforts to remove him from Florida's governorship was also bad. On November 6, 1776, Lord Germain had sent him a letter that greatly disturbed him. Not only was he depressed by the fact that Turnbull's complaints were before the Board of Trade and that no one knew what would be the verdict of their lordships, but even worse was Lord Germain's opinion about the whole affair: "I am extremely sorry to find that at a time when the greatest Harmony among the King's Servants is so highly necessary, and the utmost Exertions in supporting of the Constitution the indispensible Duty of every faithful Subject, that Party Prejudices, and private Animosities, are suffered to mix themselves in public proceedings, and the King's Service deprived of the Support, which it would receive from the united Assistance of the Inhabitants, through the Prevalence of a factious Disposition among the Officers of the Crown, which will ever be more likely to be fomented, than allayed, by a Conduct in the Governor that appears to be rather the effect of sudden Passion than Meditation & sound Policy."[56] Thus had spoken the Principal Secretary of State, Lord George Germain, and Tonyn understood only too well what he meant. He answered: "Your Lordships disapprobation of my Conduct respecting the suspension of Mr. Drayton, and Doctor Turnbull, gives me the greatest concern; although my Lord, the uprightness of my intentions are a justification to me, in my own mind."[57]

In a short time, however, the situation changed, and New Smyrna entered its last dramatic phase. No one knows exactly how things happened, but for more than 150 years an account about it has been transmitted orally and unchanged from generation to generation among the decendants of these settlers, an account repeated also by all contemporary authors who dealt with the story of the colony.[58]

It seems that a party of Englishmen from St. Augustine "on an excursion down the coast, called at New Smyrna, to see the improvements, especially a very large stone building that was commenced for a mansion house."[59] They were impressed by the oppressive conditions under which the settlers were living, and some of the visitors remarked that if these people knew their rights, they would not suffer this kind of slavery. It just happened that an intelligent boy was present and heard this conversation. He went to his mother and told her all about it, whereupon that night the woman invited some of her friends to discuss the matter. They decided to find out more about it, and they made plans which they kept secret.

On March 25, 1777, three of them asked for permission to go down the coast and to fish for turtle. This was granted to them as a special favor, and the three colonists went fishing, but they continued northwards on the coastal road toward St. Augustine. When they came opposite the town on Anastasia Island, they took their clothes off, put them on their heads, and swam the dangerous tidal waters of the Matanzas River. Once in St. Augustine, they appeared before the authorities and asked for justice, "alledging their time of servitude was expired, and that the terms of Mr. Turnbull's part had not been complied with; they were persuaded to return" as Tonyn reported to Whitehall. And so they did. It seems, however, that what "persuaded" them was Tonyn's promise that their rights would be protected by the provincial government.

Back in New Smyrna, those petty tyrants, the overseers, had probably not noticed the prolonged absence of the three men, since they knew that they had gone fishing; and under the tight silence that wrapped the colonists, they were unable to detect the anxiety and anticipation of these men. When the three settlers returned, they made everybody happy with the good news. They immediately made secret plans for the departure of a large number of colonists for St. Augustine, and they elected as the leader of this operation the Minorcan Pallicier, who was the head carpenter of the mansion house. When everybody was ready, one day toward the end of April they left New Smyrna, the women and children with the old men placed in the center, while the strongest men, "armed with wooden spears," were placed front and rear. "In this order, they set off like the children of Israel from a place that had proved an Egypt to them."[60] A veritable exodus!

They had gone a long way from the colony when their cruel overseers realized what had happened. The Lord surely had "heard their cry by reason of their taskmasters."[61] Andrew Turnbull, Jr., was notified and rode after them, he reached them before their arrival in St. Augustine, but he tried in vain to persuade them to return.

Silently this column of tortured people continued its northward march without paying attention to their master's nephew. On the third day they arrived in town. They saw the Governor, who sent them to the Attorney General, Henry Yonge, Jr., who happened also to be one of Turnbull's attorneys. When the colonists made clear that they wanted to be released from their bondage because they had fulfilled the terms of their contracts, the Governor asked the Chief Justice, William Drayton, to hear their complaints and to administer justice.[62] But the latter refused to do so; instead, he directed the colonists to Spencer Man, a Justice of the Peace.

It was decided then that the colonists should make written depositions under oath on the basis of which judicial procedures would be initiated. The deponents had to dictate their statements to a clerk of the Attorney General and then take an oath to the truth of them before the Justice of the Peace. In most cases an interpreter helped with the translation of the Minorcan dialect. When the Attorney General found that there were about 90 deponents, he thought that the number was large and the examination would be long and troublesome, so he asked them to appoint a few who would represent their grievances.[63] Eighteen of them performed this duty. To the rest Tonyn talked and again managed to persuade them to return to New Smyrna in order to secure the crop.[64] Most of them had their families there, and since their troubles were now in the hands of the courts and the East Florida government was sympathetic to their claims, they did not hesitate to return; moreover, they were going for one task only—to secure the crops.

It was, however, quite peculiar for Tonyn to ask them to return to New Smyrna. Certainly it was not an interest in Turnbull's affairs that made him take this step. It seems rather that he was thinking of the food shortage, then quite acute in Florida on account of the Revolution, and the relief he could expect from New Smyrna's output. Since he had repeatedly assured Lord Germain of the care he took of Turnbull's colony during the latter's absence, perhaps he thought that he could now make this gesture, which looked gallant but still could not save the doomed New Smyrna.

When all depositions were made, even those among the officials who were well informed of New Smyrna's gruesome conditions were shocked. There was an account of oppression and sufferings, of torture and murder. The deponents, one by one, had told moving stories that expressed the anguish of their last ten years. In simple words and with a profound human warmth they narrated their lives in New Smyrna and unfolded the story of their starvation and deprivation, incredible working conditions, abandonment in sickness, and ruthless punishments. They told especially of how their indentures had expired and how they were illegally detained in the colony.[65] When Henry Yonge, Jr., the Attorney General who had friendly relations with Dr. Turnbull, read these depositions, he immediately wrote to the Governor: "I observe a number of Cruelties & indeed Murders committed by some of the Doctor's Servants, (which from his Character certainly could never have come to his Knowledge) I therefore think it my Duty to lay a Copy of the Several Depositions before your Excellency, for your Perusal. I am confident that Justice will be done to those People."[66]

No one could agree with him more than Tonyn himself. In a long report to Lord Germain, he assured him once again about the attention he had paid to the New Smyrna Colony. Then he told him about the settlers' exodus, which he asserted was the result of "Injustice and Tyranny and Oppression," and how he sent them back to secure the crops, with the exception of those who stayed to represent them before the courts and that "there is reason to believe, that many and shoking and unjustifiable actions will come to light, for by the affidavits of some of these people, besides the distress, tyranny and cruelties they have suffered, not less than six Murders have been committed, at least six people have lost their lives and no inquiry has been made into it."[67] About what he planned to do, Tonyn explained to his government: "I am inclined to see that Justice is done these poor people, not only from a principle of humanity, but from Policy as I am credibly informed, that they have invited the Rebels in Georgia to come to their relief, and deliverance, and have promised their assistance, and Mr. Bisset acquaints me that they are not to be trusted with Arms, and has requested me in case of an invasion, to bring the most turbulent of them to town."[68] Tonyn further repeated what he already had stated in previous reports, that he had always doubted the success of this colony, and he added: "I will venture my Lord to affirm, and I am confident, that the discharging of the White People will be no real loss to them, as the expense of their and their Families maintenance will equal the value of their labour, when the produce will come into other hands than their own, yet, my Lord, these may individually and unconnected prove industrious Settlers in the Province."[69]

Tonyn, closing his report, thought that the time had come for his government at Whitehall to decide whom they wanted to support in East Florida, him or Turnbull. The argument of the Revolution was used now by him in the same manner as it had previously been used by Andrew Turnbull. The Scottish doctor had thought that at such a time, when all British colonies in America but one had revolted, the government in London would do anything, even replace Florida's Governor, in order to appease people there and save at least this one colony for the Crown. With this thought in mind, Turnbull had risked his expensive trip to England, and he had failed. Tonyn now used the revolutionary situation in order to secure the wholehearted support of the British government: "The American levelling principles have not been less alive here, than in other Provinces, [with] Governors pulled down, and Government trampled upon; the attempts to that end in this Province, thank God have failed in their completion; and I am happy, my Lord, in my own conscience that I have preserved this Province in its allegiance to my most gracious Sovereign, and I trust and hope I may be permitted to mention to your Lordship, what has been found and proved by experience, that the American Governments have been in themselves too weak to stand, and without Governors are powerfully supported my Lord by His Majesty's Ministers, their Government cannot escape being brought into contempt by the turbulent and factious."[70] In such an excited way that his words were penned not according to grammatical rules but as they came up in his mind, Tonyn asked for the "powerful support of His Majesty's Ministers." He succeeded.

In the eyes of most colonists, Tonyn was an authority that had brought justice and liberated them from an unbearable slavery. They no longer had to join the Georgian revolutionists in order to find freedom. The Governor had given it to them. In fact they soon forgot about the American patriots, and a number of them, especially among the younger, joined Florida's militia. There they asserted themselves, acquired a sense of security to a degree they never had before, possessed arms, and associated themselves with the defense of a great empire.

Thus, finally, Tonyn succeeded in having the men he needed from New Smyrna. For Turnbull, this was terrible, because Tonyn had "added to his favorite corps of Rangers by it, who, with some Indians, are employed in destroying and scalping some of the frontier Georgians. Gov. Tonyn has engaged as many of the young men from the Smyrnea Settlement as he wanted for this horrid Service, which he gives out as highly agreeable to Administration: if that is the case, I cannot expect any redress."[71]

During May and June of 1777 most of the people of New Smyrna had migrated to St. Augustine. Their cases had been determined by the courts. By July 17, 1777, Doctor Turnbull's attorneys had set all of the colonists free.[72] A few of them stayed back for the harvest, and when this was over, they too joined their families and friends. On November 9, 1777, the man who had stayed last of all in New Smyrna moved to St. Augustine; he was the ailing Father Pedro Camps.

In this way, the colony which started with so many hopes and in such grandiose manner, the colony which the celebrated *philosophe*, Abbé Raynal, thought would some day revive Athens and Lacedaemon in North America and would become "the residence of politeness, of the fine arts, and of elegance" had come to an end. On November 10, 1777, Turnbull was afraid that Tonyn "will not even leave [me] the liberty of mourning over the *deserted village*."[73]

NOTES — Chapter Ten

1. Tonyn to Dartmouth, St. Augustine, Sept. 15, 1775, C.O. 5/555, pp. 341-42.
2. *Ibid.*, p. 343. Also, in Tonyn to Dartmouth, Sept. 20, 1775, St. Augustine, C.O. 5/555, p. 389.
3. Tonyn to Dartmouth, St. Augustine, Aug. 24, 1775, C.O. 5/555, pp. 323-24, also enclosures Nos. 1 and 2.
4. *Ibid.*, p. 325.
5. *Ibid.*, p. 341.
6. St. Augustine, Dec. 27, 1775, C.O. 5/556, pp. 2-3.
7. Tonyn to Germain, St. Augustine, Mar. 22, 1776, C.O. 5/556, p. 74.
8. "To the King's Most Excellent Majesty the Humble Address of the Inhabitants of the Province of East Florida," St. Augustine, Feb. 27, 1776, C.O. 5/556, pp. 113-15.
9. *Ibid.*, p. 115.
10. Tonyn to Germain, St. Augustine, Mar. 22, 1776, C.O. 5/556, p. 75.
11. *Ibid.*, enclosures No. 3 and 4.
12. *Ibid.*, p. 76.
13. C.O. 5/546, p. 82.
14. Minutes of the Council, Feb. 2-13, 1776, C. O. 5/571.
15. New Smyrna, Mar. 7, 1776, C.O. 5/556, p. 105.
16. New Smyrna, Mar. 15, 1776, C.O. 5/556, pp. 89-93.
17. St. Augustine, Mar. 18, 1776, C.O. 5/556, p. 97.
18. *Ibid.*, p. 100.
19. Defense of Andrew Turnbull to the charge brought against him by Governor Tonyn, C.O. 5/554, p. 83.

20. Board of Trade Meetings of May 24, 1776, C.O. 391/83, p. 97.
21. *Ibid.*
22. William Drayton's Petition to the Board of Trade, C.O. 5/546, pp. 25-44.
23. *Ibid.*, p. 26.
24. Board of Trade Meetings of June 3 and 10, 1776, C.O. 391/83, pp. 108-13.
25. Whitehall, June 14, 1776, C.O. 5/556, p. 234.
26. *Ibid.*, p. 235.
27. London, May 10, 1776, C.O. 5/556.
28. Board of Trade Meetings of June 3, 1776, C.O. 391/83, p. 109.
29. C.O. 5/556, p. 118.
30. Minutes of Council of East Florida, Mar. 30, 1776, C.O. 5/556, pp. 505-12.
31. St. Augustine, Apr. 2, 1776, C.O. 5/556, pp. 495-98.
32. C.O. 5/546, p. 85.
33. *Ibid.*
34. *Ibid.*, pp. 84-85.
35. *Ibid.*
36. C.O. 324/43, p. 413.
37. C.O. 5/546, pp. 49-52.
38. *Ibid.*
39. Board of Trade meetings of Sept. 20, 1776, C.O. 391/83, p. 161.
40. C.O. 5/546, pp. 53 f.
41. *Ibid.*
42. Board of Trade Meetings of Dec. 10, 1776, C.O. 391/83, p. 200.
43. C.O. 5/546, pp. 75-85.
44. Whitehall, Apr. 14, 1777, C.O. 5/557, pp. 114-21.
45. Turnbull to Shelburne, New York, Nov. 10, 1777, Lansdowne MSS, Vol. 88, f. 163.
46. Enclosures of St. Augustine Custom House in C.O. 5/558.
47. A. Turnbull, "The Refutation etc.," p. 668.
48. Tonyn to Germain, St. Augustine, July 19, 1776, C.O. 5/568, pp. 337-38.
49. *Ibid.*, p. 338.
50. New Smyrna, Sept. 1, 1776, C.O. 5/556, p. 767.
51. Bisset to Tonyn, Palmernia, Sept. 1, 1776, C.O. 5/556, pp. 771-72.
52. *Ibid.*, p. 772.
53. St. Augustine, Aug. 21, 1776, C.O. 5/556, p. 774.
54. St. Augustine, Sept. 8, 1776, C.O. 5/556, p. 763.
55. Tonyn to Drayton, St. Augustine, Nov. 28, 1777, enclosure "C" in C.O. 5/546.
56. Whitehall, Nov. 6, 1776, C.O. 5/556.
57. St. Augustine, Apr. 7, 1777, C.O. 5/557.
58. Corse, *op. cit.*, pp. 157 f, attributes this story to Romans. This account, however, does not come in conflict with the version given by the relative documents. It only fills in gaps, perhaps accurately, since they have been repeated by so many contemporaries, and since anyway they do not change the succession of events given by the official records.
59. Williams, *op. cit.*, p. 189. It is interesting to note the reference to the unfinished stone mansion of Turnbull, his *casa fuerta*, which must have been an object exciting the curiosity of St. Augustinians and which, more than a century after Lee Williams' book, misinformed enthusiasts label as a fort.

60. *Ibid.*, p. 190.

61. Exodus 3:7.

62. Tonyn to Germain, St. Augustine, May 8, 1777, C.O. 5/557, p. 421.

63. Henry Yonge, Jr., to Tonyn, St. Augustine, May 8, 1777, C.O. 5/557, p. 425.

64. Tonyn to Germain, St. Augustine, May 8, 1777, C.O. 5/557, p. 420.

65. Enclosures in C.O. 5/557, pp. 429-79.

66. St. Augustine, May 8, 1777, C.O. 5/557, pp. 425-26.

67. St. Augustine, May 8, 1777, C. O. 5/557, p. 421.

68. *Ibid.*, p. 420.

69. *Ibid.*, p. 422.

70. *Ibid.*, pp. 422-23.

71. Turnbull to Shelburne, New York, Nov. 10, 1777, Lansdowne MSS, Vol. 88, f. 163.

72. Tonyn to Germain, St. Augustine, July 17, 1777, C.O. 5/557.

73. Turnbull to Shelburne, New York, Nov. 10, 1777, Lansdowne MSS, Vol. 88, f. 163.

Epilogue

THUS, THE LAST PAGE OF THIS STORY has been opened with the coming of New Smyrna's end. The cause of it was perhaps Turnbull himself. His greedy, irresponsible transportation of so many Europeans to a remote subtropical coast of the New World without providing the means for their support; his lack of consideration for their lives; his view of them as mere tools for the success of his venture; his arrogance, despotism, and cruelty had all contributed to making these settlers abandon the colony.

But perhaps it was not Turnbull but rather Tonyn who was responsible for the fall of New Smyrna. Turnbull had his limitations and had made grave mistakes. But he had supported the colony through the first years of anguish and despair and placed it on the road to recovery with the successful production of indigo and other products. No, perhaps it was not Turnbull, but the Governor himself who brought the colony's end. Perhaps it was Tonyn's ruthless revenge against his most powerful political opponent, his efforts to lure the able men of the colony into the ranks of his Rangers, the encouragement and promises for justice and help, without which it is doubtful they would have dared desert the settlement. For they remembered only too well their disastrous attempt nine years earlier, when the British authorities of St. Augustine had crushed them, chased them like wild animals, captured them finally, and punished and executed their leaders. And they had lived with a garrison installed at New Smyrna ever since, to watch them and to remind them of the consequences of rebellion. How could they have dared turn against Turnbull again without having a powerful support, the support of the Governor himself?

And yet was Turnbull or was Tonyn powerful enough to bring the downfall of a colony whose settlers persistently clung to their determination for a new life in a New World? Perhaps it was still another, more formidable, element: the mighty American wilderness, which resented its taming and sought to destroy those who attempted it. The struggle between the white man and the wilderness was not a new one. Sometime between 1587 and 1590 the "second colonie" of Sir Walter Raleigh on Roanoke Island was completely exterminated, leaving no trace of its over 100 men and women. Later, in 1607, a colony close to the mouth of the Kennebec River suffered the same fate: the extremely "frosty" weather, the lack of food, and Indian raids had wiped out most of its original 100 colonists and forced the remainder to leave for England. Again, during the same time, in May of 1607, 104 colonists had established Jamestown in "Virginia, Earth's only paradise." Four months later, in September, only 46 were still alive; before the year was over two-thirds of the original number had lost their lives from malaria and other diseases, starvation, and Indians. Colonists continued to be pumped into Virginia and for the next six years after 1618 4,000 persons came there from England. But when, six years later, in 1624, a census was taken, only 1,275 were still alive. Lord George Calvert's "Ferryland," his first attempt to colonize Newfoundland, passed through similar experiences. The colonists there survived the attacks of Frenchmen, but not the "sad fare of winter upon all this land": the disease and the deprivation. Lord Calvert, in 1629, just managed to save a handful of them, after they had fought a losing battle for almost six years. And farther to the south, as Governor Bradford said, the "Hidious and desolated wilderness, full of wild beasts and wild men" killed in 1620, during the first winter of his colony at Plymouth, 51 of the 101 who had landed.

Again and again this story was repeated. It was the persistent fight of many men for many years; it was the blood and lives of thousands who came from the other side of the Atlantic that finally made the charms and riches of this country available for millions. In New Smyrna, malaria and other diseases, starvation, and hardships had reduced the number of colonists to less than a third of those who first arrived. The Mosquito Coast had become for the survivors the City of Dis in the Inferno. No matter what Turnbull and Tonyn had done, perhaps nothing could have kept the settlers in New Smyrna. As had happened before in other areas, the wilderness had pushed them out.

And yet, when the deaths of the settlers approached an almost normal rate, when indigo and other products began to bring considerable profits, it was then that disaster came to New Smyrna! Remote and varied causes, though they clarify the background and show the inherent limitations of the colony, fail to explain its untimely end. The quest for a more immediate explanation reveals that the single event which, more than any other, brought about New Smyrna's breakup was, without doubt, the American Revolution. Because of it, of course, all British property, plantations, settlements, and interests had to be abandoned in 1783, when Florida again passed into Spanish hands. It made no difference then if a settlement were under the supervision of a Turnbull, a Tonyn, a Moultrie, or a Bisset, if in the past it had successfully faced the wrath of the wilderness or was still struggling for survival. In 1783, with the conclusion of the Revolutionary War, all British subjects had to go from Florida, leaving everything behind. By that time, however, New Smyrna had ceased to exist.

The American Revolution had acted in the province like a catalytic agent that changed personal feelings into meaningful attitudes, gave direction to sympathies and antipathies, brought some people together and separated others. Moreover it had made large numbers of settlers conscious of their political rights, emboldened them to raise their voice, and intensified their reaction against the royal government. The outcome of these developments was the premature death of New Smyrna, which would have come naturally five years later, in 1783, with the end of all British settlements in Florida.

Without the revolutionary fermentation in the northern colonies and the emotional tension it created, without the contacts with the near-by Georgian rebels and the raids of the Carolina privateers upon their coast, the colonists of New Smyrna might have prolonged their period of inertness. But the wind from the north made their hearts leap, their spirits restless. Their quest for freedom was forcibly revived, and they did not care if this blessing should come to them from Georgia with the raiding parties, or from South Carolina with the daring privateers. As it happened, it finally came from St. Augustine with a decree of the royal government that freed them from their bonds. Seizing the opportunity, they embraced it!

NEW SMYRNA

It is difficult to say whether events at New Smyrna would have eventually led to its abandonment without the concurrent events to the north. Without the revolutionary activities in the other colonies, Turnbull's feelings could have been expressed only as a personal dislike toward Moultrie, whose appointment to the office of the Lieutenant Governor in place of himself, had once hurt him; and he could have entertained an aversion to the person of Tonyn (not a rare sentiment for a Scotsman toward an Irishman); but the Revolution roused these personal feelings into general issues. His antipathy was channelled into a fight against the royal Governor who did not have a "due regard to the just Rights of His Majesty's Subjects,"¹ who was a "Man of Morocco . . . a Tyrant and Oppressor."² And he was able to accuse Tonyn of "Measures highly oppressive, and of various Acts of Despotism against the British Constitution, the Laws of the Land and Liberty of the Subjects."³ The Revolution gave Turnbull the arguments, the phraseology, and a mode of action. Despite his anxious defense of his loyalty, Turnbull combined his activities with those of others and participated in the struggle for a representative legislature; for reinstatement of the Governor's victims, such as Chief Justice Drayton; for a just land policy; for the protection of the freedoms and property of the British subjects in Florida. In fact, he became so involved that he was soon considered one of the leaders of Florida's movement against the royal Governor! His efforts in London for the removal of Tonyn were projected against the revolutionary background in America. But by being in London for more than a year, engaged in a Herculean task, he had left New Smyrna in inexperienced hands, exposed, and unprotected from the vengeful plans of the Governor. The result for the colony was fatal.

As for Tonyn, it is probable that without the alarming situation created by the American Revolution he would have entertained only an aversion to the person of Turnbull (not a rare sentiment for an Irishman toward a Scotsman); but the Revolution made him nervous and suspicious. He thought that everyone who was not with him was against him. Moreover, he considered an attack against his government as being an attack against the defense of the empire. Tonyn was positive that Turnbull was a leader of a pro-American faction, and thus a dangerous enemy who should be exterminated. Also, without the Revolution and the dispatch of the British forces stationed at St. Augustine to the various fronts, Tonyn would not have felt the need to organize his Rangers. When he found that he wanted recruits to fill the Rangers' ranks, he did not hesitate to take advantage of the colony's manpower. Under normal circumstances it is doubtful if Tonyn could have gone so far in destroying not only Turnbull, but also everything that was related to him.

With the coming of the colonists to St. Augustine, the last page of this story was opened indeed. On it is written the fate of the proprietors, Turnbull and his associates, after the fall of New Smyrna; the fate of the colonists, all those who had survived in their new homes; and the fate of the land at the Mosquitoes, upon its abandonment.

The Proprietors

While still in New York, waiting for the removal of the embargo, Turnbull was advised by his Florida friends to stay there, because by returning to his colony he would expose himself to the vindictiveness of Governor Tonyn. To this suggestion Turnbull answered that "this advice cannot be attended to, for my family is in his province, & there is not any danger which I would not face to protect them."[4] By the end of the month, he had returned to New Smyrna.

En route home, he stopped in St. Augustine, on November 29, 1777,[5] where he heard more details about the destruction of New Smyrna. There his friends informed him about the undermining role of the crafty Governor, who applied every art he knew in order to break up the settlement: "He [Tonyn] had established a firm belief among these [New Smyrna] Men (being all brought from despotick Governments) that the Governor of the Province had all power over them and not the Propriators, which encouraged the idle and mutinous."[6] Tonyn then had attempted to frighten the colonists into abandoning the settlement; on the one hand he disarmed them, on the other he alarmed them with messages about pending attacks of Georgian rebels. He thought that in this way they would decide to move to St. Augustine. Moreover, with his attitude it was as if he wanted to encourage the Indians to visit New Smyrna. Indeed, during Turnbull's absence, a war party of nearby Creeks, after "having robbed and insulted some of the neighbouring Plantations, came to Smyrnia and loaded their Horses with Cloaths and effects of some Families there. They also presented their Fire-locks and drew their Scalping knives on some Men, who endeavoured to hinder this open Insult and Robbery." By the end of the fall of 1776, another Indian party encamped on the colony's lands "and lived all winter on the

Cattle belonging to that Settlement, which they shot down to a great amount." But the colonists, despite their fear, did not abandon New Smyrna. Then Tonyn employed the services of "one Spaniard and another half Spaniard" who "opened a Correspondence with some of the worst of the People at Smyrnia," trying to induce them to come to St. Augustine where the Governor would offer them asylum. It was in this way that the first three settlers were persuaded to go and complain to the St. Augustine authorities.

This disquieting news greeted Turnbull upon his return to Florida, and it was then clear in his mind that Governor Tonyn wanted to break up the colony not only because he needed the able settlers for his Rangers, but also because "he and his Connections would have the Advantage of putting some of the most industrious of these Families to cultivate their Plantations." In St. Augustine, also, Turnbull found out that when approximately 100 settlers, who had abandoned New Smyrna, appeared before two Justices, they were ordered "back to their Labour, which they refused, and consequently were committed to Custody to live on Bread and Water, 'til they became sensible of their Error. This order of the Justices was frustrated by Governor Tonyn, who took two of the Prisoners into his House and Service, and also sent Hams, Pies, and other Meats to the other Prisoners, which to them was a convincing Proof of his Power and Authority being superior to the Laws and to the order of the Justices, and it was also an avowal of his Intentions in their Favour. The Consequences of which were that the others, who till then remained on the Settlement, left it also, and all appealed from the Sentence of the Justices to the Court of Sessions." Tracing also the Governor's influence not only upon the attorneys' attitudes, but even upon the judges' decisions was, for Turnbull, an easy task. When he heard all these stories, he anxiously continued his journey to New Smyrna. Before leaving St. Augustine, however, Turnbull saw his former servants abandoned and suffering. But it was too late to interfere.

Back in his colony, Turnbull found a very sad situation. With the white servants gone, all that was left were the Negro slaves, a few overseers, and his family. He was happy to see his wife and seven children again, but he soon realized that with the settlement deserted, everything had changed. One could no longer live safely in New Smyrna. The Governor had taken away the two ship guns, which were mounted on specially made carriages and which were important items in the defense of the colony; the small garrison that had been stationed there, originally a force of one officer and twenty-two men, was now gone; the strong double stockade which had been constructed around the magazines at the expense of the settlement, as it was left unmanned had been rendered useless. Then, early in December, 1777, only a few days after he had arrived home, a party of 40 Indians raided New Smyrna, broke open one of the storehouses, and loaded their horses with corn. When a man went to inquire about their intentions, the Indians threatened him with a tomahawk. Turnbull thought that these attacks and robberies were the beginning of an Indian war, which would come as the result of the Governor's unsuccessful Indian policy. "The total Destruction of all Plantations is the certain and first Hostility in a War with them and the most excruciating Torments are always inflicted on the unhappy Victims of Indian Rage, which may soon be the Fate of some of us, if the Superintendent Mr. Stewart does not, by his Conduct and Prudence, counterbalance Governor Tonyn's bad management. At any Rate we do not live in any kind of Security at present for everything we have is at the will of these Savages." For this reason he removed his family to St. Augustine, where his losing battle entered a desperate phase.

The small capital of East Florida was in turmoil again during those days because of Tonyn's announced intention to rid his government of the reinstated Chief Justice. The Governor blamed Drayton for the renewal of the movement for a representative legislature in the province; and he was particularly angry with him, because he thought that Drayton was the author of a strong petition to the Crown in which members of Florida's Grand Jury, other property holders in the province, and refugees from among the Loyalists who had recently swarmed into St. Augustine, had used an emphatic tone to assert their rights:

We Declare, that we hold it to be our Indubitable Right to make such Inquirys and Presentments of Public Grievances as we judge proper, and to Deliver the same in our own Terms, without being Dictated to, or obliged to alter the same by Order of the Court or any Person or Persons whatever. And we all agree that these our Sentiments under our Hands and Seals shall be made Publick for our own Justification.[7]

Tonyn could not stand the expression of this disloyalty. He probably thought that William Drayton, the mastermind behind this opposition, ought to be neutralized. Thus, Tonyn first inspired an "address to the Governor of East Florida," signed by 229 refugees, in which an effort was made to counterbalance the assertions of Drayton's petition to the Crown and show that the Governor's policies had the support of the inhabitants. In this "address" a special emphasis was placed, of course, upon the importance of Tonyn's defense measures as well as upon the consideration and relief he had offered to the refugees.[8]

Tonyn personally undertook an attack against Drayton before the Council to which he submitted a new set of accusations against him. This time Tonyn maintained that the Chief Justice had refused to aid the provincial government; that he had disapproved of the defense measures taken by the Governor; that he had questioned the latter's right to grant letters of marque; that in the past, during an expedition of Florida's forces at St. Marys River, the Chief Justice had recommended a capitulation with the rebels at that area. To this he also added several other minor charges making Drayton's defense very difficult. The latter submitted as evidence the fact that a few months earlier he had offered 22 of his Negroes to work for the fortifications and that he himself had enlisted in Colonel Fuser's battalion of the 60th Regiment. Despite this convincing answer showing Drayton's loyalty, on December 16, 1777, the Council decided to suspend Drayton from his office until the Crown's wish could be made known.[9]

The Chief Justice knew only too well what he might expect from this attack. Therefore, a month before Tonyn officially announced his dismissal, Drayton sold his beloved Oak Park, the 300-acre estate in the outskirts of St. Augustine, where he had lived since 1767. Shortly thereafter, he and his wife and his year-and-a-half-old son, William, moved to South Carolina. There, close to Charleston, at Magnolia Gardens, known then as the Drayton House, he found peace of mind among relatives and friends. Even there, however, Tonyn tried to harm him and wrote, on April 4, 1778, to General Sir William Howe about Drayton's disloyal attitudes. But with the war taking a grave turn for the British forces, the General could not pay attention to such minor affairs. When the subsequent British evacuation of Charleston took place, Drayton decided to stay. During that period he finally made up his mind and subscribed to the patriotic cause. A year before his death in 1790, he became first a judge of the admiralty court and then successively Associate Justice of the State of South Carolina and District Judge of the United States of America.

Epilogue

At the end of this happy year, William Drayton died as an American in the place where he was born.[10]

It was in this manner that Andrew Turnbull, moving to St. Augustine, found himself alone and deprived of the company and advice of his most intimate friend. He immediately felt the atmosphere of terror that prevailed in town, which made almost impossible for him the collection of evidence showing the part played by Governor Tonyn in the breaking up of New Smyrna, "for there is not a man in the Province," he wrote to Lord Germain, "who dares give an Affidavit, nor scarcely a Justice of Peace who can safely take an Affidavit against Govr. Tonyn's Interest or Mr. Moultrie's, as every man who does not support all their Measures tho' frequently unjustifiable and malicious to a great Degree, is immediately branded with the Epithet of a factitious Man, and is made an object of their Resentment and Enmity. . . . all live in a continual apprehension of his [Tonyn's] Spies and Informers, who warp and mutilate every conversation where his Name is mentioned into Disaffection and I do not know what."[11]

For this reason, Turnbull requested Lord Germain that Tonyn and Moultrie be withdrawn from East Florida's government and in their place "a cool, judicious, and unprejudiced Man be appointed to superintend the Province. . . . Such a Man will be easily found by Your Lordship in England."[12] The justification for such a request was that New Smyrna was a concern of great magnitude which, among other things, could be used as a source of food supply for the Crown's army during that period of imperial crisis. This favor, of course, was never granted, and Lord Germain never answered this letter, just as he never answered Turnbull's earlier letters or those of a later period.[13]

With Drayton out of the way, Tonyn concentrated his fire against Turnbull and several others who opposed his iron rule. The difficulty he faced was the fact that his opponents were all among the most distinguished inhabitants of the province. As he explained to Lord Germain: "They are Gentlemen but, my Lord, in all Colonies, Georgia excepted, the principle people have been at the head of this rebellion."[14]

For several months the tension between the Governor and Turnbull continued, with the latter accusing Tonyn of negligence toward the people of New Smyrna, who continued suffering in St. Augustine, and also for prejudice and partiality toward the handling of the colony's affairs in the past.[15] But the Governor's reactions were very

163

cautious. Even Turnbull was surprised and in a letter to Lord Shelburne he wrote that despite the fact that in reproaching Tonyn he used "tone and terms as [he] never made use of before to any Gentleman," the Governor "contrary to his usual manner, . . . took [the insult] very tamely." Turnbull, of course, could not be fooled by the Governor's self-control: "But I hear he is meditating more mischief against me, and a few days ago he sent a big man of his connections to insult me, but he proved so much of a bully, that he put up with the reproof of a good Cane for his Impertinence."[16]

It seems, indeed, that Tonyn was "meditating" on the most appropriate way to exterminate his opponent. He wanted, however, to have undisputable proof of Whitehall's confidence and support. Then he could advance with his plans. Soon these assurances came from London. On February 19, 1778, Lord Germain wrote to him: "It must give you particular pleasure to be informed, that His Majesty approves of the Measures you took for the defence of the Province, & of the spirit & good conduct of the Officers & Troops employed in that service. . . . The authority vested in you and the Council of East Florida by the Instruction, is a proof of His Majesty's entire confidence in your integrity & attention to the public advantage, without being swayed by motives of prejudice or partiality, & I have no doubt that this very delicate trust will be executed in such a manner as shall fulfill the King's gracious Intentions."[17]

In this way the London government approved not only of his defense measures, his Rangers and their raids and scalpings in Georgia, but also his refugee policy and the land grants to them. As far as New Smyrna was concerned, Lord Germain coolly expressed his government's opinion: "The desertion of the Smyrnea settlement by the People, is an unfortunate circumstance for the Province, & must occasion a severe loss to the Proprietors. If it be in your power to lessen that loss, or to give the many assistance in retrieving their Affairs, I must desire you will exert your Endeavours on their behalf."[18] By "propriators" Lord Germain meant Turnbull's London partners and not Turnbull himself who was, to him, the manager of the company's property in Florida.

Now Tonyn could start an open fight against his opponent. In August of the same year 1778, he denied Turnbull the privilege of personally occupying his office as Secretary and Clerk of the Council.[19] The blow was heavy. The suffering Turnbull saw that the only regular income with which he supported his large family was threatened. He knew that he could expect more from the determined Governor. And as had happened a few months earlier with his friend Drayton, he too decided to leave the province and go somewhere else. He wrote to Lord Shelburne: "I am now employed in collecting the scattered remains of the settlement; and I shall remain here, if I can, till I hear from England; but if this Governor is continued, I must quit the Province and shall probably carry my family to the English, Spanish or French West Indies till the War is over."[20] His decision to leave Florida became final, but soon it was almost impossible for him to implement it.

When Tonyn realized that more than £40,000 sterling had been spent for the development of New Smyrna,[21] that in England there were partners anxious to save as much as they could from their vanishing investment, and that Lord Germain wanted him to protect their interests, he immediately adopted a new policy. He came in contact with Turnbull's former partners, who resided in London and became their official representative in Florida. Then, on February 17, 1780, he issued a writ of *ne exeat vel provincia,* by which he prohibited Turnbull's departure from the province of Florida. The reason was, as the writ stated, "that he the said Andrew Turnbull is greatly indebted to the said Complainants, and designs quickly to go into parts beyond & out of the Limits and Jurisdiction of our said Province, which tends to the great injury and damage of the said Complainants."[22] In order to make certain that Turnbull would not escape, he demanded a bail of £4,000 sterling and he instructed the Provost Marshal that "in case the said Andrew Turnbull shall refuse to give such bail or security then you are to commit him the said Andrew Turnbull to our Prison in our said Province there to be kept in safe Custody until he shall do it of his own Account."[23]

Turnbull, of course, did not have that enormous sum of money. The period that had passed since his recent arrival from London was marked by an uninterrupted succession of property losses. When a few months earlier, in August, 1778, a rover privateer landed at the Mosquito coast and carried off from New Smyrna 30 Negro slaves, the last blow had been struck against him. The St. Augustine authorities expended every effort to recover them, but without success. The two ships sent after the privateer, the sloop *Otter* and an armed schooner *George,* were lost during the chase in the rough waters off Cape Canaveral. When this writ was issued, Turnbull was in desperate financial straits. Not being able to offer the £4,000 sterling for bail, he became the prisoner of Alexander Forrester, the acting Provost Marshal.[24]

After Turnbull's commitment to jail, Governor Tonyn filed a Bill in Chancery against him, acting as the representative of Turnbull's partners. It seems that originally Lady Mary Duncan, the widow of Sir William, and also Richard Earl Temple, the only executor of Grenville's last will and testament, both had expressed a desire to settle the New Smyrna accounts in a speedy and amicable way. Governor Tonyn, however, chose the most costly procedure of a suit in Chancery, which could virtually crush Turnbull. The latter demurred to it. In an unorthodox court procedure the demurrer was overruled by the Governor himself.

The irregularities which took place during this court hearing showed once again how determined Tonyn was to destroy Turnbull. The Governor was unable to produce any written evidence that he was the legal representative of Turnbull's partners. Then, during the procedure he spoke in behalf of Richard Earl Temple, although the latter had in the meantime died; the actual heirs of Turnbull's original partner, George Grenville, were his sons William Grenville, an infant, and Thomas Grenville of Lincoln's Inn in the County of Middlesex. But what was extremely odd was that Tonyn appeared during this trial in many roles at the same time: he was the "legal representative" of Turnbull's copartners, a witness in the case, the judge of it, and the executive authority whose organs kept Turnbull in custody. At a later time, William Drayton, Florida's former Chief Justice, called this combination of roles a "most glaring Impropriety, which militates against all Law and Justice";[25] and Turnbull, narrating the incident to Lord Shelburne, wrote, "the demurrer was overruled and the Court dismissed after Tonyn had made a speech most glaring and false and injurious to me, to which I began to reply but was ordered to be silent."[26]

Turnbull had to return to the Provost Marshal under whose custody he remained for more than a year.[27] Then on May 7, 1781, the Governor decided to take off the writ of *ne exeat vel provincia,* in order to permit Turnbull to show before the Court of Chancery that this writ "was not only illegal in every circumstance, but highly oppressive on the whole,"[28] as the prisoner maintained. Tonyn wanted perhaps to give this chance to Turnbull in order to show impartiality toward the case, being at the same time positive that Turnbull would not be able to prove his assertion.

The latter, however, suspected these plans and since he was technically free to depart from the province, "being apprehensive of a further imprisonment on some other frivolous pretext,"[29] he immediately hired two small sloops;[30] in one of them he put his large family and in the other as many of his possessions as he could, and he left in a hurry for Charleston, where it was rumored the British headquarters would be established.

While a prisoner, Turnbull had frequently thought of Charleston as a possible place to escape, and he had already asked his friend Lord Shelburne to write an introductory letter to Lord Cornwallis. He had seen the General in the Shelburne home but had not been formally introduced. He decided to ask Lord Shelburne for this favor being aware of the difficulties which civilians encounter in a military area; in fact, only recently he had experienced a situation passing through New York when returning from London. Therefore he assured Lord Shelburne that an introduction would be very helpful in a new place and that he did not plan to bother General Cornwallis with a request for a civilian post or something similar. "I can live everywhere by my profession, my Lord," Turnbull had written, "I do not therefore mean to give trouble to Lord Cornwallis."[31]

It was an agonizing trip from St. Augustine to Charleston. Sailing for six days on the open ocean the Turnbull family, together with James Penman who followed them, were constantly on the alert trying to avoid the numerous privateers and rebel rowboats that cruised the coast. The sloop that carried them finally arrived at Charleston, but not the other, which fell into the hands of the patrolling Americans.[32]

Tired and destitute they arrived in Charleston on May 13, 1781.[33] They had left behind every earthly possession except the few belongings they had attempted to take with them, and even these they had lost during their voyage. "This loss, however," Turnbull stoically remarked, "seemed to me to be highly compensated by the satisfaction I had of being out of the Grip of Tonyn's Talons."[34] The calamities they had suffered, however, during the last years, the tension of the voyage, and the difficulties they met in wartime Charleston made them all feel very unhappy. Maria Gracia, the beautiful Greek wife of Dr. Turnbull, felt particularly depressed and suffered a nervous breakdown. A year after their arrival in Charleston she finally recovered "her health and usual placid Temper of Mind," and she was relieved of the "continual uneasiness and Anxiety" from which she had suffered.[35]

Perhaps Cornwallis was never informed by Lord Shelburne about Turnbull's character; but he was so by Tonyn, who, as soon as he realized that his bird had flown from the cage, immediately notified both General Cornwallis and the British Commandant of Charleston about Turnbull's disloyalty. He asked them to drive Turnbull out of the city.[36] Two years earlier he had also sent a lengthy confidential report to General Sir Henry Clinton in which he had accused Andrew Turnbull, William Drayton, James Penman, and Spencer Mann as the leaders of Florida's rebellious faction, and he had even implied that General Provost and Lieutenant Colonel Fuser were sympathetic to this faction's views.[37] Again, Tonyn was not very successful. Turnbull's friends in Charleston explained to General Cornwallis and to Brigadier General Alexander Leslie that the Governor's request was the product of a personal vengeance. Turnbull too wrote to them offering counterevidence proving his loyalty.[38] As a consequence, he and his family were left undisturbed by the British authorities.

A year had passed in Charleston and the situation had not improved for the Turnbulls. During the hasty escape from St. Augustine, Turnbull had left everything behind, among other things his papers and vouchers without which he could not obtain a satisfactory settlement with the heirs of his former partners. These papers were now in Tonyn's hands, and he would not return them to their rightful owner.[39] This action upset Turnbull, a condition aggravated by several other calamities that befell the family. The eldest son had remained in St. Augustine where "after having had a regular and classical education [he] had accepted with thankfulness of being Assistant to a Deputy Commissary of Provisions, and cheerfully undertook to serve Beef, Pork &c. to the Garrison in Saint Augustine in order to ease of a part of the Burden of a large Family, he received five shillings a day for this Labour with a Ration."[40] Of his three daughters, two were married by 1778, but within four years they both were widows while still young, not even twenty years of age. Soon after their arrival at Charleston, one of them was married again "to a Practitioner in the Law, a good Man and able in his Profession"; the other, however, still a very young widow with two children, was living with her parents. The three younger boys, of whom the oldest was eleven, were all in school at Charleston. There was also an addition to the family, a little orphan left to the Turnbulls when he was one year old by a "worthy mother," who "died of grief from Tonyn's oppressions and enmity to her husband."[41]

Epilogue

While Turnbull struggled in a strange town to establish himself in the medical profession, he received the news that Tonyn refused to pay his salary as Secretary of the Province, considering him as having resigned. Turnbull protested and stated that he had never expressed such an intention, but to no avail; he never received his salary.[42]

Now, at this trying time, the evacuation of Charleston by the British forces was decided upon by the London government. The year was 1782, and what had happened during the past few months justified the contemporary popular song "The World Turned Upside Down!" On October 19, 1781, General Cornwallis had surrendered at Yorktown. The war was lost for the British, and now the evacuation of the American towns was taking place. For a while Turnbull did not know what to do, but he finally decided to leave America. For this purpose he wrote again to his friend, Lord Shelburne, who was now a very important member of the government in England. He asked him for a "trifling Employment," until he could establish himself in the medical profession either in England or in Jamaica.[43] He explained to Lord Shelburne that he could not stay in Charleston, because he was afraid that the American government would be a "rude almost savage Democracy."[44]

But the "trifling Employment" was never offered to Turnbull, and when the orders for evacuation were given, he decided to remain with the British merchants, who could prolong their stay at Charleston for six months until they could dispose of their merchandise. It was during this time that distinguished members of the Charleston officials asked him to become a resident of South Carolina and practice medicine. As Turnbull interpreted their offer, "they thought me a valuable Acquisition in a sickly Country."[45]

By that time he had thought a great deal about his situation. As he explained to Lord Shelburne, in a way he was forced to stay, because both his papers and vouchers were in Tonyn's hands and therefore he was unable to settle his accounts with the heirs of his partners. "My papers thus being detained by Governor Tonyn prevents me to present from pursuing my Interest elsewhere, and obliges me to exile myself from Country, for without Vouchers I cannot give that Satisfaction which I wish, and is expected from me by the Men I was concerned with, I am also deprived of a Sum of Money due by the other Partners to me considerable."[46]

To the leading men of Charleston who had asked him to remain there he answered that he would do so, but under the condition that he would remain a British subject. They accepted his terms, though later he was again asked to become an American citizen and again he refused. George Miller, a resident of Charleston during this time, described this incident as follows: "After the evacuation of Charleston, Doctor Turnbull and Mr. James Penman were required to become Citizens, which they refused to do, and being men of respectable character, the matter was left to the decision of a Committee of the Legislature then sitting, who agreed they should remain as His Majesty's subjects; the only instance, I believe, of the kind that happened between the Evacuation of the Province and the peace, which redounds much to their honour, since it is at once a proof of their steady Loyalty, and the high respect in which their Characters were held."[47]

A year later, in May 30, 1783, he was almost certain that he would never leave America again. "It is now probable," he wrote to Lord Shelburne, "that I shall end my days here . . . I am apprehensive, therefore, my Lord, that I shall never have the Honour of seeing you more."[48] He blamed this state of affairs upon the cruelty of his partners' heirs, who did not want to reach a settlement and close the accounts of New Smyrna. Perhaps he had also realized that, uprooted as he had become from Europe, he had more reason to stay in this New World than to return to England or elsewhere. Almost all his children and grandchildren were born in this country. In Charleston, though a newcomer, he had already a number of good friends, while others sympathized with him as a victim of a ruthless royal governor or revered him as a member of the highly respected medical profession.

Many years later, January 20, 1830, his heirs applied to the United States Commission of Private Land Claims for the title to lands which Andrew Turnbull had received from the Crown. They presented as grounds for their claim their assertion that the "said Andrew Turnbull joined the Revolutionary forces and became an American citizen in consequence of which neither he nor any of his children received any compensation from the British Government."[49] The above assertion is completely inaccurate. Andrew Turnbull never joined the Revolutionary forces, although he did support the forces that fought the Americans; moreover, he and his children had received a small compensation from the British government for the losses they suffered in New Smyrna.

The claim that Turnbull became an American citizen was also far from the truth. Despite the fact that he disagreed with and strongly criticized members of the British government, and despite also Tonyn's opinion that he was one of the leaders of a rebellious faction, Turnbull down to the last day of his life remained a loyal subject of Great Britain. While in St. Augustine, being still a prisoner of Tonyn, he had written to Lord Germain that "it is probable that Gov.ʳ Tonyn flatters himself of being able to drive me, thro' Despair, to such a step [of becoming disloyal], but he will find himself grossly mistaken, for the Amor Patriae and of the British Constitution, while it lasts, will always hold me fast as a British Subject which, however, is not meant to imply that I am in Love with the Present Ministers, nor with their Measures."[50]

Thus, the claim of Andrew Turnbull's heirs in 1830 was simply in the climate of opinion of the Jacksonian era, which was characterized by many remarkable developments but not by the honesty of its land claims. Turnbull remained a British subject because of his *amor patriae* or because of his uninterrupted efforts to recover the value of his lost property in New Smyrna from the British Treasury, efforts made by virtue of his "being His Majesty's subject and in no sense citizen of any of the United States."[51]

In the meantime, better days came for him and his family. His medical profession provided a comfortable living and a distinguished place in Charleston society. Turnbull's activities were now oriented toward medicine and he is believed to have been one of the founders of the South Carolina Medical Society. Thus, living a completely different life from the one he had lived in Florida, Turnbull ended his days in Charleston, on March 13, 1792, being then seventy-three years of age.[52]

Somewhere in Saint Philip's cemetery in Charleston, in an unmarked grave, lie today the remains of one of the most extraordinary men who ever came to colonize America, Andrew Turnbull. He was a true "baroque" man—dynamic, restless, imaginative, arrogant, unsentimental, daring, a persistent fighter. His plans had a sweeping perspective and a grandiose character; his relationships, outside his family and a very restricted circle of acquaintances, were completely devoid of emotionalism; his strong attachment to a distant, fixed goal, made him deal ruthlessly with everything that obstructed, delayed, or jeopardized his final success. No distance was too far, no objective too difficult, no enemy too big for him. Andrew Turnbull was of the same timber as all empire builders.

A few years later, on August 2, 1798, the beautiful Grecian lady,

Maria Gracia, "relict and consort of Dr. Andrew Turnbull," followed him to the grave. She was sixty-eight years of age when she died, and she was interred in the same Saint Philip's yard as was her husband.

In the second half of the twentieth century, more than 150 years after Turnbull's death, his descendants proudly honor the founder of their family in America, ready to defend the memory and acts of their remarkable ancestor.

The Colonists

The first few weeks of residence in the capital of East Florida were enough to persuade the former New Smyrna settlers that the exodus from the colony was not destined to change their unhappy condition. Fear, famine, disease, and death, their inseparable companions for almost ten years, were still with them and remained for quite a long time.

From the balmy tranquillity of New Smyrna, these people suddenly found themselves in the middle of a crowded, noisy, and nervous St. Augustine. The "little town of the deep" was now full of strangers from the North, who had come there to escape the disastrous effects of the Revolution. Most of them had suffered human and property losses in their colonies and, though lucky to be alive, were in a depressed mood, restless, embittered, and demanding. Isolated St. Augustine was not prepared for such a crisis and the result was an acute housing problem and a dangerous food shortage.

Then, to all these difficulties created by the influx of the loyalists, the New Smyrna refugees were added. Destitute and confused as they were, they depended upon the largess of the Governor. But Tonyn was not anxious to exert himself in offering relief to these people. His goal had been attained. With the desertion of New Smyrna, the destruction of his archenemy, Dr. Andrew Turnbull, had been accomplished; and with the recruitment from among the former colonists of all able men for the Rangers, his plan for the augmentation of his favorite military unit had been successful. In the old men, women, and children of the New Smyrna crowd, the Governor did not have any particular interest; he merely assigned to them an area to the north of the town for their temporary settlement. And there, toward the city gate, close to the walls and under the trees, the New Smyrna people improvised shelters and started a desperate struggle for survival.

COLONEL JAMES GRANT, FLORIDA'S FIRST BRITISH GOVERNOR, 1764-1771

VIEW of the GOVERNORS house at St AUGUSTINE in E. FLORIDA. Novr 1764

Left: LIEUTENANT GOVERNOR JOHN MOULTRIE

Below: GOVERNOR PATRICK TONYN

Above: CHIEF JUSTICE WILLIAM ▌

St. George Street as it appeared in the nineteenth century. The Minorcan Chapel was on the second floor of the first house to the left.

A nineteenth-century view of the so-called "Oldest School House"

A TYPICAL NEW SMYRNA LANDSCAPE DURING THE NINETEENTH CENTURY. *(Courtesy J. Carver Harris)*

THE FERNANDEZ-LLAMBIAS HOUSE—RESTORED AND MAINTAINED BY THE SAINT AUGUSTINE HISTORICAL SOCIETY. *(Courtesy the Society)*

The months of late spring and summer of 1777 passed without major calamities. But when later, in August and September of that year, the seasonal heavy rains came with their violent torrents and strong winds, the weakened refugees could not resist any longer and died. According to the official reports, within eight months after they had left New Smyrna, from May to December of 1777, 53 men and women and 16 children lost their lives.[53] In this horrifying report, Tonyn stated that the total number of deaths for the year 1777 was 84. When he had completed the enumeration of all the losses, Tonyn added separately the death of "34 Greeks," who indeed must have had the greatest rate of mortality in comparison with the other ethnic groups in New Smyrna.[54]

The great number of deaths in St. Augustine was attributed to the sickly condition of the settlers before the desertion of the colony: "Many of them came to town with dropsies and other disorders, of which several have died," Tonyn reported to Lord Germain on December 29, 1777.[55] But Turnbull thought that the opposite was the truth, and during the same month of December, 1777, he gave Lord Germain his own version of what had happened. He did not neglect, of course, first to describe the "good" life of these men back in his colony, a fact which by that time even Lord Germain knew was untrue. Thus Turnbull weakened the otherwise very interesting description in which he stated that "these People (having been accustomed for years to a regular and wholesome Diet and to comfortable and dry Habitations with such Exercise by Agriculture as contributed to their Health) on being removed to St. Augustine, they became so sickly, that sixty five of them died in the last two months [October and November of 1777] from what I see of their Deseases, Want, and Misery, I think that a few months more will bury the greatest Part of them." He thought that one of the main causes of the many deaths was their exposure "in the Rains of August and September, which deseased and dropsied them in such a manner as must end in Death, a few of the young and robust excepted, whose Constitutions have stood the Shock of the complicated Misery, and Wretchedness into which they were deluded; for their want is now so great, that above a hundred of the women and Children went to the Governour's House some Days ago, and demanded sustenance in the most clamorous Manner."[56]

Tonyn, in July, 1777,[57] had already thought about granting small plots of land to each family. But it took him several months to put his ideas into action. Only in December of that year did he report to his government in London that he had "alloted Lands between this [town of St. Augustine] and St. John's river, and must give them some assistance in that provision way."[58] In this area was established the "Greek Settlement," as the British used to call it, which extended approximately from Hypolita Street north to the city gates, and from St. George Street to the San Sebastian River.[59] Within these boundaries those who survived from among the former settlers of New Smyrna built their homes, cultivated small plots of land, and after some time opened their small business enterprises. When Father Pedro Camps came to St. Augustine from New Smyrna in November, 1777, he established a Roman Catholic church on the second floor of a house on St. George Street, next to a building subsequently called the "Spanish Inn." It was also known as "the Greek Church," or "the Church of the Mahonese," and sometimes "the Minorcan chapel."

Despite the many calamities that befell the New Smyrna refugees, by January 15, 1778, 419 of them were still alive. From the Governor's report it is evident that of this number about 128 were children born in New Smyrna.[60] Of the remaining 291 adults, a few were women, and several young men served either in the Rangers or in the navy manning the ships used by the East Florida government. The rest of them were busy in St. Augustine, mostly in farming and fishing.

Then the time came when the British decided to abandon St. Augustine. Their 20-year interregnum in Florida, from 1763 to 1783, had now come to an end, and by the Treaty of Paris they returned the whole province back to Spain.

Tonyn was promptly notified by the London government about this change and received his instructions concerning the evacuation of the British population. By the end of September, 1783, his superiors in London had dispatched to him a copy of the definitive treaty, as well as the Royal Sign Manual, which authorized him to deliver up the province to the Spanish according to the terms of the treaty.[61] All the British subjects in Florida had to leave within the next 18 months. For this purpose the home officials provided 4,000 tons of shipping and ordered the officers commanding the Leeward Islands and Jamaica to contribute to that service. They also instructed Tonyn to remain in St. Augustine until evacuation was completed.[62]

Once again the former colonists of New Smyrna had to make up their minds whether they would follow the British or remain in St. Augustine with the Spanish. By that time, Greeks, Minorcans, Italians, Corsicans, all of them, had had enough "evacuations" during the last 15 years, so that there were many who were not willing to move again, pass through new adventures, and start their life anew in another land.

Tonyn's ambition was to take away every single inhabitant of East Florida. By doing so, he hoped to transfer a deserted area to the Spaniards, the repeopling of which might prove a Herculean task for the new masters. Thus, Tonyn thought that for a long time East Florida would not offer any competition to the British interests; moreover, by taking away over 16,000 people, he could enrich with experienced colonists several of the British possessions in the Caribbean and the Atlantic.

With these thoughts in mind, Tonyn had a conference with Father Pedro Camps who expressed his desire of returning to Europe. There was no doubt that such a move of the beloved prelate would be followed by most of his parishioners.[68] The Minorcans also had several meetings with the Governor and expressed their determination to leave either for Europe, mostly for Gibraltar, which was close to their island, or for various British colonies, especially the Bahamas, where finally several did go. As Tonyn explained the situation to Lord Sydney, who had become the Principal Secretary of State by that time, "The intentions of the Minorcans were my Lord to emigrate, they had carefully consulted me thereupon, and solicited to be sent the Major part to Gibraltar, others to Dominica and the Bahamas, to the latter of which, a considerable number have gone a few to Dominica, and some to Europe."[64]

Then Father Camps changed his mind and decided to stay in Florida, and so did most of the former New Smyrna people. Tonyn attributed this change to the fact that with the coming of the Spanish, Father Camps was promoted and highly honored, and this moral and material reward had influenced his attitude. Moreover, the three Roman Catholic priests—of whom two were Irish—who arrived in the meantime, had managed to persuade not only him but also his parishioners to stay; "they impressed on the Minorcan women the ideas, that their children must be left behind, as the Church was the sole Guardian of the Souls of their children, and it was her duty to prevent their being brought up Hereticks, which those that emigrated would be, and would incur eternal damnation: these steps in my

175

opinion were my Lord, infringments of the treaty of Peace, and were however of such a nature, as could not be animadverted upon."[65]

Thus the new Spanish Governor, Vicente Manuel de Zéspedes, on July 12, 1784, the same day that he formally received the town and the fortress of San Marcos from Governor Tonyn, also received a memorial which greatly added to the happiness of the day. It was signed by 29 Greeks and Italians who, with all due respect submitted to him their congratulations and assured him that they were happy to pass under the Spanish dominion; then they added: "We humbly beg Your Excellency to represent us to His Majesty as desirous of being recognized as natural-born subjects, and we declare our readiness as such to sacrifice our lives in the royal service and to obey with especial pleasure and zeal your Excellency's orders."[66]

The next day, Governor Zéspedes received a second memorial, signed by 50 Minorcans who, after congratulating the new Governor, assured him that "as Catholics and natural born Spanish subjects we rejoice in finding ourselves restored to the dominion of our legitimate lord and sovereign, whom We humbly beg Your Excellency to acquaint that we are desirous of offering ourselves to the royal service. Your Excellency also may count upon all our powers, obedience, and devotion."[67]

Governor Zéspedes was satisfied. The two memorials were an expression of loyalty not only of the 29 Greeks and Italians and the 50 Minorcans who had signed them but also of their families, who during those days comprised the most solid and most numerous part of East Florida's population. Zéspedes explained to his superiors that "the number of individuals joining in this memorial, and in the accompanying one of the Italians and Greeks, is in excess of the number who signed; they total 460, including all persons of both sexes, according to the list which their priest, Father Pedro Campos, says he has."[68]

These people had made a remarkable recovery within six years without having received any particular care by anyone, as if their freedom alone were enough to improve their health and elevate their standard of living. In January of 1778, their community had 419 members. Since then several had departed, together with the other British subjects, for various parts of the Empire, and it is certain that a few others must have died. And yet their numbers instead of decreasing, actually increased. Intermarriages between the Greek, Minorcan, and Italian families and the births that followed augmented their numbers which, in the summer of 1784, reached 460 persons.[69] The frequent Spanish censuses which followed from that year on showed an amazing development of these people.

The Spanish rule was a welcome change for the Minorcans. Their identity as "natural-born Spanish subjects" gave them a feeling of security and hopes for preferred treatment. But this was not the case with the Greeks and the Italians. They were uncertain about what would happen to them under the new regime. Some of them had remained in Florida, because they could do nothing better at that time. For instance, the Greek Petro Cozifaccy [Petros Cotsifakis] was, according to a contemporary English report, "an industrious man, who after being on board a Vessel in order to settle under a British Government at Domenica was detained by Authority . . . until falling sick." Thus, he was obliged to disembark and finally "he was constrained to settle under the Spanish Government."[70] His name appears first in the memorial submitted to Governor Zéspedes by the Greeks and Italians in which with pomp and enthusiasm they declared their "readiness as such to sacrifice our lives in the royal service."

It is not clear why a man like Cotsifakis, who was forced by circumstances to stay behind, would subscribe to such a strong statement. Perhaps he, as well as several others, having recently changed masters, one after another, tried to make the best of an uncertain situation. However, they all were afraid that under the Spanish domination they might lose at least two of the most cherished blessings which they had thoroughly enjoyed during the past few years: the property rights over the small piece of land granted to them by the British within the periphery of St. Augustine and the right of locomotion. Not that they really planned to transfer themselves somewhere else, but it seems that after the years they had spent tied to the land of New Smyrna, it was a wonderful feeling for them to know that they could move from place to place freely.

Thus, six months after the arrival of Governor Zéspedes, 14 from among the same Greeks and Italians who had signed the memorial submitted a petition in which they explained to him the manner in which they had become owners of their little plots and they also exp.essed their deep concern because "they have heard it said that as soon as they become vassals of His Catholic Majesty they will not be free to retire to their own country or to any other that may be agreeable to them, when the term designated by the treaty has elapsed;

therefore," they concluded, "your supplicants humbly beg that Your Honor, taking all these things into consideration, will, as an act of generosity and in recognition of the uncertain status of your supplicants, confirm them in the possession of their lands and in the liberty which they ought to have to retire from the province."[71]

Zéspedes was willing to grant this request immediately. The cultivation of these lands could contribute to the economic development of Florida. He had already asked for the approval of such confirmation of those property rights.[72] But the reply had not yet come and in order to pacify the anxious petitioners, he issued a decree in which he asserted that: "As soon as the happy dominion of His Catholic Majesty was established, the Minorcans, Italians and Greeks were notified that I would ask (as I have in effect asked) permission of His Majesty to divide among them land in proportion to the number of families and the energy and good behavior of each individual, to which request I have as yet received no reply, though I am daily expecting a favorable one. Until it arrives, and even afterwards, to no one will the free and unmolested departure from the province be interfered with."[73] The Greeks and Italians realized that they did not have serious reasons to worry, and so together with their fellow Minorcans continued striving to improve their lands.

When Turnbull saw, in December of 1777, the "Deseases, Want, and Misery" of these people, he predicted that "a few months more will bury the greatest Part of them." But six years later, in 1783, a preliminary Spanish census revealed not only that the former New Smyrna colonists had increased their numbers but also that they had settled in quite well. "The greatest Part of them" were proprietors of small pieces of land, owned houses, or sometimes schooners and fishing boats; they had established themselves as specialized artisans, and in some cases they owned not only stores and other real estate but, ironically, they even owned slaves.

The rapid change in their lives is dramatically reflected in a number of censuses taken in a relatively short time. Immediately after the census of 1783, the Spanish authorities took another more complete accounting in 1784, in order to supply their government with the needed information for revenue purposes. Then in 1786, the newcomer Father Thomas Hassett, who was profoundly interested in the education of the Roman Catholics of St. Augustine, took his own census in order to clarify the synthesis of the town's population and their educational needs.[74] A year later, in 1787, and

Epilogue

again in 1798, other revenue censuses were taken which illuminate the development of the property and relationships of these people. In this case, the reading of otherwise cold statistical data reveals a warming human effort and produces an evidence of the long due reward to their labor and pains.

Their stories perhaps are not impressive, but the speedy recovery of the former New Smyrna colonists under conditions of freedom is. For instance, Petros Cotsifakis, the Greek from Corsica who had decided to leave with the British and go to the Leeward Island of Dominica and who finally was obliged to stay in Florida, by 1783 was well established in St. Augustine. In that year he was thirty-three years old and was married to the Minorcan Agnes Cabedo, who was the same age.[75] Agnes was a widow, and from her previous marriage she had a little daughter. After their marriage in 1778,[76] two more daughters were added to the Cotsifakis family,[77] and during the year of 1783 a son was born to them.[78] On the way to the so-called "Minorcan Chapel," there was the lot which was owned by Cotsifakis, and on it he had built a house, which was also his property, in which he lived with his family. His stated occupation was "storekeeper," but besides his store he owned a schooner, and it is not difficult for one to imagine his joy when he used to cut the rolling Atlantic on his own vessel with its swelling sails, "pursuing his happiness."

Since he came from New Smyrna, he had tightened his relationships with former fellow colonists, such as the Segui, the Buxanis, the Llambias,[79] by becoming godfather to their children at their baptisms; in this manner, to several families he had become *koumbaros*, the time-honored relationship which in Greece bound entire communities together. As did most of the other respectable property owners of St. Augustine, Cotsifakis owned Negro Slaves, one male and two females. All this change in his life happened within six years, since 1777, when he came to town starving and naked like all his fellow settlers from New Smyrna. In the years to come he continued increasing both his property and his family.

Gaspar Papi, from Smyrna, Asia Minor, started his free life in St. Augustine as a farmer. In 1781, the thirty-three-year-old Greek married Anna Pons, from Mercadal of Minorca, twelve years his junior and his best men were two fellow Greeks, Ioannis Giannopoulos from Mani and Ioannis Koluminas from Corsica.[80] By 1783, he owned four acres of land beyond the City Gates, close to the

179

Shrine of Our Lady of La Leche, on which he had built a cottage. He lived, however, with his family in another little house, which he also owned, within the city limits, in the Greek settlement. After some time, Papi shifted his occupation and became a storekeeper. His business grew, as well as his family,[81] and when in July 1817, he made an inventory of his property in his last will and testament,[82] he showed that he was a man of substance. His store carried a quantity and variety of merchandise from material for clothes and shoes to table silver, from books to commodities such as tobacco, rice, sugar, butter, and salt; he had lent money to people; he had two houses, one old and one new "of wood," much furniture, and an orange grove that had 75 trees producing sweet oranges. He owned two female and three male Negro slaves and a great deal of other property, also four horses and 138 head of cattle. Down to the middle of the nineteenth century his main house downtown was one of the most beautiful in St. Augustine.

The Cretan Demetrios Fudulakis is the only one appearing in any document as adhering to "the Greek church."[83] Six years after 1777, when he arrived in St. Augustine, he also was well established. He was then thirty-seven years old. His wife, Maria Bross, from the Aegean island of Santorini, was forty-seven years old. They lived together with the two grown-up sons of Maria from her previous marriage to Domingo Costa, a Greek from Corsica, and with their own son, who was born in New Smyrna. In that year of 1783, Fudulakis had already three acres of land and he owned a house close to the Shrine of Our Lady of La Leche. He was both a farmer and a fisherman. Ten years later, he with his stepson, Yorge Costa, bought a schooner. By that time, Fudulakis was a man of property.

Anastasios Mavromatis,[84] who was born in the Greek island of Melos, was living, six years after his arrival in St. Augustine, in his own small house "of boards" in the Greek settlement, with his wife and his two little children. He was then thirty-two years old and his wife, Francesca Llebres from Minorca, twenty-two. He was a farmer and cultivated two acres of land as a tenant, but he had on it a cottage, which was his own property. He also had two slaves, one his own and another whom he rented. A few years later he owned four acres of land and three horses, and he had increased his family by one more daughter.

The above are not unusual "success stories," but are average cases that exemplify the "big change" in the lives of the former New Smyrna settlers. According to Father Thomas Hassett, in 1786 there were in St. Augustine a total of 469 of them—241 males and 228 females, among whom there were 97 married couples. The total number of slaves owned by them was 70.[85]

Some of the New Smyrna people had occupations which kept them in town, such as Elias Medici or Francisco Marin who were shoemakers, or Petros Drimarachis, Nicolas Stephanopoli, Antonio Llambias, Domingo Exarcopoulos, and Gabriel Triay, who were carpenters. Others were engaged in activities that carried them away, like Antonios Stephanopoli, who already in 1783 was the owner of a schooner, "in which," according to the census of that year, "he makes voyages to the United States." Some of them made a livelihood through occupations which appeared natural to them, such as Juan Francisco Arnau, Francisco Stacoly, Marcos Andreu, Nicolas Salada,[86] Luis Sochy, and many others who were all mariners; and some made a livelihood through the most unexpected occupations, such as Michael (Miguel) Costa, who in 1783 was registered as a "Medical Doctor," or Ioannis Giannopoulos (Juan Janopoli) who at first was known in St. Augustine as a carpenter and later became a teacher.

It seems that Miguel Costa had either learned through hard experience or somehow had been initiated in the treatment of some of the "fevers" and "distempers" with medicinal herbs and roots and "nostrums," and he had perhaps acquired a surgical dexterity, or he knew all about the time-honored methods of "bleeding and purging and sweating," and so he became the only known person among the New Smyrna people who "practiced physick." It is almost certain that during that time the harm he might have caused could not be greater than the harm caused by more "learned" physicians. Medicine, however, was a kind of paraprofessional occupation for Miguel Costa, because after 1783 he appeared in official documents as a mariner.

The educational activities of Giannopoulos in St. Augustine, though not exceptional for Greeks abroad, left deep traces in the history of the town. He was about eighteen years old when he came from Mani of Greece to New Smyrna, and there despite the difficulties he managed to survive. When in 1777 the colony was abandoned, he arrived in St. Augustine as miserable as the other colonists. He was then a widower with no other possessions but his youth and the few rags on his back. The end of the first year of freedom found him still alive and with an optimistic outlook for the future. So, on November 1, 1778, he married Antonia Rosello, a widow from Mercadal,

A receipt from the educational accounts of John Gianopoli (Giannopoulos).

Minorca.[87] Working hard for the next few years, he acquired some property. In 1783 he was cultivating, as a tenant, three acres of land, which he had rented from an Englishman for "72½ pessos"; but he also had as his own property three slaves, two horses, and his own house, which was "situated further up than the Minorcan chapel."[88] In the meantime, he had increased the circle of his relations among his former fellow colonists by becoming a godfather to children in the families of Drimarachi, Andreu, Alsina, Medici, Andes, Llopis, Reis, and Llorens.[89]

Unfortunately, the year 1786 found him a widower again, living alone in his house and extending his hospitality to his *koumbaros,* Petros Drimarachis; the latter had also become a widower and lived at the home of Giannopoulos with his daughter and little son. Giannopoulos remained unmarried for four years and then, on January 13, 1790, he married a widow, Geronima Pesso de Burgos.[90] Two years later, however, Giannopoulos was once again a widower. A number of men might have been discouraged by similar marital experiences, but not Giannopoulos. He was evidently a staunch believer in the institution of marriage. He might have thought that he had married enough Mediterranean women, all widows and older than himself, so perhaps for this reason, on December 2, 1793, when he married for a fourth time, he chose an American girl, Ann Maria Barbara Simpson,[91] 24 years his junior.[92] Ann was a Roman Catholic from St. Augustine whose mother was born in Baltimore, Maryland, and her father in London. It seems that she made Giannopoulos a very happy man; and their family increased at a rapid pace. Within five years after their marriage, they had three children: one daughter, Maria Manuela Barbara, and two sons the younger, George Pedro Pasqual, and the older, Manuel de Jesus Domingo. Evidently it was during this time that Giannopoulos started teaching, thus becoming one of the very first teachers in the "oldest city" of the United States. Though no details are known about his school, receipts of tuition paid by his pupils indicate that he might have had a sizable income from it.

With the passing of the years, the former colonists of New Smyrna saw their numbers increasing and their property acquiring respectable dimensions. In 1821, when Florida had become part of the United States, they claimed title to 48,956 acres of land and their claims were all confirmed by the United States Land Commissioners.[93] By that time they had become the oldest and most solid group of inhabitants in St. Augustine. Their descendants—settled, better educated, and more numerous—played an important role in the local political life, filling a number of municipal and federal offices and at times being able to elect the mayor of the town from their own ranks.

In later periods of nationalistic upheavals in the country, such as the Jacksonian era or the last years of the nineteenth century, when nativistic trends were mixed with interest of local politicians, the off-spring of the New Smyrna settlers suffered from the effects of unjustified discrimination. But these brief, unfortunate moments were not enough to hinder the further development of these people. From among them came statesmen and bishops, literary men and scholars, West-Pointers, businessmen, farmers, fishermen and a great number of other honest, sensitive, and hard-working men and women.[94]

In the second half of the twentieth century every corner in St. Augustine, every inch of the city, testifies to the part which the colonists of New Smyrna and their descendants played in the life of the town. There are still the beautiful eighteenth-century houses of Llambias, Triay, and others, as well as the building that housed the "Minorcan" chapel on St. George Street. There is also an aged wooden structure, the "oldest wooden schoolhouse in the United States," which is pointed out to visitors as the original Giannopoulos' school-house; and the grateful town has given his name to one of her streets, a tribute to a Greek who "lambadan diedosen,"[95] a task most highly prized in his former country. The city directory with all the Minorcan, Greek, and Italian names reads like a list of the Turnbull ships which carried the first settlers to the shores of New Smyrna. There are the numerous members of the Mauncy, Benét, Pelicer, Arnau, Capella, Andreu, Capo, Genovar, Leonardy, Pacetti, Lopez, Pappy, Sabate, Pomar, Segui, Usina, Ponce, and many, many other families. In their houses one can eat the same tasty dishes which their forefathers used to prepare, especially the Minorcan shrimp *pilau,* which originated in Arabia and was carried to Spain and the Balearics by the Moors; from there, enriched with shrimps and other sea-food, it was brought to Florida by the Minorcans. In these closing decades of the twentieth century, the same excitement occurs among these children of the old New Smyrna generation as prevailed all those years ago when they heard that "mullet is on the beach"; and they rush either to the Vilano or to the St. Augustine beach, many of them carrying the same kind of round net which in Greece is called *pezóvoli* and in St. Augustine, "Minorcan net;" and with the same dexterity as their forefathers, they skillfully cast the net by hand over the schools of silver mullet.

Epilogue

When in the narrow lanes of St. Augustine the stranger meets the dark eyes and expressive Mediterranean faces of these descendants, his mind travels back almost 200 years to the first New Smyrna colonists who came from cosmopolitan Smyrna and the white islands of the Aegean, from the rocky shoulders of Mani and the mild Italian valleys, from manly Corsica and charming Minorca, all places strung like beads in a rosary stretched from one end to the other of the blue Mediterranean. And he feels, on reading the verses written by Stephen Vincent Benét, himself a descendant of this Minorcan generation:

> *Thy came here, they toiled here*
> *They broke their hearts afar*
> *· · · · · · · ·*
> *It was not so to be*
> *Let us still remember them,*
> *Men from oversea*
> *· · · · · · · ·*
> *They lived here, and died here*
> *They left singing names.*[96]

The Land

When Turnbull left Florida in 1781, New Smyrna became a ghost town. The empty buildings, the abandoned plantation, the deserted docks, the fast-growing weeds in the neglected fields, all gave a very melancholy picture of what once was a busy and populous place. But New Smyrna did not long remain in this condition. The pressure of the swarming loyalists made Tonyn distribute some of its land to them, and a few of these refugees remained there until the evacuation of the province was completed.[97]

With the coming of the Spanish into Florida, the sons of George Grenville and Lady Mary Duncan, who were the only heirs of Turnbull's deceased partners, abandoned every idea of repossessing the actual land of the colony. So they submitted claims to the Land Commissioners appointed by British Parliament asking for indemnification for the losses suffered in their property as a consequence of the cession of Florida to the king of Spain. They claimed the sum of £28,991 15s 0d.[98] Of this amount they were finally awarded £12,144.[99]

Turnbull did the same. In 1783, in Charleston, South Carolina, he had already lost hope that he would some day return to New Smyrna.[100] Three years later, on May 12, 1786, he appointed as his

185

attorney his friend, James Penman, who was by then a resident of London, and authorized him to claim from the British government an indemnity for his lost property.[101]

Turnbull had received his land under both systems used by the British government for the distribution of land in Florida between 1763 and 1783. Under the first, the Provincial Council granted small tracts to settlers through the so-called "family right." Thus, the head of a family could obtain 100 acres for himself and 50 additional acres for every white or black man, woman, or child, member of his family.[102] The size of these grants could be increased to 1,000 acres if the settlers could cultivate it and meet the conditions of the grant. In order also to secure a just distribution of the best locations, grants were laid out in parallelograms, the front measuring one-third of the length, which would be extended inland rather than along a highway, river, or creek.[103] The second system involved grants of 20,000 acres or more, which were made after a petition to the Board of Trade by Orders of the King in Council. The number of families to be settled in these tracts, in a given time, was carefully specified.[104]

Turnbull, in 1786, submitted two claims, one under his name asking for an indemnity of £6,462 10s 0d, and another one as "Dr. Andrew Turnbull and children" for £15,057 10s 0d. The first claim was completely rejected, and for the second the British government allowed only £916 13s 4d.[105]

In the meantime, during the years of the Spanish occupation of Florida, no spectacular development took place in the land of New Smyrna. For a long time the population of Florida remained very small[106] and those who wanted to establish themselves on the land of Turnbull's colony were not numerous. Finally, a few non-Spanish inhabitants of East Florida received grants in the so-called "Turnbull's back swamp," which was known for its fertile soil, particularly adapted for the cultivation of sugar cane, cotton, and corn. In this way, life and a small-scale agriculture continued in the area of the old colony, especially after 1816 when the Spanish governor, José Coppinger, endeavored to foster settlement there.

Thus, when Florida became a United States territory, there were several Americans holding Spanish titles on sections of the Turnbull swamp, such as James Darley for 500 acres;[107] James Dell for 5,000 acres;[108] Charles Sibbard for 4,000 acres;[109] Ralph King for 5,000 acres;[110] as well as William Mills for 16,000 acres on the Mosquitoes, and the trustees of Robert McHarly for 600 acres on

Turnbull's plantation.[111] Soon the United States government appointed a Board of Land Commissioners which held its first meeting in St. Augustine on August 4, 1823.[112] Its authority was to examine the validity not only of the Spanish but also of the British land titles. Then, a number of people presented their claims, among whom the children of Dr. Andrew Turnbull petitioned for the confirmation of their titles on an extensive body of land amounting to 43,301 acres, the one acre being not in New Smyrna, but in St. Augustine; it had been granted to Dr. Andrew Turnbull on January 15, 1767.

Turnbull's heirs endeavored to avail themselves of the *jus post-liminium,* asking for the restoration of their rights to the land as they were before the coming of the Spanish to Florida. But unfortunately for them the fate of almost all the claims based on British titles was identical. The Land Commissioners failed to uphold or confirm them.[113] But the children of Dr. Turnbull returned after some time to claim 70,000 acres of land. On January 20, 1830, Commissioner Burnet, of the Committee on Private Land Claims, reported to the United States Senate on the Turnbull question and asked the rejection of their new claims.[114] He did so without knowing that several basic arguments raised by the Turnbulls were erroneously presented.

One of them, for instance, affirmed that Andrew Turnbull's heirs had the right to petition for the confirmation of their titles because their father had not been compensated by the British government when the Spanish came to Florida. Burnet answered that the Treaty of 1783 enabled Turnbull to reclaim his property and that he had neglected to do so.[115] But what Burnet did not know was that "Dr. Andrew Turnbull and children" had not neglected to do so and that the British government had awarded them £916 13s 4d.

Then Turnbull's heirs maintained that the United States ought to confirm their title, because their father had joined the Americans at the beginning of the Revolutionary War. On this point, Commissioner Burnet remarked that "although that course entitles him to the most favorable consideration"[116] still this claim of his heirs ought to be rejected. The Commissioner did not know, of course, that Dr. Andrew Turnbull, despite the fact that he lived the last ten years of his life in the United States, preferred to pay the Alien Duty rather than to become an American citizen as he was asked to by the Charleston authorities and that he died a British subject.

By 1835 the heirs of Dr. Turnbull had restricted their ambitions and claimed only 57,000 acres. The Board of Land Commissioners, however, gave them again the same stereotyped answer: "Resolved: That it is inexpedient to grant the prayer of the petitioners."[117]

For Turnbull, his associates, and their heirs, New Smyrna was an "adventure," an investment that was to produce a profitable return. But for the hundreds of colonists who left their homes in Europe and came to America to find freedom in one form or another, it was "the land of promise." No matter if the piece of land which they were to receive after the end of their service was 50 or 100 acres, they had set their hearts on it.[118] This was the one and only concrete reward for the hard work of some of the best years of their lives, the span of which during those days was very short indeed. This was the land on which they could stand and build a new life in the New World. But not one of all these people ever received even one acre of this "promised" land—even though most of the time it had been promised in writing.

It seems that John Lee Williams is quite accurate when he asserts that to the settlers who escaped to St. Augustine, besides their freedom "lands were offered . . . [by the British Courts] at New Smyrna, but they suspected some trick was on foot, to get them into Turnbull's hands, and besides, they detested the place, where they had suffered so much."[119] Thus, the bulk of the survivors from the New Smyrna Colony remained in St. Augustine, although some of them went to other parts of the world. But none returned to the colony.

When Florida became American in 1821, there were a few planters in Turnbull's back swamp and in the periphery of the old colony. But the actual area where the settlement of New Smyrna was thriving, once upon a time, was completely deserted. This is how it looked in 1821 to an anonymous correspondent of the *Charleston Courier*:

Musquito Inlet: a snug and safe inlet for small vessels, affording from ten to twelve feet of water on its bar. . . . The insect called the Musquito, is said by some prejudiced or not well informed persons, to be intolerable in this section of the province; but I know that they are not worse here than they are generally along the sea coast of the southern states. . . . On the west side of the Hillsborough, about four miles from the inlet, and situated on a quarry of the stone above mentioned [coquina] formerly stood the town of New Smyrna. Many of its ruins are still visible. It sunk to ruins in consequence of the effect of the despotic security of their landlord.[120]

Williams again in 1837 gives the following information: "New Smyrna: The site of this old town, that once contained 1,800 inhabitants, has been purchased by Col. Andrews and Major Lytle of the army, and we learn that it is their intention to resurvey it in town lots."[121] This may be considered the date of the rebirth of New Smyrna.

In the second half of the twentieth century, on the area where the greatest colonization of North America was ever attempted—with the arrival of 1,255 settlers at one time, the acquisition of more than 100,000 acres of land and the investment of more than 40,000 pounds—there is a beautiful little town, where people live and enjoy the charms of a semitropical land. Under the pavement on the side of its streets still run Dr. Andrew Turnbull's irrigation canals, lined with ancient coquina rocks and built "in the Egyptian's mode of watering," in the very way he had seen them by the Nile. The place names and a few ruins of the old colony's structures certify the past of this dramatic site. But one can hear now the happy laughter of the youth who play on the sandy shores and in the water of sunny New Smyrna. No one would suspect the pain of the bloody birth of this enchanting place.

N O T E S — Epilogue

1. Memorial of Turnbull to the Board of Trade, London, Dec. 6, 1776, C.O. 5/546, p. 53.

2. Turnbull to Shelburne, St. Augustine, Mar. 14, 1780, Lansdowne MSS, Vol. 1219, f. 36-60.

3. Turnbull to Germain, St. Augustine, Mar. 16, 1780, Lansdowne MSS, Vol. 1219, f. 40.

4. Turnbull to Shelburne, New York, Nov. 10, 1777, Lansdowne MSS, Vol. 88, f. 163.

5. Turnbull to Germain, St. Augustine, Dec. 29, 1777, C.O. 5/558, p. 101.

6. The following facts are taken from: Turnbull to Germain, St. Augustine, Dec. 8, 1777, Sackville MSS, II, 82 ff., private collection of Mrs. Stopford Sackville MSS, Drayton House, Northamptonshire, England.

7. C.O. 5/556.

8. C.O. 5/546; Siebert, I, 63-66, 316-17.

9. *Ibid.*

10. Siebert, *op. cit.*, I, 317.

11. Turnbull to Germain, St. Augustine, Dec. 8, 1777, Sackville MSS, II, 82 ff.

12. *Ibid.*

13. Turnbull to Germain, St. Augustine, Mar. 16, 1780, Lansdowne MSS, Vol. 1219, f. 40.

14. St. Augustine, Dec. 29, 1777, C.O. 5/558, p. 103.

15. *Ibid.*

16. St. Augustine, Dec. 16, 1777, Lansdowne MSS, Vol. 88, p. 173.

17. Whitehall, Feb. 19, 1778, C.O. 5/558, pp. 2-8.
18. *Ibid.*, p. 8.
19. Official Notice, St. Augustine, Aug. 11, 1778, C.O. 5/158, p. 469.
20. St. Augustine, December 16, 1777, Lansdowne MSS., Vol. 88, p. 174; also, Mar. 14, 1780, Vol. 1219, f. 47.
21. C.O. 5/558, p. 104.
22. East Florida, Feb. 17, 1780, Lansdowne MSS, Vol. 1219, f. 47.
23. *Ibid.*
24. Tonyn to Germain, St. Augustine, Aug. 20, 1778, C.O. 5/569; Minutes of the Council, St. Augustine, Aug. 27, 1778, and Tonyn to Brigadier General Prevost, St. Augustine, Aug. 27, 1778, C.O. 5/559, pp. 40-42; Turnbull to Shelburne, St. Augustine, Mar. 14, 1780, Lansdowne MSS, Vol. 1219, f. 36-60; Statement by Forrester, St. Augustine, Mar. 3, 1780, Lansdowne MSS, Vol. 1219, f. 47.
25. Drayton, *op. cit.*, Postscript.
26. St. Augustine, Mar. 14, 1780, Lansdowne MSS, Vol. 1219, f. 36-60.
27. Turnbull to Germain, Charleston, S.C., June 15, 1781, C.O. 5/158, pp. 465-68; Turnbull to Shelburne, Charleston, S.C., July 31, 1782, Lansdowne MSS, Vol. 66. pp. 753-56.
28. *Ibid*, Lansdowne MSS.
29. *Ibid.*
30. *Ibid.*
31. St. Augustine, Mar. 14, 1780, Lansdowne MSS, Vol. 1219, f. 36-60.
32. Turnbull to Shelburne, Charleston, S.C., July 31, 1782, Lansdowne MSS, Vol. 66, pp. 753-56.
33. *Ibid.*
34. *Ibid.*
35. Turnbull to Shelburne, Charleston, S.C., May 23, 1782, Lansdowne MSS, Vol. 66, p. 714.
36. Turnbull to Shelburne, Charleston, S.C., July 31, 1782, Lansdowne MSS, Vol. 66, p. 753-56.
37. St. Augustine, May 27, 1780, American MSS in Royal Institute, II, 127-28.
38. Turnbull to Shelburne, Charleston, S.C., July 31, 1782, Lansdowne MSS, Vol. 66, pp. 753-56.
39. Turnbull to Shelburne, Charleston, S.C., Dec. 6, 1782, Lansdowne MSS, Vol. 66, pp. 757-59.
40. Turnbull to Shelburne, Charleston, S.C., June 21, 1782, Lansdowne MSS, Vol. 66, pp. 718-19.
41. *Ibid.*
42. Turnbull to Shelburne, Charleston, S.C., July 7, 1782, Lansdowne MSS, Vol. 66, pp. 749-51.
43. Charleston, S.C., June 21, 1782, *ibid.*, pp. 718-19.
44. *Ibid.*
45. Turnbull to Shelburne, Charleston, S.C., Dec. 6, 1782, *ibid.*, pp. 757-59.
46. *Ibid.*
47. Statement by George Miller on Nov. 15, 1787, in Treasury 77-204.
48. Charleston, S. C., May 30, 1783, Lansdowne MSS, Vol. 88, f. 189.
49. *American State Papers*, V, 13, claim 591.
50. St. Augustine, Mar. 16, 1780, Lansdowne MSS, Vol. 1219, f. 40.
51. Corse, *op. cit.*, p. 187.
52. *Ibid.*, pp. 194 ff.

NOTES — Epilogue

53. C. O. 5/558, p. 107.
54. *Ibid.*
55. St. Augustine, Dec. 29, 1777, C. O. 5/558, p. 104.
56. St. Augustine, Dec. 8, 1777, Sackville MSS, II, 82 ff. Turnbull to Shelburne, Charleston, S.C., July 3, 1782, Lansdowne MSS, Vol. 66, pp. 725-27.
57. Tonyn to Germain, St. Augustine, July 26, 1777, C. O. 5/557, p. 517.
58. C. O. 5/558, p. 104.
59. Lawson, *op. cit.*
60. C. O. 5/558, p. 107. These 128 are the only survivors of 258 persons born in New Smyrna from Aug. 25, 1768 to Sept. 16, 1777, as recorded in Father Camps' Register of Baptisms.
61. C. O. 5/560, pp. 721-33.
62. *Ibid.*
63. Tonyn to Lord Sydney, St. Augustine, Apr. 4, 1785, C.O. 5/561, p. 360.
64. *Ibid.*, pp. 359-60.
65. *Ibid.*, pp. 360-61.
66. Memorial of the Italians and Greeks, St. Augustine, July 12, 1784, enclosure in Zéspedes to Conde de Gálvez, St. Augustine, July 16, 1784, Archivo General de Indias, Audencia de Santo Domingo, leg. 2660, pp. 1-10, translated into English in Joseph Byrne Lockey, edited with a foreword by John Walton Caughey, *East Florida, 1783-1785, A File of Documents Assembled and Many of them Translated* (Berkeley: University of California Press, 1949), pp. 232-33. This work will be hereafter designated as Lockey. The names of the 29 Greeks and Italians in the spelling of the document are the following: Pietro Cozifaccy; Roco Leonardy; Domenico Martinelli; Juan Columynas; Francesco Staccoli; Giuseppe Giannelli; Ferdinando Fallini; Giuseppe Rossi; Francesco Pezzo di Borgo; Luigi Bruciantiny; Guiseppe Bonnelly; Andrew Pacetti; Giovanni Gianopoli; Pietro Damiralli; Diacinto Pou; Giuseppe Buisany; Giorgi Coleuralli; Francesco Condioli; Giuseppe Battaglini; Anastasy Mauromati; Pietro Truppe; Elia Medici; Juan Cabado; Luigi Soccy; Michel Grazies; Pietro Pasqua; Nicola Salata; Matheo Peregrini; Michele Costa.
67. Memorial of the Minorcans, St. Augustine, July 13, 1784, *ibid.* The names of the Minorcans, in the document's spellings, are the following: Lorenzo Capo; Francisco Pelliser; Martin Arnandis; Juan Alsina; Francisco Marin; Juan Yuanedas; Antonio Alsina; Sebastian Ortegas; Roberto Roger; Juan Villalonga; Miguel Serni; Juan Triay; Juan Selom; Diego Segui; Mathias Pons; Santiago Prats; Juan Carrera; Rafael Rimena; Francisco Selord; Bartolomé Llafrui; Juan Capo; Bernat Harnau; Josef Pons; Antonio Andreu; Juan Pons; Juan Segui; Bartolomé Lopis; Pable Zapetero; Josef Hernández; Diego Hernández; Miguel Gracias; Juan Jerrero; Georgio Olaz; Juan Triay y Pons; Antonio Reyo; Josef Hernández Cardona; Bartolomé Alsina; Francisco Arnau; Juan Llorens; Josef Torró; Josef Hernández; Francisco Bila; Pere Cruay; Lorenzo Capella; Lazaro Ortegas; Antonio Grimaldi; Juan Portella; Juan Colominas; Domingo Malblo; Marcos Andres.
68. *Ibid.*
69. C. 1784.
70. Statement by George Miller, Charleston, S.C., Nov. 15, 1787, Treassury 77-204.
71. Petition of the Greeks and Italians submitted to Governor Zéspedes, St. Augustine, Jan. 27, 1785, Enclosure in *East Florida Papers*, Library of Congress, 640, translated into English in Lockey, pp. 462-63.

NOTES — Epilogue

72. Zéspedes to Bernardo de Gálvez, St. Augustine, Feb. 28, 1785, *ibid.*, p. 461.

73. Decree, St. Augustine, Jan. 28, 1785, *ibid.*, p. 463.

74. On Hassett's census see Joseph B. Lockey, "Public Education in Spanish St. Augustine," *Florida Historical Quarterly*, XV, 3 (January, 1937), pp. 152-54. A copy of this census, together with all censuses of the second Spanish period in Florida, are found in "Census Returns 1784-1814," among the *East Florida Papers*. They can also be found, together with their English translations in the Archives of the St. Augustine Historical Society.

75. All information on these brief biographical sketches is found in the above mentioned Spanish censuses, including Father Hassett's census; Father Camps' Register is also used and in those cases the exact reference to it is given. Agnes' name in Hassett's census appears as Ynes Queredo.

76. Father Camps' Register, entry 4, of 1778.

77. *Ibid.*, entry 6, of 1779; entry 9, of 1781.

78. *Ibid.*, entry 22, of 1783.

79. *Ibid.*, entry 2, of 1779; entry 14, of 1781; entry 6, of 1782.

80. *Ibid.*, entry 2, of 1781.

81. *Ibid.*, WPA I, entries 171, 285, 443; *ibid.*, II, entry 12.

82. Deposited at the Archives of the St. Augustine Historical Society.

83. Census of 1783.

84. In the census of 1783, he appears as "Antonio Mabromati." This is evidently a mistake of the census taker, who confused the name of Anastasios with the name of his father deceased by that time, which was Antonios.

85. Hassett, p. 25.

86. The Census of 1783 states that Nicolas Salada was a "native of Esclavonia," which is either the area between the Drava and Sava rivers of present day Croatia in Yugoslavia, or a district in Northeastern Thrace called by the Byzantine "Sclavonia."

87. Marriages of Father Camps' Register, entry 12, of 1778.

88. Census of 1783.

89. Father Camps' Register, entries 16, 17, 28, 29, of 1780; 6, 8, 18 of 1781; 3 of 1782.

90. WPA, White Marriages, 1764-1801, I, entry of Jan. 13, 1790.

91. *Ibid.*, entry of Dec. 2, 1793.

92. White Baptisms, Vol. I, entry No. 252.

93. *St. Augustine Record*, Apr. 22, 1948.

94. *Ibid.*

95. "He carried on the torch."

96. Rosemary and Stephen Vincent Benét, *A Book of Americans* (New York: Farrar and Rinehart, Inc., 1933), p. 26.

97. Schedule and Valuation of Lady Mary Duncan's estate, statement attached to the description of Grant, A., Treasury 77/7.

98. East Florida Claims, Memorial Grenville, Lady Mary Duncan, Dec. 30, 1786, Treasury 77/7.

99. Mowat, *East Florida*, p. 72; Siebert, *op. cit.*, II, 297 ff.

100. Turnbull to Shelburne, Charleston, S.C., May 30, 1783, Lansdowne MSS, Vol. 88, f. 189.

101. Deposition of May 12, 1786, Treasury 77/7.

102. British Ordinance of Nov. 1765, in *American State Papers, Documents of the Congress of the United States in Relation to the Public Lands* (Washington: Gales and Seaton), V, 756-57.

103. *Ibid.*

104. The Historical Records Survey, Division of Professional and Service Projects, Works Progress Administration, *Spanish Land Grants in Florida* (Tallahassee, Florida: State Library Board, 1940), I, Unconfirmed Claims, xvi.

105. Siebert, *op. cit.*, II, 308.

106. For instance, in 1787 the total population of East Florida was a little over 900 whites and 490 negro slaves. The numbers of whites from the point of view of national origin were as follows: 31 from Spain; 25 from the Canaries; 62 natives of Florida; 448 Minorcans, Greeks and Italians; 342 British. Troops and government employees are not included. From Zéspedes to Crown, St. Augustine, Apr. 15, 1787, in Brooks MSS, in Library of Congress.

107. *Spanish Land Grants*, Unc. D. 4.

108. *American State Papers, Public Lands*, V, 427.

109. *Ibid.*

110. *Spanish Land Grants*, Unc. K. 2.

111. *American State Papers, Public Lands*, V, 427.

112. Sidney Walter Martin, *Florida during the Territorial Days*, (Athens: University of Georgia Press, 1944), p. 69 ff.

113. A complete analysis of the whole question can be found in the Report submitted to Congress in 1825, by the Commissioners Samuel R. Overton and Joseph N. White in *American State Papers, Public Lands*, IV, 251 ff., and V, 13, 757 ff.

114. *Ibid.*, VI, 126.

115. *Ibid.*

116. *Ibid.*

117. Statement by General Clark, Assistant Counsel of the United States, submitted to the Secretary of the Treasury Nov. 4, 1835, *ibid.*, VIII.

118. It has been already explained in Chapter III that there is lack of agreement in the sources of the length of the service and on the amount of the land which the settlers were to receive after the termination of their contracts. Turnbull, also, in his "Refutation," remains silent on this matter, and this attitude of his is quite understandable. Nevertheless, almost all the sources agree that a piece of land had been promised to the settlers, the amount of which varies between the minimum mentioned by Mrs. Corse, who states that: "After they [the settlers] had paid off their indebtedness to the Company by from seven to eight years' labor, each was to receive fifty acres of land, with five additional acres for each child in his family," *op. cit.*, p. 31 (on this point Mrs. Corse has partially adopted the information given by the German traveller Johann David Schoepf, *op. cit.*, pp. 233-36), and the maximum contained in the copy of the contract between the Minorcans and Dr. Turnbull, which is signed only by the latter and found in the Public Archives of Mahón, Minorca: "when the contract with Mr. Turnbull is finished, each head of a family will have one hundred English quarters of land for himself, and fifty for each person of his family, male or female, and it will be as his property, and as land established in ownership forever, being a royal grant. N. B. One hundred and sixty quarters of land have a perimeter of two English miles." (For its English translation, see the *St. Augustine Record*, Sept. 2, 1953.)

119. Williams, *op. cit.*, p. 190.

120. In *Darby*, 1821, pp. 76-77.

121. Williams, *op. cit.*, p. 302.

Bibliography

T HE documents related to the History of the New Smyrna Colony can be found in the British Public Record Office, as well as in collections, libraries, and public archives of several other countries. The following list indicates only material to which direct reference is made in this book. The British documents are indicated in the usual manner, i.e., their category (such as C. [olonial] O. [ffice]; T. [reasury]; S. [tate] P. [apers]; P. [rivy] C. [ouncil] R. [egister]), the number of class, and the number of volume. Thus, C.O. 5/540 means: Colonial Office, class 5, volume 540. The documents in public archives of other countries are indicated with the number of bundle and/or volume, or in the particular way adopted by those archives. Page references to all documents are not given in the following list, but in the footnotes to the text. A few published collections of documents are also listed below.

UNPUBLISHED DOCUMENTS

British Public Record Office: C.O. 5/540, 541, 544, 545, 546, 548, 549, 550-561, 563, 568, 569, 571; C.O. 174/ 4-5; C.O. 324/ 43; C.O. 391/ 83; P.C.R. Vol. 112; S.P. 97/ 32-43; S.P. 105/ 119; T. 77/7 and 204.
Royal Institute: American MSS, Vol. II.
Collection of Mrs. Stopferd Sackville, Drayton House, Northhamptonshire, England: Sackville Historical MSS, Vol. II.
Archivo General de Indias, Seville, Spain: Audiencia de Santo Domingo, legajos 2594, 2660, 2673.
William L. Clements Library, University of Michigan: Knox MSS; Lansdowne MSS, Vols. 52, 66, 88; Folios 139, 147, 157, 163, 189; Vol. 1219, Folios 36-60.
Archive de la Corse, Ajaccio, Corsica, 68/c 76; 69/c 77; 70/c 77; 71/c 77.
Archive de France: Affaires Etrangères, B I 1058.
Municipal Archives of Mahón, Minorca: Files of Notaries: Antonio Flaquer, Bk. 363, Fo. 27; Bartholomé Deyá, Bk. 3, Fos. 94, 103, 129; Ramon Ballester, Bk. 86, Fos. 143, 147, 148, 149, 150, 152; Andrés Vila, Bk. 265, Fos. 229, 231, 233, 246.

Bibliography

Library of Congress, Manuscripts Division: East Florida Papers; Brooks MSS.
Library of Roman Catholic Bishop of St. Augustine, Florida; Father Pedro
Camps' Register, "The Golden Rule Book of the Minorcans"; White
Marriages, 1784-1801.
Library of St. Augustine Historical Society, St. Augustine, Florida: Copy of
the form of contract between Andrew Turnbull and Minorcan indenture
servant; translations of East Florida Papers, and Father Pedro Camps'
Register; material related to property acquired in St. Augustine by the
New Smyrna colonists; documents on the St. Augustine history related to
New Smyrna.
Stetson Collection, 1752-64, University of Florida: AI 87-1-14/2.

PUBLISHED DOCUMENTS

American State Papers. Documents of the Congress of the United States in
Relation to the Public Lands, Vols. IV and V.
Averette, Annie, transl., [Collection of translated Spanish documents] The
Unwritten History of Old St. Augustine. St. Augustine, Florida: Record
Company, 1909.
Historical Records Survey, Division of Professional and Service Projects, Works
Progress Administration, Spanish Land Grants in Florida, Vol. I, Uncon-
firmed Claims. Tallahassee, Florida: State Library Board, 1940.
Historical Records Survey, Division of Community Service Programs, Works
Progress Administration, Translation and Transcription of Church Ar-
chives in Florida, Roman Catholic Records, St. Augustine Parish, White
Baptisms, 1784-1792, Vol. 1 and 2. Tallahassee, Florida: State Library
Board, 1941.
Lambros, Spyridon P., "The Migration of Maniates to Tuscany during the
seventeenth Century." [Transcripts from Florence Real Archivio di Stato,
Miscellanea Medicea, Doc. di Corredo Filza XXVI, No. 11: Trattati e
Capitoli corsi tra in Ser^{mo} Gran Duca Ferdinando 2°: et i Greci de
Braccio di Maina nel 1663 rinovati poi da medesimi con Cosimo 3: nel
1670 per transferirsi molte delle loro Famiglie nel Dominio di Toscana.
Also, transcripts of original Italian and Greek documents from the Ar-
chives of Venice], Neos Hellenomnemon, Vol. II. Athens: 1905.
Lockey, Joseph Byrne, edited by John Walton Caughey, East Florida 1783-
1785: A File of Documents Assembled and Many of them Translated.
Berkeley: University of California Press, 1949.
Sanz, Francisco Hernandez, "La Colognia Griega Establecida en Mahon
durante el Siglo XVIII," [Collection of 26 documents] in Revista de
Menorca, Vol. XX. Mahón, Minorca. 1925.
Whitaker, Arthur Preston, Documents Relating to the Commercial Policy of
Spain in the Floridas. Florida: 1931.

SECONDARY SOURCES

The following list includes only works referred to in the text.

Works related to the background of the colonists from Greece:
Daskalakis, Apostolos V., Mane kai e Othomanike Aftokratoria 1453-1821
[Mani and the Ottoman Empire, 1453-1821]. Athens: 1925.
Eschavannes, E. d', Histoire de Corinth, relation des principaux événements
de la Morée. Paris: 1854.

Bibliography

Fremor, Pat Leigh, *Mani*. New York: Harpers, 1960.

Goudas, Anastasios. *Bioi Paralleloi ton Andron tes Epanastaseos* [Parallel Lives of the Man of the Revolution], Vol. VIII. Athens: 1875.

Kandeloros, Take Ch., *Ho Harmatolismos tes Peloponnesou* [The "Harmatolism" of Peloponnesos, 1500-1821]. Athens: 1924.

Leake, Col. William Martin, *Travels in the Morea*, Vol. I. London: 1830.

Malafouris, M., *Greeks in America, 1529-1948*. New York: 1948.

Melirrytos, Kyriakos, *Chronologia Historike* [Historical Chronology]. Odessa, Russia: 1836.

Paparregopoulos, Constantine, *Istoria tou Ellenikou Ethnous* [History of the Greek Nation], Vol. V, part II. Athens: 1925.

Politopoulos, Takes E., "Maniates in America," *Nea Estia*, Vol. L, p. 580 (Sept., 1951).

Pouqueville, F. C. H. L., *Voyage de la Grèce*. 2nd ed., Vol. IV. Paris: 1826.

Rozakos, N. I., "Unemployment in Mani and Migration," *Nea Estia*, Vol. L, p. 578 (Aug., 1951).

Sakellariou, Michael B., *He Peloponnesos kata ten Defteran Tourkokratian, 1715-1821* [Peloponnesos Under the Second Period of Turkish Rule, 1715-1821]. Athens: Byzantinisch-Neugriechische Yahrbücher, 1939.

Sathas, Constantine N., *Tourkokratoumene Hellas* [Greece under Turkish Rule, A Historical Essay on the Revolutions against the Ottoman Yoke, 1453-1821]. Athens: 1869.

Stavrianos, L. S., *The Balkans since 1453*. New York: Rinehart & Co., 1958.

Works related to the background of the colonists from Corsica:

Blanken, Gerard, *Les Grècs de Cargése (Corse)*, *Recherches sur leur langue et sur leur histoire*. Levden, Holland: 1951.

Buchon, Jean A., *Nouvelles recherches historique sur la Principauté francaise de Morée et ses hautes baronies*, Vol. I. Paris: 1845.

Fardys, Nicholas B., *Yle kai Skarifema Istorias tes en Korsike Ellenikes Paroikias* [Material and Draft of a History of the Greek Colony in Corsica]. Athens: 1888.

Gregorovius, Ferdinand, *Istoria tes Poleos Athenon kata tous Mesous Aionas* [History of the City of Athens during the Middle Ages], translated into Greek by S. P. Lambros, Vol. II. Athens: 1904.

Kambouroglou, Demetrios Gr., "Peri apo tes Manes eis ten Neson Kyrnon Ellenikes Apoikias," [About the Greek Colony from Mani in the island of Corsica], *Hebdomas*, Vol. II, No. 61 (April, 1885).

Miclosich-Muller, Fr., *Acta et diplomata Graeca medii aevi*, Vol. III. Vindobonae: 1865.

Mostratou, Smaragda D., *Kargeze, to Elleniko Horio tes Korsikes* [Cargese, the Greek Village of Corsica]. Athens: 1963.

Papadopoulos, G. G., "Asmata Demotika ton en Korsike Ellenon" [Folk-songs of the Greeks in Corsica], *Pandora*, Vol. XV, No. 353 (Dec., 1864).

Papadopoulos, G. G., *Chronographia peri tes Katagoges ton en Mane Stephanopoulon, tes aftothen eis Korsiken Apoikeseos &c.* [Chronography on the Origin of the Stephanopoli of Mani and their Migration from there to Corsica]. Athens: 1845.

Sathas, Constantine N., *Monumenta Hellenicae Historiae*, Vol. VIII. Paris: 1880-90.

Stephanopoli, Nicolas, *Histoire de la colonie grèque établie en Corse*. Paris: 1826.

Stephanopoli, P., *Histoire de la colonie grèque établie en Corse*. Pise: 1836.

Bibliography

Works related to the background of the colonists from Minorca:

Chamberlain, Frederick, *The Balearics and their People.* London: 1908.
Cleghorn, George, *Observations of the Epidemical Diseases in Minorca from the Year 1744 to 1749.* London: 1779.
Markham, Clements R., *The Story of Majorca and Minorca.* London: 1908.
Marshall, F. H., "A Greek Community in Minorca," *The Slavonic and East European Review,* Vol. XI (1932-33).
Pasarius, J. Mascaro, *Mapa de la Isla de Menorca.* Mahón: 1953.
Pons, Maria Rosa Lafuente Vanrell y, *Account of the Deplorable State of the Island of Minorca and the many Injuries Inflicted on its Inhabitants under the Command of Deputy Governor Johnston.* London: 1766.
Svoronos, Nicholas G., *E Ellenike Paroikia tes Minorkas* [The Greek Colony of Minorca. A Contribution to the History of the Greek Merchant Marine during the 18th Century], Mélanges offers à Octave et Melpo Merlier. Athens: 1953.
Victory, Juan, *Guide of Minorca.* Mahón: 1948.

OTHER SECONDARY SOURCES

Arana, Eugenia B. and Wiles, Doris, "Burials in the Cathedral," *El Escribano* (A St. Augustine Historical Society Quarterly) Vol. III, (Jan., 1966).
Bandelier, F., transl., *The Journey of Alvar Nuñez Cabeza de Vaca and his Companions, from Florida to the Pacific 1528-1536.* New York: 1822.
Bartram, William, *Travels through North and South Carolina.* Philadelphia: 1791.
Beer, George L., *British Colonial Policy, 1754-1765.* New York: The Macmillan Company, 1907.
Beeson, Jr., Kenneth H., unpublished thesis for the Degree of Master of Arts on the New Smyrna Colony, presented at the University of Florida: Jan., 1959.
Benét, Stephen and Rosemary, *A Book of Americans.* New York: Farrar and Rinehart, 1933.
Corse, Carita Doggett, *Dr. Andrew Turnbull and the New Smyrna Colony in Florida.* Florida: 1919.
Curley, Michael J., *Church and State in the Spanish Floridas, 1783-1822.* Washington, D.C.: The Catholic University of America Press, 1940.
de Brahm, William Gerard, *History of the Three Provinces, South Carolina, Georgia and East Florida.* Unpublished MSS, c. 1772, Harvard College Library.
Drayton, William, *An Inquiry into the Present State and Administration of Affairs in the Province of East Florida; with some Observations on the Case of the late Ch. Justice there.* Florida: 1778. Unpublished MSS in the Manuscript Division of the Library of Congress.
Gannon, Michael V., *The Cross in the Sand, the Early Catholic Church in Florida, 1513-1870.* Gainesville, Florida: University of Florida Press, 1965.
Grant, Alastair MacPherson, *General James Grant of Ballindalloch, 1720-1806.* London: 1930.
"Journal of Lieutenant Colonel James Grant, Commanding an Expedition against the Cherokee Indians, June-July, 1761," *Florida Historical Quarterly,* Vol. XII, No. 1 (July, 1933).
Lawson, Edward W., "Minorcans of Saint Augustine," Paper read before the St. Augustine Historical Society, Dec. 14, 1948.

Bibliography

Lockey, Joseph B., "Public Education in Spanish St. Augustine," *Florida Historical Quarterly*, Vol. XV, No. 3 (Jan., 1937).

Martin, Sidney Walter, *Florida during the Territorial Days*. Athens, Georgia: University of Georgia Press, 1944.

Menzies, Archibald, *Proposal for Peopling his Majesty's Southern Colonies on the Continent of America*. Megerby Castle, Perthshire: 1763.

Mowat, Charles Loch, *East Florida as a British Province, 1763-1784*. Berkeley: University of California Press, 1943.

Mowat, Charles Loch, "The First Campaign of Publicity for Florida," *Mississippi Valley Historical Review*, Vol. XXX, (Dec., 1943).

Pennington, Edgar Legare, "The Church in Florida, 1763-1892," *Historical Magazine of the Protestant Episcopal Church*, Vol. III (Mar., 1938).

Phillips, P. Lee, *Notes on the Life and Works of Bernard Romans*. Florida: The Florida State Historical Society, 1924.

Postlethwayt, Malachy, *The Universal Dictionary of Trade and Commerce*. London: 1757.

Raynal, Abbé, *A Philosophical and Political History of the Settlements and Trade of the Europeans in the East and West Indies*, Vol. VI. London: 1798.

Schoepf, Johann David, *Travels in the Confederation*. Philadelphia: 1911.

Siebert, Wilbur Henry, *Loyalists in East Florida, 1774-1785*. Florida: The Florida Historical Society, 1929.

Siebert, Wilbur Henry, "The Departure of the Spaniards and other Groups from East Florida, 1763-1764," *Florida Historical Quarterly*, Vol. XIX (Oct., 1940).

Stork, William, *A Description of East Florida*. London: 1769.

Tucker, Philip C., "Notes on the Life of James Grant prior and subsequent to his Governorship of East Florida," *Florida Historical Quarterly*, Vol. VIII, No. 2 (Oct., 1929).

Turnbull, Andrew, "The Refutation of Late Account of New Smyrna," *The Columbian Magazine*, (Nov., 1788).

Vignoles, Charles, *The History of the Floridas with Observations on the Climate, Soil, and Productions*. Brooklyn, N.Y.: 1824.

William, John Lee, *The Territory of Florida*. New York: A. T. Goodrich, 1837.

ADDITIONAL SOURCES

Darby, 1821, pp. 76-77.

Boston Chronicle, July 18, 1768.

The Gentlemen's Magazine, Vol. XXXVII (London: 1767), pp. 21-22.

Scots Magazine, Vol. XXVIII (May, 1766), p. 271.

South Carolina and American Gazette, March 2, 1765; Nov. 10, 1776; Aug. 10, 1767.

South Carolina Gazette, July 4, 1768.

Index

Index

Catherine the Great: 30

Charleston, S.C.: 84, 124, 130, 162, 167-71, 185, 187

Cherokee War: 14

Clearwater, Fla.: 55

Clinton, Sir Henry: 168

Cochineal: 15, 67

Colon, Minorca: 44

Columbus, Christopher: 55

Constantinople, Turkey: 27

Cooper, William: 26, 27

Coppinger, José: 186

Corn: 72, 84

Cornwallis, Lord Charles: 167, 168, 169

Coron, Greece: Port of embarkation, 37n32; mentioned, 9, 30, 31, 33, 105

Corona, Clatha: 61, 62

Corsica: 1, 30, 33, 36n22, 40-43, 81, 179, 180

Corsicans: revolt against Genoese, 42, 43; Greeks among, 51n13, 16, 19; mentioned, 1, 21n2; 44, 49, 82, 104, 175

Cosifachis, Petros: 40, 50n9; 85, 87, 90, 91, 177, 179

Cosimo III, de Medici: 41

Costa, Domingo (Kyriakos): 33, 40, 180

Costa, Michael (Miguel): 181

Costa, Yorge: 180

Cotton: 11, 12, 15, 20

Cowkeeper, Indian Chief: 96, 97, 116

Creek Indians: 94, 96, 129, 145, 159. See Indians

Crete: 33, 41

Cuba: fishermen from, 107; mentioned, 10.

Darley, James: 186

Dartmouth, 2nd Earl of (William Legge): 100, 110, 118, 125, 127, 131

Dell, James: 186

Demalachis, Peter: 88

Dominica: 179

Drimarachis, Petros: 40, 50n8, 181, 183

Duncan, Lady Mary: 166, 185

Duncan, Sir William: signs new indenture, 68; mentioned, 13, 14, 18, 68, 98, 166

Drayton, William: resigns from Council, 114; Inquiry &c. by, 121; the Bryan affair and, 117-19, 121; American Revolution and, 131; visits London, 136; reinstatement in Council of, 146; final dismissal from Council, 162; leaves for South Carolina, 162; death of, 163; mentioned, 102, 114, 116, 120, 123, 125-27, 131-38, 140, 147, 149, 158, 161-63, 165-66, 168

Drayton, William Henry: 126, 136

Dunmore, 4th Earl of (John Murray): 127, 131

Dura Bin, Gracia Maria: 13. See Turnbull, Gracia Maria

East Florida: description of, 11, 78n33; climate of, 81; Council of, 17, 109, 121, 125, 131, 133-34, 138-39, 143-64, 186; struggle for Colonial Legislature in, 122; Grand Jury of, 122, 123, 127, 131, 140, 161; mentioned, 13, 17-20, 25-28, 47, 61, 67, 68, 73, 74, 88, 94, 95, 99-102, 104-6, 110, 114, 122-26, 129, 135, 140, 143, 151, 162, 174-76, 186

East India: 101

Echevarria, Bishop Joseph: 107, 108

Edinburgh, Scotland: 14

Egypt: 189

England: 10, 17, 28, 61, 62, 74, 76, 80, 100, 111, 118, 119, 124, 136, 139, 151, 165, 169. See Great Britain, Whitehall

Esclavonia: 192n86

Exarcopoulos, Kyriakos (Domingo): 37n32, 181

Ferryland, Newfoundland: 156

Florence, Italy: 41

Forbes, Rev. John: career of, 109-10; mentioned, 116, 119, 132

Fornells, Minorca: 44

Forni, Carlo: 59, 61

Forrester, Alexander: 166

Fort Duquesne: 14

Fort Picolata: 94

France: reaction against New Smyrna's company by, 28; mentioned, 2, 25, 28, 43, 44, 50n4

Franklin, Benjamin: 118

Frazer, Rev. John: 110

Index

Fundulakis, Demetrios: 33, 37n29, 180

Fuser, Lt. Colonel: 162, 168

Gage, General Thomas: 99, 127

Garcia, Michael: 83

Generina, Anthony: 91

Genoese Republic: 25, 42, 43

Georgia: patriots from, 130, 145, 146, 150, 151, 157, 159; mentioned, 11, 17, 19, 115-17, 124, 129, 138, 157, 163, 164

Germain, Lord George: 5, 67, 137, 138, 140-44, 146, 147, 149, 150, 163, 164, 173

Germany: 27

Giannopoulos, George Pedro Pasqual: 183

Giannopoulos, Ioannis: background of, 38n32; life in St. Augustine, 179, 181, 183

Giannopoulos, Manuel de Jesus Domingo: 183

Giannopoulos, Maria Manuela Barbara: 183

Gibraltar: 45, 47, 54, 64, 175

Gimell's Place, Florida: 119

Gordon, Arthur: 145

Grammatos, John: records about, 52n25; 45

Grand Seignior: 34. See Porte, Ottoman

Grant, Gov. James: proclamation of, 10, 114; surveys Mosquito Inlet, 57; Indian policy of, 94, 95; leaves Florida, 100; mentioned, 5, 14, 15, 18, 19, 28, 55-58, 60-64, 68-73, 75, 81-86, 95-101, 109, 110, 117, 139

Grant, Robert: 15, 99

Great Britain: 10, 17, 28, 45, 67, 120, 131, 132. See England

Greece: 1, 2, 20, 30, 31, 33, 34, 49, 105, 181, 184

Greek Orthodox: priests, 19, 33, 105; church, 20, 42, 78n16; 174, 180; mentioned, 30, 45, 56, 104, 105

Greeks: departure from Coron, 9, 21n2; number of settlers, 51n20; in Minorca, 45; mortality of, 92; names of, 191n66-71; mentioned, 1, 6, 11-15, 17, 19, 20, 26, 28, 32, 33, 42-45, 49, 55, 58, 60, 70, 99, 105, 118, 132, 173-79, 184

Grenville, Lord George: 18, 45, 68, 166, 185

Grenville, Thomas: 166

Grenville, William: 166

Grunulons, James: 87

Guidadela, Minorca: 44

Halifax River: 15, 63

Hancock, John: 114

Hasset, Father Thomas: 37n30, 178, 181

Havana, Cuba: 10, 11, 15, 57, 59, 61

Hayes, Anthony: 37n31

Hemp: 15, 67

Hernandes, Rafel: 86

Hillsborough, 1st Earl of: receives disquietening reports about New Smyrna, 58; approves plans for New Smyrna's fort, 63, 64; forwards a relief grant to A. Turnbull, 70; receives report on Indian raid, 98; displeased with Turnbull, 99; agrees on Moultrie's nomination for Lt. Governor, 101; mentioned, 49, 62, 67, 69, 75, 86, 100, 114

Hillsborough River: 15, 56, 57, 71, 97, 188

Holy See: 106, 108. See Vatican, Roman Catholic Church

Howe, Sir William: 162

Iatros family: 41

Indian River: 145

Indians: first visit to New Smyrna by, 96-98; New Smyrna raided by, 145, 161; satisfied with Grant's policy, 94, 95; Bryan and the, 117-19; used against American patriots, 129-31, 33; mentioned, 156

Indigo: 11, 15, 67, 72, 74, 101

Ionian Islands: 30

Ionians: 42

Ireland: 26

Italians: overseers from among the, 58; names of, 191n66, 71; mentioned, 1, 26, 44, 82, 87, 175-78

Italy: 2, 25, 42, 44, 55, 185

Janopoli, Juan: See Giannopoulos

Johnston, James: 24, 25, 35n2, 46

Johnston, Lady Cecil: 24

Jolly (or Jollie), Martin: 100, 139

Jurados of Minorca: 24

203

Index